MW00487513

G. HOUTEKAMER, P. ARTIS • *MVS I/O Subsystem: Configuration Management & Performance Analysis* 0-07-002553-3

A. KAPOOR • *SNA: Architecture, Protocols, and Implementation* 0-07-033727-6

R. CROWNHART • *IBM's Workstation CICS* 0-07-014770-1

R. LAMB • *Cooperative Processing Using CICS* 0-07-036111-8

C. DANEY • *Programming in REXX* 0-07-015305-1

P. KIESEL • *REXX: Advanced Techniques for Programmers* 0-07-034600-3

J. KNEILING • *Understanding CICS Internals* 0-07-037040-0

A. FRIEND • *COBOL Application Debugging Under MVS: COBOL and COBOL II* 0-07-022453-6

H. BOOKMAN • *COBOL/370: For VS COBOL and COBOL II Programmers* 0-07-006583-7

L. BRUMBAUGH • *VSAM: Architecture, Theory, and Applications* 0-07-008606-6

B. MERROW • *VSE/ESA: Performance Management & Fine Tuning* 0-07-041793-9

J. SAVIT • *VM/CMS: Concepts and Facilities* 0-07-054977-X

T. EDDOLLS • *ASO: Automated Systems Operations for MVS* 0-07-018994-3

T. KELLER • *CICS: Capacity Planning and Performance Management* 0-07-033783-9

T. BARITZ, D. DUNNE • *AS/400: Concepts and Facilities, 2/e* 0-07-018303-1

J. LEBERT • *CICS Essentials for Application Developers and Programmers* 0-07-035869-9

L. TRINDELL • *NetView: A Professional's Guide to SNA Network Management* 0-07-041984-1

To order or receive additional information on these or any other McGraw-Hill titles, in the United States please call 1-800-822-8158. In the other countries, contact your local McGraw-Hill representative.

AS/400
Information Engineering

AS/400
Information Engineering

John Porter

McGraw-Hill, Inc.

New York   San Francisco   Washington, D.C.   Auckland   Bogotá
Caracas   Lisbon   London   Madrid   Mexico City   Milan
Montreal   New Delhi   San Juan   Singapore
Sydney   Tokyo   Toronto

Library of Congress Cataloging-in-Publication Data

Porter, John (John Hubert)
AS/400 information engineering / John Porter.
    p.   cm.
Includes index.
ISBN 0-07-050623-X
1. IBM AS/400 (Computer).   2. Computer software—Development.
I. Title.
QA76.8.I25919P67   1993   93-2127
005.245—dc20   CIP

1 2 3 4 5 6 7 8 9 0   DOC/DOC   9 9   8 7 6 5 4 3

ISBN 0-07-050623-X

The sponsoring editor for this book was Jerry Papke, the editing supervisor was Fred Dahl, and the production supervisor was Suzanne W. Babeuf. This book was set in Century Schoolbook by Inkwell Publishing Services.

Printed and bound by R.R. Donnelley & Sons Company.

Contents

Preface

The changing realities for business have resulted in an examination of many of the traditional ways of doing things. Business literature is filled with a lexicon of new terms and concepts: Just-in-Time Inventory, Total Quality, the Theory of Constraints, Activity-Based Cost Accounting, etc. In many ways the significance of these new terms and concepts is not that they offer the solution to competitive problems, but that they challenge traditional ways of doing things and help to institutionalize a process of ongoing improvement.

In the world of Information Services, ongoing improvement has always been a part of our culture, but we have traditionally looked to technical advances as the basis for this improvement. More "bang for the buck" in hardware and more effective languages and compilers have typically been the source of productivity gains in Information Services. But after a certain point technical advances alone are not the answer, and how we use technology becomes the issue.

I have always been fascinated by technology and its impact on society. In my own view, the invention of the steam engine and the subsequent invention of the electric motor completely revolutionized society by bringing unlimited power to the producer of goods, freeing workers from the limits of their own physical strength. But it was not until the development of the concepts of interchangeable parts by the Springfield Armory and the assembly line by Henry Ford that consumers started to realize the benefits of low-cost goods that were produced through mass production.

Of the two innovations, certainly the more radical for the individual worker was the concept of interchangeable parts. Until the Springfield Armory and the War Department introduced the concept of interchangeability to the manufacture of muskets in the nineteenth century, all gun manufacture was performed by craftsmen. As with any craft activity, planning (design) and production were intertwined activities, and the details of the design were not completed until the production was finished. Parts interchangeability was accomplished by formalizing design specifications prior to production. This provided the ability to establish a formal production process whose individual elements could be studied and optimized. It also meant that a complex product could be broken down into components, and that many specialists could be organized to accomplish a common goal rather than limit the scope of a task to the capabilities of one craftsman.

Software development for midrange computers has typically been a craft activity. The mind-set for many of us in the midrange arena might best be expressed by the adage "Real men code first." While this emphasis on production over planning has served us well in the early days of the midrange, the needs of our customers/users dictate a reexamination of this philosophy. Early midrange computers were of limited capability, and were used to serve the needs of small businesses. The focus was typically on accounting applications. Packages provided us with a starting point, and software development frequently consisted of programming enhancements that were accomplished within the architectural framework provided by the package. New skills are required because the capability of the midrange has increased so that it can be used to displace mainframes and the emphasis has changed from accounting to mission-critical applications such as customer service, production, and inventory planning. The new skills that are needed are in the effective managing and planning of either the development or acquisition of software.

It is partially the purpose of this book to assist the practitioner in acquiring these skills. A more basic purpose, however, is to impact the culture in which we work so that the emphasis is on planning, and to assist the practitioner in creating an environment in which we have the opportunity to "do things right the first time." The experience of the automobile industry in recent years provides tangible evidence that the key to improved productivity is to not just throw technology at the problem.

Rather, the concepts of "Lean Production" emphasize quality over quantity, the use of multiskilled teams in product design, a "Just-in-Time" philosophy applied to both planning and production, and an emphasis on product design and process design rather than on inspection as the solution to both quality and productivity problems. Many of these concepts, which are recognized as the keys to improving hard goods productivity, are equally significant in the production of software. The concepts of "Lean Production" have for the most part already been adapted to the special needs of software development. But in many instances there is a significant gap between the "best" of these practices and the practices in use in many organizations. Closing this gap becomes an issue of understanding the practices, and of obtaining a management buy-in to the cultural changes required. In the main part of this book, the emphasis is on the practices. In the appendix, a section discusses a Metrics program to assist in evaluating the effectiveness and productivity of an Information Services Department. This latter section is intended to assist the IS Department in developing the information needed to stimulate a management buy-in to the cultural changes which have been discussed in the main section of the book.

Various portions of this book are intended to serve the needs of three audiences: management, the software professional, and the user. The sections intended for management address basic issues in organizing the software effort: setting of strategic goals, a focus on high-impact process automation, the use of group development techniques, and control techniques such as timeboxes and iterative development.

Sections intended for the practitioner include an explanation of structured analysis and design techniques, an overview of relational database design concepts, an explanation of several of the CASE tools available for the AS/400 developer, and criteria that might be useful in determining the appropriateness of a CASE (Computer-Aided Software Engineering) tool for your environment.

For the user who participates in business process reengineering and in the development of the basic information infrastructure of the organization, several of the sections on structured analysis and design contain explanations of the graphic techniques that are evolving as the way of expressing the design of a new system. These graphic techniques are advocated as the appropriate deliverables for the group development sessions in which the user is the primary participant. The section in the appendix which discusses application software packages is intended for all three audiences. It is the basic premise of this section that current approaches used in developing and using software packages can be significantly improved. It is also suggested that a make-or-buy decision on package software should follow a preliminary design effort, not precede it.

The specific ideas discussed in this book do not represent any original scientific breakthrough on the part of the author. Instead, this book represents an attempt to organize and present the ideas and concepts of many pioneers in a useful manner. My background is engineering, and the role of the engineer is not to perform the research necessary to make scientific breakthroughs. Rather, the engineer's role is to use the scientific discoveries of others to create something useful for society. In writing this book, which organizes the ideas of others, I hope that I have accomplished the basic goal of an engineer—to do something that is useful.

I would be very appreciative of any feedback concerning the approaches and material covered, as well as suggestions for later publications. I can be reached at the following address:

99 Eastlawn Street
Fairfield, CT 06430

Acknowledgments

Many friends have assisted me in the preparation of this material. I would like to thank, in particular, Gary Robinson of Moor Medical who had the patience to read the initial draft and provide many valuable suggestions. I would also like to thank Karen Forster who did the content editing of the manuscript, and significantly improved the readability. Other thanks go to Ron Hiner of Ambrose Consulting, Hal Leahy of Information Management Associates, Darrel Voitik of Data-Wright, Joe Sebik of Management Solutions Group, and Jim Kahn of Protege Consulting. I would also like to thank Dale Agger and the staff at *News 3X/400* for the opportunity to initially present part of this material as articles in the magazine.

John Porter

AS/400
Information Engineering

Introduction

When an Information Services (IS) Department is considering ways to improve software development productivity, a first issue that should be addressed is quality. Industry statistics on the development or purchase of software systems indicate that there are major problems in satisfying a company's needs. Consider that:

Fifteen percent of all software projects never deliver anything—that is, they utterly fail to achieve their established goals. (1)*

Overruns of 100 to 200 percent are common in software projects. (1)

In one study of a company's software efforts, 64 percent of the errors were in analysis and design, even though the users had formally signed off on the documentation. (2)

Can these problems be avoided by buying a software package to meet your company's needs? A recent survey of 90 users of four midrange manufacturing packages (with the names supplied by the package vendors) provided the following results: (3)

Fifty percent felt that their original objectives were not met.

---

*Numerals in parentheses refer to references at the end of each chapter.

Thirty-three percent would not buy the same package again.

Ten percent failed in their first implementation.

In looking at our success rate, it is hard to visualize another industry or profession surviving with a comparable level of consumer satisfaction. Can you imagine the home building industry with 15 percent of their clients feeling that the contractor never delivered anything, or an appliance company with 33 percent of their customers reporting that they would not buy the same product again?

Is there a solution to these quality problems? Perhaps the place to start is with the term *software*. The implication of this term has always been that programs, or "software," are complete flexible, and that any changes needed to adapt a computer to a specific need of a user can be readily accomplished. This was certainly true in the early days of computers, when programs focused on a specific task and were typically independent of other programs. And it is still true if the user's request involves a straightforward program, such as a display or report that uses existing files. But if a user request involves a basic change to the files, this could affect hundreds of programs and be a major task. Changing software is almost like moving a wall in an office building. If the wall to be moved is a partition, it is a minor problem. But if the wall is a load-bearing support, this is typically a major construction project.

So the start of a solution to both productivity and quality problems might be to no longer talk about "software" per se, but to think in terms of structural software and peripheral software. *Structural software changes* tend to be major problems, while *peripheral software changes* are minor tasks. As a consequence, getting the structural software "right" should be the primary emphasis when new systems are built or purchased. It has long been recognized that, for major building projects, planning and design skills are needed in addition to construction skills. In major software projects, we also need to recognize that construction (or programming) skills are not enough, and that, to deal with the structural elements of software, planning skills are needed.

When we start to think of the planning skills required to deal with the structural software part of a large system, a number of specifics can be identified.

Project planning and control skills

Software design and system integration skills

Business process redesign skills

"Effecting change" skills

Are these skills normally part of a midrange Information Services Department's inventory? If you look at the tasks that this department traditionally performs, most projects involve maintenance to established systems. Frequently projects are only of several months' duration, involving a single programmer/analyst working along. But if a major software system is to be built, consider these differences:

The size of the project typically requires a team approach, making team coordination and systems integration more of a problem.

Frequently the starting point for a major system effort is a business strategic objective. So the scope and boundaries of the new system must be defined.

The reengineering of business processes, which is frequently the goal of a new system, involves the crossing of organizational boundaries and the restructuring of traditional responsibilities.

A successful effort to improve software maintenance productivity frequently involves the updating of old legacy database designs that were based on previous database technology.

The impact of change on the user can be much more significant.

If a new software system is to be successful, how to handle these differences must be planned for. And for this planning to be effective, it typically means that the midrange IS Department must acquire new skills.

But how necessary are these new skills if the intended solution is a purchased software package? Looking at the satisfaction level for package purchases, it's obvious that we need to do something different. If the package vendor does a good selling job and the customer makes a poor purchasing decision, the onus is on the customer to change. Review again the differences previously cited for a major internal development effort. Most of these conditions also apply to a major software package purchase except for "designing the new system." But, instead of designing a system, we must define our needs properly so that we have a basis for purchasing.

The typical software package demonstration stresses functionality, and purchasing decisions are frequently made without evaluating the structure of the package. It's almost like buying a house after seeing only unrelated pictures of furniture displays of each room. Unfortunately these pictures will not tell you how the rooms relate to each other, if there is an expansion attic that could be converted to bedrooms, and so on. During the normal life of a software system, two to four times the original cost will be spent on maintenance. This expenditure is typically necessary in order to evolve and enhance the system as the needs of the business grow, laws are changed, personalities change, and other factors come to bear. So the ability to enhance the purchased software package is an important criterion.

A more significant consideration, when a software package is purchase based on a "functionality" review, is the ability of the user to determine requirements. As we will discuss more thoroughly in Chap. 3, having computers in the environment affects the requirements. Consider the significance of the statistic (cited in the beginning of this chapter) that 64 percent of the errors in a software effort were in requirements, even though the user had formally signed off on the documentation. Thus, even though the user has signed off on the package purchase, there will be a strong need to revise the package in the future. How easily these revisions can be accomplished is based on the structure of the package and on how closely it conforms to the underlying information structure of the company.

To compare a package structure with the basic information structure of a business, the basic information used to run the business must be defined. As we will discuss in more detail in later chapters, this definition involves many of the initial steps involved in designing a system that is to be custom-built. So a package can be a shortcut, but it is a construction shortcut, not a planning shortcut.

As you proceed through this book, you will note that I consider the issue of software development productivity to be in many instances an issue of quality. I also hold that the solution to quality problems lies with improving the development process. For the midrange computer environment, improving the process usually means improving the planning out part of the process.

In addition to improving the process as a way of increasing software development productivity, new tools can also be an important factor. These tools, called *CASE tools (Computer-Aided Software Engineering),* have been developed to support both the planning and the construction phases of the process. But an important perspective when the acquisition of these tools is considered, is that the success rate in using them has been spotty. Perhaps the major reason for this indifferent success rate is that they were purchased as a new silver bullet to improve productivity, rather than in support of the new development processes which we will discuss in this book.

One of the first major successes in the use of new tools to make major improvements in productivity was by Ford in the early days of mass production. But the significant contribution of these tools was not that they performed a machining step faster, but that they held tighter machining tolerances. This permitted true parts interchangeability, the foundation of mass production.

So too with the new CASE tools. While they might do a specific job such as coding faster, their greater significance is to support improved processes. As an example, it is now generally accepted that an iterative approach to software development is a better way to do things. This approach emphasizes getting a first working version that includes the basic functionality done as quickly as possible. This initial version is then expanded to include additional functionality.

The problem with an iterative approach using conventional programming languages is that continual changes to a program lead to structural degradation, making future changes more difficult. Using the newer CASE tools, a program is easily rebuilt each time it is changed, thus avoiding structural degradation. Changing and rebuilding the program are significantly easier than making program changes using conventional languages. Thus the significance of the CASE tool in this instance is not that the programming itself is faster, but that it is an "enabler" that permits a fundamental change in the process used to build software.

So, with improving the process and the quality as potential keys to improving software development productivity, let's take a look at how software might be developed.

REFERENCES

1. Abel-Hamid, Tarek and Madnick, Stuart. "How We Fail to Learn from Software Development Failures," *Sloan Management Review,* Fall 1990.

2. Martin, James. *Systems Design from Provable Correct Constraints.* Prentice-Hall: Englewood Cliffs, N.J., 1985.

3. Capron, William. "Follow the Rules to Avoid Failure," *3X/400 Information Management,* December 1991.

Towards an
Engineering Discipline

CRAFT VERSUS ENGINEERING

Ken Follett's novel, *Pillars of the Earth,* describes the building of a 12th-century cathedral in England. The master builder for the cathedral was a craftsman who was initially trained as a stone mason. Because of his background, the construction method described in the narrative is the typical medieval craft approach, which intermingles the design and construction activities as the building progresses. A dramatic point in the narrative occurs when the master builder realizes that the height of the walls might produce a torsion effect during high winds and that the cathedral might collapse during a storm. Fortunately, a solution is available: Flying buttresses will support the walls. But the problem is not discovered until well into the construction process. What if a solution had not been available or the problem had not been discovered before a storm caused the cathedral to collapse? That's the problem with a craft approach: In a large building project of any type, when construction proceeds without any formal plans and evaluations, it's hard to foresee problems.

Today, the disciplines of architecture and structural engineering are separate from the craft skills used in construction. As a consequence, a structural design for a new building can be prepared in advance. Using strength-of-materials formulas, the design can then be evaluated prior to construction. This permits construction of a building to proceed with reasonable confidence that major problems will not occur unexpectedly. This design capability also permits new types of buildings to be built without relying on the craftsman's empirical wisdom that a design has worked previously.

And what does building a cathedral have to do with software development? A basic assumption in many IS Departments is that the craft-oriented approaches adequate for small software projects can be scaled up and used for large projects. But by analogy, the evolution of physical construction does not support this assumption.

In software development, we can learn a number of lessons from the evolution of construction. First, for any system (be it a building or business software), a structural component can be designed and evaluated prior to physical construction. Second, the design and evaluation of this structural component typically involve technical skills and disciplines that are different from those involved in physical construction. Third, to minimize risk, the structural design should be prepared before construction begins. Then, within the framework and limits of a sound structural design, a detailed component design can evolve to permit customization and completion of the structure or system to meet specific temporary or permanent needs.

Yet software developers have not learned from the experiences of such disciplines as architecture, as suggested in Capers Jones' book, *Applied Software Measurement.* (1) The reason is that the early computers were used to solve mathematical problems for the military, particularly complex ballistic and scientific calculations. As a result, computer science started as a subdiscipline of a science primarily interested in final results and with no history of a formal process to achieve these results.

Before computers, solving mathematical problems required substantial mental effort but did not involve much formal planning or design. Problems were typically small and self-contained, and they usually involved only one or two people. When computers arrived on the scene, early software dealt with a single process or a small number of processes. System complexities arising from the need to integrate many software components were not a factor. The early uses of IBM midrange computers to solve small-business problems permitted the mind set of the early computer days to continue. Business problems were small and self-contained and often involved modifying or enhancing ready-made software packages for accounting. However, such modifications could be only cosmetic. The architectural structure of these software packages was inviolate. A new report or display could be prepared, or a new subsystem with additional functionality added. But if the original package was changed, this frequently invalidated the warranty.

But the types of systems business management is now demanding of the midrange IS Department no longer involve small, back office automation efforts. And the increased horsepower of the midrange makes it viable as the hardware solution for medium-sized companies and divisions of larger companies, areas that formerly were the domain of mainframe computers.

In these new environments, it is no longer easy to adapt the business to the capabilities of the "closest fit" software package; rather a software solution must meet the specific needs of the business. An accounts receivable package that is less than perfect for the $5-million-per-year company might result in an extra hour per week of clerical time. But an inventory tracking system that does not provide the proper information for the $50-million-per-year company might change an order fulfillment cycle from an hour to a week, or result in the production of unneeded goods. Unacceptable!

In many instances, the competitive advantage that could be gained by automating a mission-critical application can only be realized with the *right* software. And this software can be obtained only if IS has the specification, design, and management skills needed to build or purchase complete systems or software components that meet users' specific needs. For the midrange IS Department that is pursuing more effective approaches to meeting the company's software needs, computer pioneers have provided the foundations for the new technical and management skill set that is required.

Clive Finkelstein and James Martin identified data as the structural foundation for software design.

Edgar F. Codd used set theory to provide a mathematical foundation for database design, and pioneered the development of relational database management systems.

The work of Phil Crosby, J. M. Juran, and others' on quality, while not originally focused on software development, nonetheless provides insights that are directly relevant to the process of developing software.

Barry Boehm and others have focused on the application development life cycle and identified a process for software development that can be studied and optimized. And IBM's development of the Joint Application Design (JAD) methodology has altered the traditional over-the-wall relationship between software producers and users.

Chris Gane, Tom DeMarco, Ed Yourdon, and many others pioneered the development of the structured analysis and design techniques that provide a formal method for designing software and a means of representing a design graphically prior to construction. These early methods have been evolving into the concepts of object-oriented design (OOD), which holds the promise for significant advances in software development productivity.

Dr. Michael Hammer has brought *lean manufacturing* lessons to the office and proposed basic tenets for designing business processes. These tenets have become the basis for the discipline called *business process reengineering*.

As a starting point in developing the skill set appropriate for an IS Department involved in mission-critical software, let us briefly review these pioneers' insights.

DATA AS THE FOUNDATION

Of all the advances in software development, the precepts of Information Engineering are perhaps the most important. By identifying the database design as the architectural structure for commercial software, Information Engineering provides the foundation for an engineering approach to software development. In the early days, when the use of computers was to solve complex mathematical problems, the formula or process the computer performed was the critical automation consideration. How to organize, store, and retrieve the data was a secondary consideration. But in business applications, complex formulas are seldom used, and the role of the computer is to store and manipulate data. Thus the emphasis in software development should be on data, and Information Engineering provides the guidance needed to use data as the structural element.

Information Engineering is a software development discipline, which James Martin defines as "the application of an interlocking set of formal techniques for the planning, analysis, design, and construction of information systems on an enterprise-wide basis or across a major section of the enterprise." (2) Martin identifies the following principles as being basic to the discipline of Information Engineering (3):

1. *Data as the foundation:* The data used in a company tends to be very stable, and as a consequence provides a more appropriate foundation for a system design than the organizational procedures which use the data.

2. *The structure of data:* Data has an inherent structure. Data Analysis, which formally identifies this structure, should be done before process logic which uses this data as designed.

3. *An enterprise perspective:* Data requires planning, defining, and structuring throughout an Enterprise or Business Area so that separately evolved systems can use this data consistently and consequently work together.

In practice, these principles identify data as the structural core of an application software system and separate the activities involved in data analysis and design from the activities in developing the processing solutions that operate on this data. The Data Model becomes the stable foundation that serves the organization's long-term needs. Specific software applications are considered transitory information solutions for current needs and are subject to frequent changes as requirements evolve.

The implementation of Information Engineering involves a top-down approach, and results in building an integrated database to be used by all processes that need this data. This integrated database, called an Enterprise Data Model, crosses the boundaries of traditional software application areas. Specific files are no longer only used by the processes within an application boundary. And by designing the enterprise Data Model early in the development process, both users and application designers are able to get a clear picture of the structural foundation for all processing software.

The focus on data analysis prior to a detailed analysis of the processes that use this data is possible because of technical progress and pragmatic insight into the nature of an enterprise's data. Two areas of technical progress are important. First, the development of inexpensive random access mass storage devices permits large amounts of data to be stored and retrieved instantaneously. Second, the development of database management software permits data to be stored in its primitive form and then retrieved and assembled quickly into a usable format.

The pragmatic insight resulting in the discipline of Information Engineering is that primitive data elements, such as a customer name or a premium rate on documents or on other media, must have an inherent rationale or they would not exist. Establishing a database design for these primitive data elements that organizes them in a coherent form leads to cohesive application systems to create, modify, or use these data primitives.

The focus on data as the structural component requires an efficient means to organize this data and software that permits its easy retrieval. In 1970, Dr. Codd of IBM presented a paper entitled, "A Relational Model of Data for Large Shared Data Banks." This paper used set theory to provide a mathematical foundation for organizing data. His rules for normalization (that is, minimizing redundancy) provide the practical basis for organizing data in its simplest form. The relational database management system that is part of the operating system on the AS/400 is based on Dr. Codd's concepts. It provides the software that facilitates the organization, retrieval, and easy use of data that has been organized according to its simplest form.

THE SIGNIFICANCE OF QUALITY

A focus on data gives us the first insight into new approaches for developing large systems. This insight is that data is the structural framework for commercial software, and this structural framework must be designed and evaluated prior to construction and prior to the detailed design of components or specific parts of the system.

In effect, this focus on the data is telling us *what* to do to more effectively develop systems. If we look at the Total Quality Movement (TQM), we can obtain insights that tell us how to do it to develop more effective systems. In particular, TQM suggests a sense of discipline in software development that is at odds with the ad hoc approaches that traditionally are part of the culture of the midrange environment.

A review of the TQM movement might start with the definitions of quality provided by two of the early pioneers, J. M. Juran and Phil Crosby.

Juran's definition of quality, *fitness for use,* is a holistic concept and provides a strategic management perspective of quality. Applying his ideas in the software world, we find two customers or users are significant: the final user who uses the software to accomplish some business task, and the intermediate user, the maintenance programmer, who is responsible for evolving the system as the needs of the business change. The definition of fitness for use addresses two strategic management goals relevant to software production:

When a product is delivered to the customer or final user, it should immediately accomplish the function for which it was intended without any extensive rework or breaking in.

The design and structure of the product must facilitate maintenance. While software doesn't break, new requirements are always a part of any dynamic business environment. If the software product does not facilitate modification or enhancement of specific elements, the long term needs of the business have not been served.

Crosby's definition of quality, *conformance to requirements,* is a tactical view and appears to stem from his long experience in dealing with manufacturing quality issues at ITT Corporation. In applying Crosby's view of quality to software development, it stresses that during the construction process, the programmer has the flexibility to determine how to do something, but does not have the flexibility to determine what to do. What to do is decided independently during a design phase, which precedes construction. The quality of the construction or programming activity is then evaluated based on how well the product conforms to the specifications developed during the earlier design phase.

Both views of quality are important to the software development world. Juran's definition is important for several reasons:

It emphasizes the need for a thorough understanding of the user's true needs before resources are used for construction.

It identifies the maintenance programmer as a user, and encourages the recognition that systems should be constructed in such a way that they can be easily maintained later.

Crosby's definition is important because it emphasizes the separation of the design and construction phases of the development process. And it encourages the discipline that the producer no longer has the right to make changes during construction without prior approval. If changes are needed, a return to the original specification process and to the individuals involved in the original process is made. This discipline is necessary in large projects, since uncoordinated changes to a design could result in a system in which the individual parts don't work together when they are finally installed.

Beyond the insights we might gain from these definitions of quality, we can gain a further perspective by reviewing the evolution of the quality movement in manufacturing. Industry generally recognizes three plateaus in the evolution of quality assurance activities:

- *Product inspection (circa 1920)*—examining intermediate and final products to detect defects.

- *Process control (circa 1960)*—monitoring defect rates to identify defective process elements.

- *Design improvement (circa 1980)*—engineering the design of the process and the product to minimize the potential for defects.

Any objective evaluation of quality in most software development environments would place the IBM midrange environment squarely at a 1920 evolutionary level. Quality is assessed by intermediate testing of programs and final testing of the system. But we are learning that a concern for quality that does not start until the end of the production or development process is too little too late. Rather quality must be built in by establishing a valid production process and designing a product that minimizes the potential for defects.

A FORMAL DEVELOPMENT PROCESS

To arrive at a starting point for a discussion of the skills and techniques needed to develop complex computer software applications, I have used two related industries, construction and manufacturing that have a long history of building complex systems. Three lessons from these industries provide that starting point.

1. Any complex system has a structural framework, and the identification, design, and evaluation of this framework prior to physical construction is absolutely necessary to minimize risk.
2. Quality is best obtained through the design of the production process and the product, not through inspection.
3. Participants in various phases of the production process must be disciplined enough to accept that their independent activities must conform to the plans of previous phases and the constraints and needs of subsequent phases of the life cycle.

When we look at these three lessons, they point in the same direction—the need for a formal development process. The high-level view of a development process is called a *Life Cycle Process Model,* and the detailed steps involved are called a *methodology.* Let's take a look at formal definitions for these two terms:

Life Cycle Process Model is a model that identifies the phases and subphases in software production and the transition criteria for progressing from one phase to the next.

A *methodology* is an elaboration of the major phases identified in the Life Cycle Process Model, producing an ordered set of detailed tasks to get from a starting point (such as a user request) to an end point (such as a deliverable product). Phases identified in the life cycle model provide the framework for identifying the more detailed tasks that comprise a methodology. For example, if enterprise modeling is an example of a life cycle phase, *defining the scope of the system* is a specific task performed as part of this enterprise modeling phase.

Some of the first attempts at developing a formal life cycle and a methodology were undertaken by such pioneers as Barry Boehm and the early Joint Application Design (JAD) specialists at IBM. In our own efforts to establish an appropriate software development process, we should be guided not only by these early efforts, but also by current efforts in other design disciplines that are emphasizing "Time to Market." The fact that Time to Market is a significant variable based on the life cycle used can be demonstrated by the experiences of two companies in manufacturing:

Ingersol Rand is a manufacturer of industrial power tools. When falling market share forced the issue of new designs for their products, the company's initial estimate was four years to design and produce a new line of tools. Management's initial reaction was that the country was able to win World War II faster. This precipitated a complete revision of the development process, and the successful introduction of a new product line in less than a year.

Chrysler Corporation's recent advertisements describing the new Design Center in Auburn Hills, Michigan also focus on the new engineering emphasis on speeding up the product development life cycle. The advertisement discusses a people reorganization that puts together designers, engineers, planners, accountants, buyers, and others to speed up Time to Market. As part of this people redeployment, a review was also made of the procedures used in development. The result of the review: a 50- to 90-percent reduction in the number of steps involved in the design and production of Chrysler products.

METHODS AND NOTATIONS

Once a formal process is established for developing software and individual tasks identified, the next step is to determine how to perform a task and how to express the results. These "how's" are called *methods and notations*.

> *Method:* A set of techniques, rules, and guidelines for tackling a problem, measuring the quality of a solution, and expressing the solution. Methods are the means of performing the tasks that make up the methodology.

Notation: A means to organize and express an idea, such as a database design. A Flow Chart is an example of a notation.

Every design discipline, whether mechanical engineering or architecture, has a formal and standardized notation, and a formal method for developing this notation. These permit the designer to organize a solution and to check the validity of ideas. But the design phase is just one part of the life cycle of a product. The product must also be produced, costed, marketed, and maintained, and the formal notation and method are also the primary means of communicating design concepts to the subsequent phases of the process.

Some of the first rules concerning the use of a formal notation might be borrowed from a profession such as mechanical engineering. In my freshman year as a mechanical engineering student, a basic course was mechanical drawing. Ideas of professionalism that were stressed in this class are appropriate for the designer of any product, and can provide some basics for software designers.

- The mechanical engineering profession has established notations for expressing ideas, and a student must learn these conventions to become a qualified professional.

- The notation serves not just the designer's needs but also the needs of others such as production, accounting, and other areas.

- Sloppy diagrams indicate a poor professional attitude and do not properly serve the needs of the other professionals and people who must use these drawings.

- Mastery of drafting skills does not make you a designer, but it is a prerequisite.

- The purpose of plans and blueprints is to organize the production process, not to document what was produced after the fact.

Beyond this set of professional standards that apply to the process of preparing design documents, we also need a set of diagrams and symbols that adequately express the parameters of a design solution. As a relatively new profession, software design has not agreed on a standard set of notations to the degree that engineering has. But since the late 1970s, such pioneers of the structured analysis and design movement as Chris Gane, Ed Yourdon, and Tom DeMarco have laid the groundwork for a formal set of graphic techniques that provide the notations needed to express a software design. And just as the architectural professions use a number of specialized techniques to express different specific design aspects such as the structural frame versus the plans for the heating and cooling system, structured analysis and design has evolved a variety of graphical techniques for various aspects of software design. As a result, the first data processing notation, the flow chart, has been replaced by a variety of graphics for software design such as the data flow diagram and the entity relationship diagram.

Established design professions demonstrate the significance and ground rules for the preparation and use of notations and methods. Software pioneers have provided directions and opportunities for notations and methods to software design. These directions and opportunities will be discussed in detail in later sections of this book.

DON'T JUST PAVE COW PATHS

Many software projects consist of routinely automating office procedures without first determining if these procedures are still appropriate. Unfortunately, many office procedures were developed according to technical limitations or management approaches of a bygone era. They are frequently based on the limitations of manual processing or on batch computer systems, and might also represent outdated practices and organizational structures. When we just automate an existing process without first assessing its validity, we are doing the same thing as the road builders who are paving a cow path. And if you spend much time in the older sections of Boston or New York, you quickly realize that cows do not make good road designers.

Dr. Hammer has popularized the idea that modern Information Technology provides the basis for a fundamental assessment of business processes. His definition of business process reengineering is:

> The radical redesign of business processes to achieve dramatic performance improvements. (4)

A frequently cited example of business process reengineering is from the Ford Motor Company. One effort to reduce costs at Ford centered on the accounts payable department. It was found that additional automation could only make a marginal improvement in efficiency. But a radical new approach which provided for automatic payment based on receiving reports rather than on invoices from the vendors resulted in a quantum improvement in efficiency.

Dr. Hammer has suggested that many concepts serving as the basis for restructuring the factory floor should also serve as the basis for reengineering the office. Following are the tenets evolving as the conceptual basis for business process reengineering (5):

- *Task integration and compression of the process:* The traditional division-of-labor principles no longer apply. Dividing up the process and assigning tasks to different people results in numerous handoffs, errors, and delays. Under the new model, one person has responsibility for an entire process when possible. A person's job is designed around an outcome or objective—a completed task, a finished component or product—instead of a single task. With this type of job consolidation, both the design of the process solution changes, and many of the coordination reports presently required are no longer necessary.

- *Decision making as part of the job:* The old model says, "A manager makes decisions. Another employee does the work." Under the new approach, the person doing the work makes many decisions. This person is, after all, the expert on this particular job. This results in faster response to problems, raises the level of quality, and helps flatten an organization. When those closest to the work are empowered to make decisions and fix problems, there is little need to manage the process—it is self-managing. From an Information Technology standpoint, this frequently means making more information available to employees so that they can make informed decisions, and the building of decisions support systems into a process solution.

- *A hybrid of centralized and decentralized approaches:* Traditionally, centralization has been the key to economies of scale and eliminating redundant resources. Decentralization has been the key to providing better customer service. And the two have often been in conflict— it's been an either/or proposition. Now, common pools of information and access to all the far-flung operations of a company permit economies of scale and hands-on expertise with customers.

- *Concurrent performance of tasks:* The sequential approach is no longer appropriate for businesses. "You do your work, and when you're done, pass it along and I'll do my work" is a thing of the past. Many processes, such as product development, become more efficient when work is done collaboratively and concurrently. "Let me see what you are doing so that I can make sure that what I'm doing fits your specifications" is the new model. This cuts down on rework and streamlines operations.

- *Capture information once, at the source:* This is a simple but important point. Information used to be difficult to transmit. So it made sense to collect and store it redundantly in various departments and business units, on distinct forms, and with differing reporting requirements. But today information is entered into a database once and used repeatedly through connected, integrated systems. Bar coding, relational databases, and electronic data interchange (EDI) are the key technologies for eliminating errors and delays and reducing clerical overhead.

A PERSPECTIVE ON CASE

Much of the current discussion in technical literature concerning improving software development productivity centers around the use of new tools. These tools are called CASE tools, and the acronym stands for Computer-Aided Software Engineering.

As a first step in understanding how these new tools assist in the efforts to improve software development productivity, let's review their history and some of the types of tools that have been developed.

Initially CASE tools focused on PC-based graphic software to automate the new diagramming techniques developed as part of structured analysis and design. Some tools included additional features, such as attribute definition and screen painting. This initial definition of CASE eventually was expanded to include most software that helped to automate the development life cycle. This expansion eventually led to a categorization of tools into upper CASE, lower CASE, and integrated CASE.

Upper CASE covers the initial concept of CASE, the support of structured analysis and design. Typically these tools are PC-based, and support a variety of graphical presentation techniques, including data flow diagrams, association matrix diagrams, entity relationship diagrams, structure charts, and action diagrams.

Lower CASE tools are primarily for the construction phase of the software life cycle. Generally there are two types: code generators, which produce third-generation language (procedural) code such as COBOL or RPG; and fourth-generation languages (4GLs), which compile machine-level programs directly from a higher-level definition.

Note: Lower CASE tools might also be classified based on their approach to automating system construction. Procedural tools, while permitting coding with fewer statements, generally still mirror the thought pattern and practices of conventional 3GL programming. Specification tools typically use a thought pattern that more closely resembles the approach taken by an engineer in designing a product from standard or customized components.

The third category of CASE tools, *integrated CASE tools,* combine the analysis and design features of upper CASE with the construction capabilities of lower CASE. In effect, instead of manually reentering specifications developed on the upper CASE tool into the front end of the lower CASE tool, an automatic linkage is provided. This linkage, called a *repository* is typically designed by the tool vendor. Specifications developed using the upper CASE tool are automatically stored in this repository. The lower CASE tool then draws from this repository, and completes the construction. Problems in defining a standard repository have meant that integrated CASE is typically provided by a vendor who has developed both upper CASE and lower CASE tools.

The power of CASE tools is a boon to software developers who lack time. (And who doesn't lack time?) But it also requires developers to obtain new skill sets to take advantage of that power.

At a demonstration of Information Engineering Workbench (IEW), an analysis and design upper CASE tool from Knowledgeware, Inc., I asked the technical representative from Knowledgeware how long it would typically take to learn IEW. Her response was, "One week if you already know structured analysis and design techniques. If you don't, probably six months to a year."

This same message came out of a number of studies. One study indicated that typical time to reach technical proficiency was three to six months. Average time to reach proficiency for structured methods was more than 18 months.

A report in *Midrange Systems* expressed the same requirement:

> Management recognizes the need for change, even if it is unsure how to achieve it. Many companies realize that they can no longer continue the craft-oriented approach to software development. They have got to start engineering. CASE as the way to start that engineering, but first they must adopt some disciplined development methods. (6)

Thus an important message about CASE is that it automates an analysis and design skill set. It does not substitute for the lack of it.

CASE is also an important enabler of new life cycles and methodologies. Some tool's provide the ability to develop an early prototype that can be evolved into a working system. This permits an early view of the system's look and feel, an important factor in eliminating misunderstandings between users and designers and in improving the quality of the software. Reduction in the labor intensity of the construction process through CASE tools also permits greater emphasis on design without changing manpower levels.

Computer Research Corporation provided the following profile of the successful CASE user:

Uses a formal life cycle process.

Uses formal structured methods.

Emphasizes quality over quantity.

Provides extensive training.

Understands both upper and lower CASE tools.

Plans to extend the use of CASE and formal methods.

Thus the important message about CASE tools is that new tools alone are not the answer to software development productivity problems. New tools should be used in conjunction with new methods, skills, and management practices. The new methods, skills, and practices are the focus of the next two sections. The final section of this book then discusses some of the tools that are appropriate for use in conjunction with these new professional approaches.

REFERENCES

1. Jones, Capers. *Applied Software Measurement*. McGraw-Hill: New York, 1991.
2. Martin, James. *Information Engineering, Book 1*. Prentice-Hall: Englewood Cliffs, N.J., 1989, p. 1.
3. Martin, James. *Structured Techniques as the Basis for CASE*. Prentice-Hall: Englewood Cliffs, N.J., 1988, p. 24.
4. Hammer, Dr. Michael. *Beyond Computing, p. 11*.
5. *Ibid.*, p. 14.
6. MacKinnon, Peter. *Midrange Systems*, May 14, 1991.

The Software Development Life Cycle

The *total quality* movement in manufacturing emphasizes that quality should be built into a product through the design of the process and of the product rather than by inspecting it after the product is built. This quality perspective is equally valid for IS, so the *process* for developing software is a place to start in discussing a new management and technical skill set. That the process to be used for software development is even an issue seems to be a reflection of the shoemaker syndrome. The shoemaker's son was the last to get a new pair of shoes because the shoemaker was so preoccupied with the needs of his customers that he ignored needs at home. Many IS departments are preoccupied with the business processes of their users. While automating these business processes, they have become the proponents of change and of new ways of doing things. But many IS departments do not seem to realize that the process used for making or purchasing application software is equally significant. And that IS needs to adopt a philosophy of continuously improving the software development process and accept a willingness to change to the same degree that we advocate the acceptance of change by our customers.

The first step in establishing a software development process is to identify the major functions that need to be accomplished. This overview, which we have previously defined as the Life Cycle Process Model, permits us to identify the major phases of the software development process, as well as the rules for progressing from one phase to the next (called *transition criteria*).

Identification of these phases then let us use the decomposition process to identify the more detailed steps: a methodology. At the methodology level, we can identify:

- What specific deliverables will result from the process.
- Who is to participate in the production of these deliverables.
- What methods are significant in producing a deliverable.
- What tools might be appropriate.

The Life Cycle Process Model has received a great deal of attention in the last few years. The most notable evaluation of various existing life cycles was performed by the Defense Science Board Task Force on Military Software. (1) Many recommendations in this report were geared to the military environment, but two recommendations stand out in terms of their applicability to software development:

Recommendation 23: Mandate the iterative setting of specifications, the rapid prototyping of specified systems, and incremental development.

Recommendation 24: Remove any dependence upon the assumptions of the *waterfall model* (a life cycle model that breaks software development into discrete phases such as requirements definition and emphasizes the completion of one phase before the next can be started) and institutionalize rapid prototyping and incremental development.

These recommendations suggest a radical departure from most of the formal software development methodologies that have been used over the last 20 years. So keeping these recommendations in mind, let's look at various approaches to software development that might be used, and discuss a new approach which includes the use of CASE Tools as an enabler for a new Life Cycle Process Model.

A LITTLE HISTORY

To develop a Life Cycle Process Model that is appropriate for a particular software development environment, an appropriate starting point is a review of various models that have been used so far. In the evolution of data processing, several life cycle models have had considerable influence.

The *code-and-fix model* was the basic model in the early days of software production (and is frequently the approach taken in maintenance-oriented midrange shops). This model is also know as the Ready-Fire-Aim model. It consists of two steps:

1. Write some code.

2. Fix the problems in the code.

This approach was popular with users, developers, and management because it led immediately to coding and a sense of something being accomplished. The origin of code-and-fix was in the mathematical problem-solving days of the early computers. This life cycle model is still effective in many midrange shops because of their focus on maintenance. For these shops, the tasks are relatively small (one to two worker months) and typically use the existing architecture of an established package or an old custom system.

This model is a craft approach. Design and production are commingled, and the shape of the product or solution is not determined until production is completed. The small scope and number of people involved does not require a planning effort to permit partitioning and coordination, which are necessary for a large team.

But this lack of planning also means that the developer has to force pieces together as they are developed. And fixes frequently are patched onto existing code almost at random because of the lack of initial organization as the basis of development. In addition, users place responsibility for the final product solely with the IS department, resulting in a lack of user input and commitment.

This model also leads to the need for a phenomenon called *documentation*, a necessity accepted in theory but seldom honored in practice. Most industries involved in the construction or production of complex products perform the construction activity according to plans and specifications produced in advance. These plans and specifications make after the fact documentation unnecessary since the initial plans adequately describe the product that has been built. Using a code-and-fix model, the product is not known until production is accomplished. As a consequence, documentation to facilitate future maintenance must occur after the fact. And since the purpose of this documentation is to help the future program maintenance activity rather than the current building project, no wonder programmers consider it a waste.

The *waterfall model,* illustrated in Fig. 2.1, superseded the code-and-fix model. As if in reaction to the avoidance of documentation the

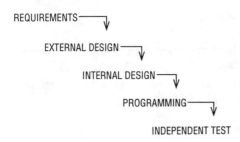

Figure 2.1 Waterfall Life Cycle Model, called the Waterfall model because you cascade through the development phases with little provision made for returning to a previous phase.

earlier model fosters, the waterfall model demands elaborate documentation as the product of each phase and as the requirement for entering the next phase. This model progressed past a strictly craft approach and formalizes specific software development phases to include an analysis phase, a design phase, a coding phase, and so on. The term waterfall became associated with this model because you progress or cascade down through the phases sequentially without formal provision for going back and repeating a phase (although limited feedback to the previous phase was considered acceptable).

Problems associated with using the waterfall model are numerous. This approach typically entails long lead times before the developer can verify a system design by demonstrating all or part of a working version to the users. Relying on the document-driven approach (and, as you know if you have purchased a formal methodology from a Big Six accounting firm, for example, this might involve a fill-in-the-blanks set of forms) makes it difficult for the user to adequately verify the look and feel of the system. And during the long lead times, users and requirements often change. Frequently, these difficulties result in an unusable system when installation time comes and in missed business opportunities.

Using a third life cycle model, the *evolutionary development model,* the developer creates a working application based on the first definition of users' requirements. This initial system then serves as the basis for evolutionary improvements in later iterations. The evolutionary model overcomes the waterfall model's inability to determine final requirements adequately and the long lead times before the user can evaluate the look and feel of the system. However, the evolutionary model presents other difficulties. One serious problem is the spaghetti code that often results when developers graft significant changes onto the initial program architecture. This type of code has no discernable logical structure, and frequently includes unreachable routines (dead code). Because of this lack of a logical structure, a maintenance programmer frequently must review an entire program to understand it well enough to make even a simple maintenance change.

A second problem is that a restricted perspective that focuses on the first working version does not typically include the planning needed to permit effective integration with other independently evolved systems. This lack of a planning perspective also frequently leads to difficulties when the new system is being installed in stages since the temporary bridging to old systems hasn't been provided for.

A fourth approach, the *transform model,* is made possible by code generators. This model is also called a rapid prototyping or a rapid application development model. It relies on a code generator's ability to convert a formal specification automatically first into a prototype first and then into a working version of the final product.

In this model, the focus of implementation moves from coding to the specification level, and the look and feel is visible to the user early on through the use of prototypes. This model thus lets a lower CASE tool serve not only as a productivity tool but also as the enabler for a specific approach to software development.

As an enhancement to the evolutionary model, the transform model resolves the spaghetti code problem because changes are made at the specification level, and then the code is completely regenerated. The evolutionary model's other problems, integration with other independently evolved systems and bridging to old systems, are not addressed.

LET'S BUILD A HOUSE

To illustrate a successful approach to design and implementation before we start to define a new Life Cycle Process Model for software development, let's return to construction. Specifically let's pursue in more detail the typical process for building a house and see what more can be learned that might be appropriate for us.

Peter Paul and his wife Mary have engaged an architect to design a house. The initial conversation and first steps might proceed in the following manner.

The couple specifies:

We want a pretty house, and our daughter is very particular about the color of her bedroom. It's got to be blue. And our son needs lots of wall space for his poster collection. I like a chintz wallpaper in my bedroom, and I have a nice antique sofa that I want near the window. I saw in Home and Gardens magazine a beautiful slate entrance foyer, and, and, and ...

The architect asks these initial questions:

Do you own a lot? How big? Does it have water and sewer, etc.? What style house do you prefer? Cape, colonial, ranch? How many bedrooms do you need? Do you want a den? What is your budget?

The architect's initial action steps are to:

1. Explain the process of building a house. First, this explanation would focus on the need to design the basic structure and to leave the transitory features, such as colors, placement of furniture, and so on, to a later stage. The initial advice would also include an explanation of the difference between wants and needs. If the budget is restricted the focus must be on basic housing requirements rather than on wants, which include all the things that they have seen or read about in other houses.

2. Prepare a contract that includes a statement of objectives, such as type of house, number of bedrooms, environment considerations (such as the availability of city water).

3. Prepare an initial architect's rendering that provides a graphic overview (a scope) of the proposed house and a floor plan (an identification of major components and how they relate to each

Figure 2.2 Architects rendering a new house—the first graphic step in preparing plans for a new house.

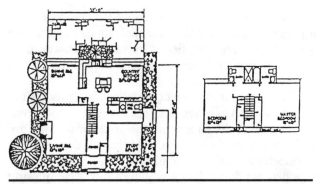

Figure 2.3 Floor plan for a new house—the second graphic step in preparing plans for a new house.

other). These two graphics (Figs. 2.2 and 2.3) are the architect's first high-level suggestions concerning the house design.

4. Prepare the first level set of plans that define the building's structure once Peter Paul and Mary accept the rendering and the floor plan.

SUBSEQUENT STEPS

Once the initial architectural plans are approved, a quote obtained from a general contractor, a building permit obtained, and all other prerequisites are in order, the architect schedules several detail design sessions with his clients. Considering purchasing lead times for material and the construction progress, the architect carefully schedules these sessions to immediately precede the relevant part of the construction activity. Typically these sessions address the look and feel of the house. For example, a visit is made to a model kitchen showroom to select the style of kitchen cabinets. Once the walls were finished, another design session was held between the couple's daughter and the painting subcontractor to select the bedroom colors.

During the construction of the hypothetical house, an issue arises that might provide some insight for software developers. The couple explain the following scheduling problems to the architect. They visited the building site while the lot was being cleared, and it rained during their visit. Would the architect schedule the construction of the roof first so that they would have immediate protection in the event of a storm? Also, the lease for their current residence expires on xxxx date. Could construction be speeded up?

The architect explains the following scheduling constraints to the clients. Building the roof first involves structural dependency. The foundation holds up the walls, and the walls hold up the roof. It is possible to build temporary supports so that the roof can be constructed first. However, this would involve significant extra cost. It would be better to put up a shelter to solve a temporary need rather than build without considering structural dependencies.

Building tradition calls for the completion of one phase, such as design, before start of the next phase, such as construction. However, a concurrent approach can be used. For example, as long as the structural plans are complete, the mason can start the foundation even though the architect has not completed the electrical and heating plans.

There is, however, a process dependency, which requires completing the appropriate step in the prior process before the equivalent step in the next process can be started. Thus, the masons can start their tasks as part of the construction phase without the electrical plans, but the electricians cannot. And concurrency does not imply a quality or professional compromise for any step of the process since a building that falls down because of an inadequate design or a construction shortcut has not sped up the process in the long run.

During the construction phase, one group of craftsmen finishes before the next group starts. But some construction activities can be done concurrently. For example, the roofers and the electricians can do their work at the same time. Again care must be taken in this scheduling, however. There is a task dependency and constraint within a phase, also. The heating contractors cannot complete their work until electricity is available so that the system can be tested. And if the sheet rock installers are closing up the walls before the electricians and plumbers are finished, costs go up.

A second discussion during the construction of the hypothetical house might also be of interest. The clients start doing their homework and suggest that significant savings might be obtained by purchasing new automation tools. They show the architect an ad for an automatic nail gun and the manufacturer's claim of a 50-percent construction savings when this new tool replaces the hammer. The architect explains that this new tool only affects a specific activity in the overall process, carpentry. Since this activity represents only 20 percent of the project, the potential 50-percent savings on the overall house cost suggested by the nail gun manufacturer was at best misleading.

A final problem arises during construction. The owners initially selected fancy electrical fixtures for which the electrician was not able to get firm price quotes. When prices were finally obtained, both the price and delivery time substantially exceeded initial estimates. The clients decided to stay with the original price and delivery estimates.

This was accomplished by refocusing on the basic functionality of the electrical fixtures rather than attempt to include gold-plated chandeliers, and other customized hardware.

Two more events occur over the next several years. After living in the house for several years, the couple decide to add a detached one-car garage that they could not afford during initial construction. When they go back to the original architect, he suggests that the complexity of the proposed enhancement does not require an architect with a CAD (computer-aided design) system, or specialized design training. Instead, they can rely completely on the services of a carpenter. Even though his primary skill set is construction, for the level of design needed for the garage, the carpenter can prepare the plans manually, get the required building permit, and so on, as well as perform the construction.

The couple eventually outgrow the house and decide to build a larger house. Since they were satisfied when the carpenter built the garage and remodeled the kitchen, they ask the carpenter to build the new house. The carpenter says he can plan for a small enhancement or maintenance project, but designing a complete house involves both academic training and experience he has not acquired in the normal course of his trade.

MORAL OF THE STORY

Before starting the definition of a Life Cycle Process Model for software development, let's stop and formalize some lessons from the story about the hypothetical house.

- The initial design process produced:

    A statement of objectives (the architect's contract).

    An overview of the proposed house, which identified both the environment and the relationship of the house to the environment (the architect's rendering).

    An identification of the major components of the proposed house and the relationship of these components to each other (the floor plan).

    A structural design (the detailed plans).

- Once the overall design had been completed, the project could be partitioned so that various tradespersons could work on the project. This partitioning also served as the basis for:

    A schedule and budget covering each phase or component.

Detailed design sessions with the clients that resolved issues such as the look and feel of individual components. These detail design sessions focused on the member of the client's family immediately affected by any look and feel issue, such as the daughter's selection of the color for her bedroom. It should also be noted that prototypes (a showroom display of model kitchens) were also used.

- Traditional scheduling and construction sequences can be accelerated to handle time to market considerations or modified to deal with short term problems (the need for shelter during a site visit). This is accomplished by allowing concurrency. The use of concurrency is constrained, however, by:

Structural dependencies.

Process dependencies.

Task dependencies and constraints.

The significance of these dependencies will be explored in further detail in Chap. 3.

- When difficulty arose concerning a component (the electrical fixtures), a viable solution was to reevaluate the initial selection and specification and to refocus on basic requirements. This is traditionally called line item budgeting by accountants. In software development, we are starting to call such an approach *timebox management*.

- Automation tools were mentioned twice in the story: an automatic nail gun to increase the productivity of the carpenter and a CAD system to aid the architect. Neither tool was a substitute for a particular professional skill, nor did the tool eliminate a process task.

A NEW LIFE CYCLE PROCESS MODEL

With the architectural model in mind, we can now describe a Life Cycle Process Model for use in the development of interactive end user applications. In this type of application, it is important to tailor the functions and the look and feel to the user's needs and perception of needs. An important step is providing prototypes and an early working version of the new system. These can subsequently be evolved to increase its functionality. This approach helps you to develop a system that meets real-world requirements.

An important feature of this life cycle model is that it lets the new system deal with business processes that are already automated to some degree (such as, when you are replacing an existing system in stages). This is accomplished by including steps for interfacing to old systems as you implement the new system in phases, thus providing for the continuity of existing systems.

In explaining this new model, we will draw on lessons from the construction of the hypothetical house. Terminology that will be used is from an evolving professional consensus in the IS community. Some of the specific terms that describe the major phases in the life cycle model are from IBM's *AD / Cycle Concepts Manual*. (2) We should note that the meaning of some of these terms is subject to interpretation, particularly the terms enterprise and business area. From a systems design perspective, these terms depart from a traditional application perspective when we are defining the scope of the initial design effort. We will discuss the determination of a design scope in detail in Chap. 3.

In describing this life cycle model, we are also taking advantage of and constrained by the CASE tools available to the IBM AS/400. The availability of inexpensive upper CASE tools means that manually preparing some of the design diagrams would not be cost effective. In the same vein, a lower CASE tool is an enabler since it permits rapid and inexpensive development of a prototype and evolution of that prototype into the first working system. An iterative approach can then be used to evolve the system to include more functionality by making the changes on the specification level. Prototyping and an iterative approach can also be accomplished using a 3GL. However, unless there is a high level of programmer discipline and adherence to the techniques of structured programming, spaghetti code might be the result.

Figure 2.4 shows an overview of the suggested software Life Cycle Process Model. This model, the structured Evolutionary Development Model, consists of several phases.

First is strategic planning, in which significant business goals and objectives relevant to the application of Information Technology are established. As in the house story, high-level and frequently unstructured customer needs must be converted into design guidelines, an overall process and phases for development must be agreed to, and design constraints must be established. An important part of the early discussion is a general agreement between client and design advisor concerning a budget which will guide subsequent activities. This strategic planning activity results in a formal text document that states objectives, constraints, and a financial overview. An example of a significant business goal for a manufacturer might be the need to reduce order fulfillment time from two weeks to one day to meet competitive pressures. This business goal then

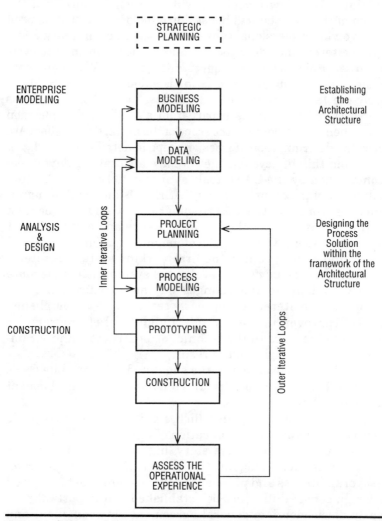

Figure 2.4 Structured Evolutionary Life Cycle Model—The software development emphasis is initially on designing the structural foundation for the system, the database. Process requirements are met by developing an early working version, and then expanding the initial functionality through an iterative process.

precipitates the need to examine and potentially redevelop systems for order entry, inventory management, shipping, and so on. A similar need currently being cited by several insurance companies is the need to reduce new policy approval time from two weeks to one day.

The completion of the strategic plan serves as the authorization for the first design phase in our life cycle, enterprise modeling. In this phase, you define the scope and boundaries of the business area targeted for development. You also establish the architectural overview that is the basis for all development activities to come. From this architectural overview, specific projects can be established in which individual parts of the system are designed, constructed, and installed.

The Enterprise Model is the product of two activities, business and data modeling.

Business Modeling means identifying the boundaries of the proposed system by first identifying the environment (what's outside the system) and the data linkages between the environment and the proposed system. Major components of the new system are then identified by documenting the flow of data and the major processes that change data as it flows within the boundaries of the system to be developed. As part of this activity, you also identify where data is at rest (a data store) between processes. Graphic documents produced as a result of this activity are high-level Data Flow Diagrams, documents analogous to the architect's rendering and the floor plan (Figs. 2.5 and 2.6). In the same way that the architect's initial drawings provide the basis for preparing a structural design of the house, the graphic documentation serves as the starting point for the structural design of the system, the Data Model.

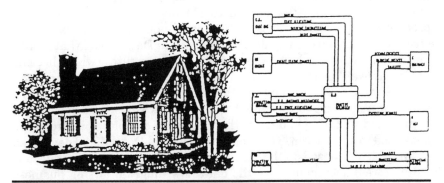

Figure 2.5 The Context level of a Data Flow Diagram is equivalent to an architect's rendering of a new house. It provides an overview of the new system and the relationship of the system to its environment.

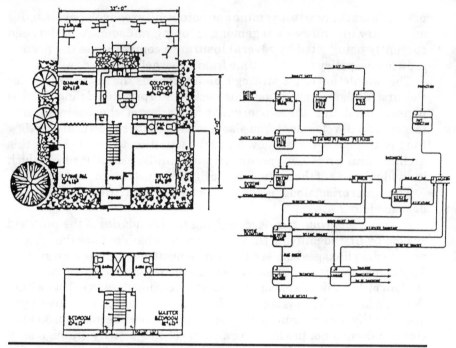

Figure 2.6 The Essential Functions level of a Data Flow Diagram is equivalent to the floor plan of a new house. It shows the major components of the new system, and the relationship of these components to each other.

Data Modeling

Information Engineering has provided the insight that data is the framework for a commercial data processing system. As a corollary, the database design serves as the structural foundation for all systems and processes that use this data. In the data modeling phase, a system structure is established by designing a logical Data Model that identifies major entities (which become files) and attributes (which become fields), as well as special field editing rules (called *domain integrity*) and the relationship among entities (called *referential integrity*). This phase is also used to document the business rules that govern the editing and updating of data so that there is a complete picture of the data used in the system. The scope of the logical Data Model developed in this phase is based on the identification of data categories or groups (data stores) documented on the data flow diagram during business modeling. The documents produced during this activity are an Entity Relationship Diagram (ERD) and an attribute listing. Figure 2.7 shows

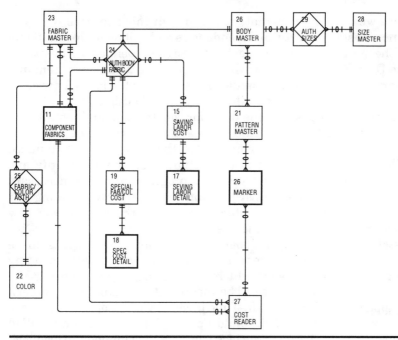

Figure 2.7 Sample Entity Relationship Diagram showing the structure of one of the component types of a system, the data.

a sample ERD. This diagram identifies the organizational structure of the major categories of data such as customer, product, and order, and establishes the significant relationships among these categories of data. For example, an ERD shows that there is a relationship between orders and customers, and that the database design should provide the user with the ability to determine which customer placed an order, and which order(s) have been placed by a specific customer.

The second step in the life cycle model is an analysis and design phase. It accomplishes project planning and process modeling.

Project Planning

Software development is not as straightforward as the house example, where various skill sets (carpentry, plumbing, and so on) provide the primary basis for breaking down an overall effort into discrete and controllable projects. The breakdown can be driven by the user (build the roof first because it might rain, or create the billing system first

because we have an immediate problem), but this approach will typically not consider structural dependencies and will result in additional
cost. The more desirable approach is to use the dependencies identified
on the Data Flow Diagram as the basis for partitioning a system into
smaller subsystems. These small subsystems are the basis for process
modeling, which includes detailed analysis and design.

This partitioning is also the basis for construction and installation
on a subsystem basis. A time standard is typically the basis for
partitioning the components identified on the DFD. The time standard
is called a *timebox*. As part of this activity, you should identify any
bridging to old systems or temporary programs that are necessary
before you can install the subsystem independently. By including this
temporary bridging to old systems as part of the project, the new
subsystem can then be installed as soon as it is ready.

Installing subsystems independently permits the benefits to be
realized immediately, and reduces the risk associated with spending
years building a new system which is then installed all at once at the
end of the development cycle. The incremental installation approach
is an application of the Just-In-Time inventory philosophy to software
development. In effect, don't build up a big inventory of uninstalled
software programs because you loose the benefit of immediate feedback
that can only be obtained by using the new software.

Process Modeling

This activity expands on the relevant details of the Business and Data
Models for each subsystem established as a separate project during the
partitioning performed during project planning. At this time relevant
processes identified in the business model are decomposed to a program level, and additional business rules and processing logic are
documented. In addition the physical database design for relevant
parts of the logical data model are finalized. You also establish a
program design for complex processes using a program structure chart.
An example is shown in Fig. 2.8.

Additional graphical techniques, such as an action diagram and
decision trees, are also used to document complex logic. This detailed design phase is similar to activities in the house building
example in which the kitchen cabinet layout is finalized, colors are
selected, the style of floor molding is selected, and all other decisions
are made.

The next step in the Life Cycle Process Model is a construction
phase, in which two major activities occur: prototyping and subsystem
construction.

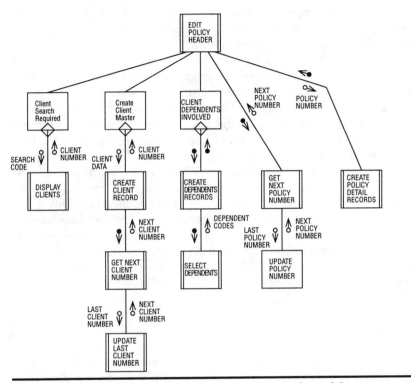

Figure 2.8 Sample Structure Chart showing the structure of one of the component types of a system, a process.

Prototyping of critical elements identified during the analysis and design phase provides the user with a preview of the proposed system. This step focuses on presenting the system's look and feel to the user early in the development process. For instance, based on the fields identified so far, this phase might generate a prototype screen to show the users.

Including prototyping as the first step in construction rather than as part of analysis and design is somewhat arbitrary, but it is based on the CASE tools presently available to the midrange practitioner. Some of the more elaborate upper CASE tools have a screen painting (formatting) facility, but the screen design typically cannot be automatically transferred to a lower CASE tool. As a consequence, prototyping is included as the first construction activity when the tool focus has already moved to lower CASE. When prototypes are developed using the lower CASE tool, they typically can be easily converted into working programs.

Construction of the subsystem initially identified during project planning is done by generating it from the system specifications.

Construction also includes producing and testing any temporary programs needed to support old files, to interface with old systems, and to convert old data to the new file system.

The Life Cycle Process Model also includes an inner iterative loop, in which you adjust and expand your specification based on the prototyping experience. Then you put the resulting prototype into use. In an outer iterative loop, you adjust specifications based on operational experience. But as with the housing example, the initial structural design constrains the ease with which an adjustment can be handled. A change in the look and feel (such as different electrical fixtures or a change in the screen format) is handled easily. Similarly, an enhancement that represents an extension (such as a new garage or additional process automation) is not significant as long as the original structure is not modified. But if the modification requires a significant alteration of the database design rather than just an extension (such as a new file) or restructures process-to-process relationships and dependencies, major costs could be incurred. In this instance, the original structural design has not served its purpose of providing a guide for subsequent detailed design.

SUMMARY

This chapter has used experiences from the construction industry to define a Life Cycle Process Model that defines the major phases of software development. As part of this definition, two feedback loops were also identified. One loop updates specifications based on a prototyping experience, and the other updates specifications based on operational experience.

In addition to the identification of the phases, a number of basic management issues are relevant at the life cycle level. These issues include how to define the scope of a project, managing the creeping expansion of this scope that typically occurs, and how to maintain an emphasis on bottom-line benefits during the course of the project. These issues are discussed in more detail in Chap. 3.

The life cycle is also the basis for a methodology that identifies the detailed tasks associated with each phase. Chapter 4 covers a suggested methodology in detail.

This chapter also mentions graphic deliverables as part of several of the phases. Methods and notations associated with these graphics are discussed in detail in Chaps. 6 and 7.

Author's note: The events described in the construction of the hypothetical house actually occurred. The significant thing (not mentioned in the story) was the fact that construction occurred using prefabricated walls and ceilings. The interesting thing about this construction technique was that the detailed panel design was accomplished using a CAD system (computer-aided design). The detailed design from the CAD system was then automatically fed into a production machine that was also controlled by a computer (computer-aided manufacturing). Thus we had the equivalent of an upper CASE tool for design and a lower CASE tool for construction. This is the same as the integrated CASE, which is talked about in software development. (1)

REFERENCES

1. Brooks, F. P. et al. *Defense Science Board Task Force Report on Military Software.* Washington D.C.: Office of the Under Secretary of Defense for Acquisition, September 1987.

2. *IBM Systems Application Architecture: AD/Cycle Concepts.* (GC26-4531-0).

FURTHER READING

Boehm, Barry M. "A Spiral Model of Software Development and Enhancement," *Computer,* May 1988, p. 61.

Connel, John L. and Shafer, Linda. *Structured Rapid Prototyping.* Prentice-Hall: Englewood Cliffs, N.J.

Porter, John H. "Systems Development and CASE Tool Integration," *NEWS 3X/400,* April 1991, p. 49.

3

Managing the Process

In one of my seminars, we reviewed plans for a new software system for the sponsoring company's distribution center. The participants in the seminar were amazed that approximately 30 percent of the anticipated programming effort was for verification and clean-up of bad inventory data that came from the company's factory.

The group suggested it might be a better investment if the project's scope included the packing station where the inventory data was prepared. But the system designers explained that this was a warehouse system, and the project covered only what happened within the warehouse. The scope of this software system was limited by the physical constraints of the building. In accepting this project scope, the designers did not stop to determine the consequences: More programming effort would be devoted to cleaning up data from outside this building than would probably have been required to automate the prior process and get the data right the first time.

This example illustrates a point: It is one thing to define a process for software development, but if the process is to be effective, you must also determine whether traditional application or organizational boundaries are an appropriate basis for defining the scope of a system and organizing a project. In the present example, users and system management didn't question the scope of the project because it conformed to an existing organizational structure that they were comfortable with and was restricted to automating existing processes. But if you apply Juran's quality criterion, *fitness for use,* to the plans for the system, you see that the data this system receives does not fill the criterion. And modern quality management shows that if you have a quality problem, the solution is not inspection and rework. The solution is to correct the source of poor quality, in this instance, the prior processes.

Many companies are realizing that Information Technology—the capabilities computers, software applications, and telecommunications offer—will not automatically provide the benefits management is seeking. The technology must be accompanied on new insights into how to apply and manage it. Perhaps the most important change needed in the application of technology is a willingness and ability to restructure the way business tasks are accomplished with the new technology. This restructuring, called *business process reengineering,* focuses on the analysis and design of work flows and processes within and among organizations.

Companies that have used the concepts of business process redesign have had some significant successes. One example is the Motorola Corporation, which reduced the number of steps in filling a customer order from 209 to 39. (1) This was done not by automating processes that have evolved from the past, but by fundamentally redesigning processes using modern technology to meet the business objectives of the future.

This chapter examines the management culture that determines how technology is applied. The goal is to improve the effectiveness of the software development process.

SOFTWARE TRIAGE

In midrange IS departments, most discussions about an organized approach to software development start with a typical reaction like, "With alligators snapping at our heels, we don't have time to worry about draining the swamp." In such a reactive mode, we let short-term user requests completely control the allocation of programming resources. And we never have enough resources to satisfy demands. The opinion is frequently expressed that a design-driven rather than a user-request-driven approach is great in theory but not very practical.

So the first management issue for most midrange IS departments is not how to design a system, but how to get the opportunity.

Perhaps the place to start looking for an answer is not in computer literature. Instead, the answer may lie in a management concept developed by the medical profession during World War I. Their problem was how to use limited resources to deal with the thousands of casualties returning from the battlefield. Our problem is similar: too much demand for too few resources. The solution was a medical management approach called "triage" that is still used today in disaster management. Webster defines *triage* as "The sorting of and allocation of treatment to patients and especially battle and disaster victims according to a system of priorities designed to maximize the number of survivors."

We can control the use of programming resources by applying a system of triage priorities to the maintenance of an existing library of software. To develop this system, we must evaluate and classify existing software. This classification should include both management and technical criteria. The management criteria are the business objectives

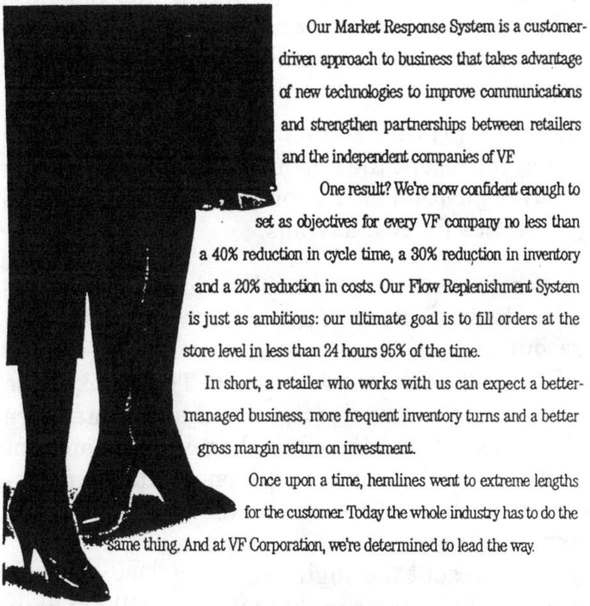

Our Market Response System is a customer-driven approach to business that takes advantage of new technologies to improve communications and strengthen partnerships between retailers and the independent companies of VF.

One result? We're now confident enough to set as objectives for every VF company no less than a 40% reduction in cycle time, a 30% reduction in inventory and a 20% reduction in costs. Our Flow Replenishment System is just as ambitious: our ultimate goal is to fill orders at the store level in less than 24 hours 95% of the time.

In short, a retailer who works with us can expect a better-managed business, more frequent inventory turns and a better gross margin return on investment.

Once upon a time, hemlines went to extreme lengths for the customer. Today the whole industry has to do the same thing. And at VF Corporation, we're determined to lead the way.

Figure 3.1 Sample of business objectives that are impacted by Information Technology (*Business Week,* October 24, 1991, p. 37).

affected by Information Technology. This is done in strategic planning, the first step in the life cycle model. See Fig. 3.1 for an example of objectives from one company, the VF Corporation.

With the business objectives established, the next step is to determine those business *processes* that are most in conflict with the business *objectives* and competitive requirements. Existing software that is part of these business processes is then identified and subjected to a technical evaluation. This evaluation consists of reviewing the software and file designs to determine whether the files use modern database design concepts, how much operator support and intervention is needed to handle error conditions and system interrupts, how much maintenance is required, and so on. The evaluation should let us classify existing software systems as follows:

Category I: High business priority, correctable software. This category covers systems that meet high priority business objectives, are essentially technically sound and can be corrected to meet new business needs.

Category II: High business priority but fatally flawed technically. This category covers systems that meet the important business objectives established by management, but have underlying technical problems that prevent upgrading or improvement in order to meet management objectives.

Category III: Low business priority software systems, that while technically viable, do not represent the opportunity for significantly improving the competitive position of the company or do not represent significant opportunities for cost savings.

Systems in Category I represent the seriously injured. Effort devoted to these systems results in a return of a system to viable service, an effective use of IS resources.

Systems in Category II represent the fatally injured. The reality to be discussed with both management and major users is that maintenance expenditures on fatally flawed systems (other than the minimum amount needed to keep them running) is throwing good money after bad. Resources that might be used to maintain these flawed systems should instead be used to reprogram or purchase replacements.

Systems in Category III represent the slightly injured. Devoting the minimum amount of attention to systems in this category will not have a significant detrimental effect on either the organizations ability to compete or on the specific software system.

ENTERPRISE MODELING

A triage evaluation can provide the opportunity to organize a design effort by freeing up resources that might otherwise be wasted in piecemeal support of software that has no long-term viability or on maintenance requests that do not represent significant business priorities. The question then becomes how to start the system design effort, the *enterprise modeling phase,* that is the first step in the software development.

The concept of enterprise modeling was first pioneered as part of an information engineering strategy. In the early books on the subject (3, 4, 5), a radical approach was suggested for enterprise modeling: Organize all data in the enterprise to provide a structural basis for automating specific business processes. Although this exhaustive approach sets a worthy goal, few organizations adopted it. Few companies have the resources to handle such a large effort, nor can they afford the lack of intermediate benefits. The exhaustive approach also violates the Just In Time concepts that are now becoming an accepted part of management practices. Applied to inventory, the Just In Time concept says: Do not produce inventory before it is needed. Doing so ties up resources unnecessarily and might result in the production of large amounts of goods with hidden flaws that can only be detected through operational use rather than by inspection. The exhaustive enterprise modeling approach produces plans for which the implementation resources might not be available and ties up resources on one activity when they could be more effectively used on another. It might also result in plans that turn out to be inadequate or inappropriate once the effort starts to use these plans to develop a system.

A more realistic alternative to the exhaustive approach is to focus on the business objectives and processes that management identified during the triage evaluation. These processes become the targets of a redesign effort and serve as the starting point for defining the scope of a new system.

Before exploring what to do from this starting point, let's first stop and make sure that we understand the nature of a *system* versus an *application.* Ben Blanchard explains a *system* as a set of logically interrelated components working toward some common purpose or objective. (6) In any particular situation, a system is defined by specifying its limits or boundaries. Everything within the boundaries is the system, everything outside is the environment. Within the system's boundaries, the components needed to accomplish the objective are then organized.

The term *application,* on the other hand, refers more to the historic partition of a business processing into subareas that conform to an organizational structure. Thus there is distinction between a system for paying vendors and a traditional accounts payable application which identifies the tasks which are performed by the accounts payable department. In the example that we previously discussed of Ford's efforts to reduce vendor payment costs, a system perspective resulted in an enhancement to Inventory Receipts processing to provide for automatic payment to vendors. An application midset would not have been able to cross a historic functional boundary to affect the order-of-magnitude savings.

As we are designing a new system in order to accomplish a business purpose or objective, we should understand that the typical business is still organized into departments and tasks that typically reflect precomputer and pretelecommunications capabilities. Consider, for example, the following business objectives: fill a customer order, develop a new product, process a new insurance policy, process a product return. To accomplish any of these business objectives, multiple organizational boundaries are crossed. If a software design effort is organization oriented it might optimize individual department activities, but this typically does not result in the optimization of an overall process.

So the design of optimized system starts with the business objective (such as, fill a customer order). Then the system must be defined based on the components needed to accomplish this objective, without regard to existing organizational boundaries. To define these components, the place to start is with the data, such as a customer order, that serves as the initial stimulus for the business objective being evaluated. Compo-

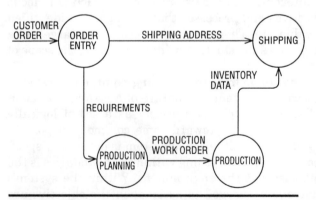

Figure 3.2 Business processes involved in accomplishing a strategic objective: Fill a customer order.

nents of the system are then identified by following this data through the processing needed until the business objective has been accomplished. As Fig. 3.2 shows, this might include the following processes: order entry, production planning, production, and shipping.

Tracking such stimulus data as a customer order lets us identify not only individual processes that transform this data but also identify related data that these processes use. A customer master, a product master, and a price file are examples of related data used by the processes for filling a customer order. This is the first cut at defining the components of the system, the initial data that initiates the system, processes that act on or transform this initial data, and related data used by the processes. Since, in all probability, the file formats for the related data will also be redesigned based on the capabilities of newer database management systems, the initial scope of the system should then be expanded to include the processing that initially creates and then maintains the related data.

The customer master provides an example of scope expansion. Since the processing in fulfilling a customer order involves a customer master, the project's scope should be expanded to include the processing needed to create and maintain the customer master. Figure 3.3 shows the scope of the proposed system being expanded to include the processes that maintain the customer master and the product masters.

And because changing the format of the customer master affects other software systems, such as accounts receivable, you might then expand the scope to include these areas. The initial definition is expanded iteratively to include all related processes that require the same data as the primary processes you started with.

The goal is to expand the scope of the design effort from the primary processes to related processes that operate on common data. The control for this expansion should be a *planning horizon*. This planning horizon is the total redevelopment effort possible in a planning period such as two years. You must use judgment based on the available software development resources to limit the processes and data that are to be systematized during the planning period. Additional processes and data not included in the scope of this development effort are part of the environment. Figure 3.3 shows an example of such exclusion. The accounts receivable and sales analysis systems are identified as part of the environment. Data requirements of these processes that are part of the environment will be handled through interfaces rather than the use of shared data files.

Thus when the term *enterprise* is used in a systems context, it has nothing to do with organizational boundaries or a legal entity. Rather

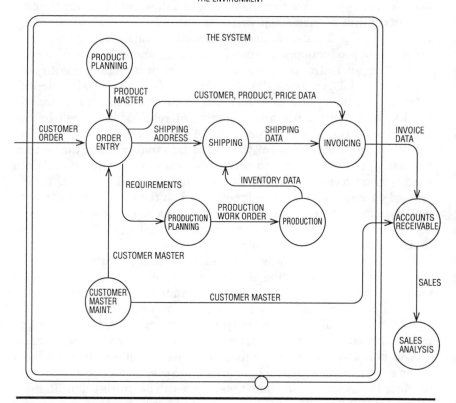

THE ENVIRONMENT

THE SYSTEM

Figure 3.3 The initial scope of the system is expanded to include related processes that share (use) the same data. Two functions, accounts receivable and sales analysis, are shown outside the scope of the new system. Including these functions within the boundaries of the development effort exceeds the Planning Horizon (the scope of the system that can be developed in a reasonable period, such as two years).

it refers to the boundaries of a business system developed to accomplish a business objective. It identifies the scope of the effort within which business processes are redesigned and data is organized so that it can be shared by the newly redesigned processes. Defining an enterprise is a judgment issue rather than an issue of the legal organization.

SCHEDULING

Once we have identified the limits of the task, we must look at how long the development of the system will take. How long is the system's time to market? Reducing time to market is a major management goal across all industries. Just as Ingersoll Rand had to accelerate product development, we need to speed up software development to meet market needs. As the business processes that Information Technology supports are integrated into a company's competitive strategy, business requirements will force us to find ways to speed up software development.

To reduce the time to market in software development, we need to examine our usual scheduling approach. Figure 3.4 illustrates the sequential scheduling approach typically followed in software development.

Using the sequential approach, the criteria for starting a given phase of the Life Cycle Process Model is the completion of the previous phase. This approach, however, has two major problems. First, there are no intermediate benefits to the systems effort. That is, users cannot take advantage of improvements during development. Second, there are no objective measures of accomplishment.

A primary advantage to a maintenance-oriented IS department is that short-term benefits are clearly visible. This certainly helps such departments survive in the corporate environment with its strong focus on the bottom line. So a switch to a design-driven approach gives the company the benefits of a business process redesign effort based on current information technology. At the same time, IS must continue delivering short-term benefits to maintain user and management support.

Sequential scheduling lacks qualitative measures to verify progress objectively until the system is finally completely installed. Breaking each life cycle phase into detailed tasks and then getting percentage completion reports for each task can be a measure of progress. The

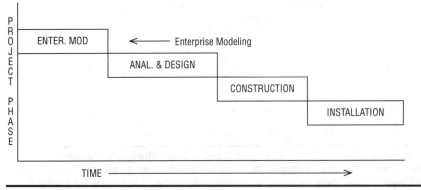

Figure 3.4 Sequential approach to scheduling. A specific phase in a development life cycle is not started until the previous phase has been completed.

problem is that a percentage completion report is a subjective measure of effort and does not include a quality evaluation. Progress reports for the first 95 percent of the project might state that everything is on schedule. When installation time comes, however, significant additional effort might be required.

The alternative to sequential scheduling is a concurrent development approach. Using this approach, life cycle phases overlap, and the overall system is broken down into subsystems that can be installed independently. Figure 3.5 illustrates this approach to scheduling.

Using this approach, we start to develop the Data Model for the first data categories without waiting for the completion of the Business Model, which identifies the scope and all the components of the system. And individual parts of the overall system are partitioned into subsystems without necessarily waiting for the completion of the Data Model. These individual subsystems are then carried through analysis, detailed design, construction, and installation as independent projects.

When the construction industry first used concurrent development, calling it *fast track construction,* they had the advantage that physical laws apply and everyone understands them. If someone suggests building the roof first, it is easy to point out that something extra would be necessary to hold it up. This acknowledgement of physical laws is called *structural dependency.* While structural dependency is not as readily apparent for information systems, it does exist and it is significant in planning for concurrent development.

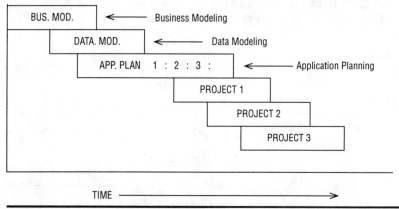

Figure 3.5 Concurrent approach to scheduling. A large software development effort is broken down into small subsystems, which are designed, programmed, and installed independently. A project covering a system can be initiated as soon as the relevant part of the Data Model has been completed.

The first step in defining the enterprise is to identify the stimulus for the business objective. In the example cited, the customer order is the stimulus for the business objective: Fill a customer order. The next step is accomplished during Business Modeling. You follow the stimulus through the various business processes until you have identified the major components. The product of this activity is a Data Flow Diagram (DFD). The generic category for this diagram is a *dependency diagram*. This term *dependency* is used because a DFD not only identifies the boundaries and the components of a system, it also shows the relationship of these components to each other. The diagram in Fig. 3.3 shows that the shipping process depends on information from the order entry and production processes.

This information dependency is the equivalent of physical dependency in the construction industry. It shows that without problems or wasted effort, you can build and install the order entry subsystem before building the shipping subsystem. But the reverse is not true.

If you build shipping first, temporary programs will be needed for entering information such as the shipping address, account information, and the like. Not only will these temporary programs eventually be discarded, but a shipping subsystem built first will probably also need significant redesign once the order entry and production subsystems are built. This redesign is necessary because the initial shipping programs that depend on independent data entry can be very different from the programs needed to extract the required information from a comprehensive database. For example, if the program is updating the status of an inventory lot record to indicate that the lot has been shipped, the processing is very different from capturing and storing the equivalent information using a stand alone procedure. These are examples of structural dependency and phase dependency, which we first discussed as scheduling constraints during the building of the house. Phase dependency is significant because we need to define the scope and boundaries of the system (the enterprise) as a prerequisite to defining the Data Model. In addition to phase dependency, the Business Model identifies the desired sequence for defining the parts of the Data Model and the structural dependencies that control the sequence in which business processes can be broken off into separate subsystems for independent development and installation.

The third type of dependency, discussed as part of the scheduling for the house, is task dependency within a life cycle phase. This dependency is typically not a significant problem in software development. Usually the same team is performing all tasks within the phase, so they can schedule these tasks in a rational way.

One major scheduling problem that frequently requires management intervention is the availability of users for the Joint Application
Design (JAD) sessions (which we will discuss in more detail in Chap.
4). Users will readily make a 50-hour commitment to participate in the
software development process. The scheduling problem arises from the
fact that the user typically prefers an hour a week for 50 weeks to a
contiguous set of eight hours per day of intensive involvement for a
short period. Since the software developers cannot proceed effectively
without the design specifications, an hour per week commitment from
the users could result in significant lost time. More important, the
developers might attempt to proceed by usurping the role of the user
and making their own decisions on the requirements and logical design
of the system.

CONTROLLING THE PROCESS

The preceding section touched lightly on the lack of qualitative measures of accomplishment with a traditional sequential scheduling approach. The suggested alternative is to divide the overall system into
small subsystems for development and installation. This partitioning
into smaller subsystems produces the significant measure of accomplishment at an early date: The user provides feedback that the new
software is doing the job or that changes are required.

The emphasis on installation and user acceptance as the only effective measure of completion is because of two major problems in software development and installation: the user's inability to define requirements and the organization's inability to manage change.

Peter DeGrace and Leslie Stahl, in their commentary on software
development, made the observations, "I think we are asking the wrong
question—. It should not be: How do we get complete requirements?
Rather it should be: Can we get complete requirements?" (7)

DeGrace and Stahl point out some reasons why we are lucky to get
90 percent of the most important requirements from users:

1. Customers often need intermediate results to make up their minds
   about what they really need in the first place.

2. People are not used to specifying things completely.

3. Customers are not entirely aware of what computing systems can do
   for them, and they see new requirements as soon as old ones are met.

4. Having computers in the environment affects the requirements.
   Until customers get the machines, they do not understand the
   computer's effect on their available work.

This inability to get complete requirements shows the first fallacy of most progress reporting schemes. Since we can't get complete requirements, attempts to measure and report progress based on the completion of tasks to automate these requirements is not very sound reasoning.

Another reason for moving from a sequential approach to concurrent development is the way change affects people. Change management is the most difficult aspect of business process redesign. Existing organizational structures are affected, and present skills are frequently made obsolete. While there is no magical solution, certainly the least disruptive approach is to implement change in small increments. Problems that arise, particularly people problems, can be isolated and dealt with on an individual basis when we implement change on an evolutionary rather than a revolutionary basis.

Incidentally, when we talk about the problems of determining requirements, the difficulties are typically in defining software processing requirements and the look and feel of the system, that is, the split of the business process between person and machine and the way that person interacts with the machine. Identifying and organizing the underlying data used by the enterprise is not the major problem. The underlying data of an organization tends to be very stable; the use of this data is the volatile element. Technology is also seldom the problem in developing new systems, although a poor understanding of technology can be disastrous. Very few projects fail for technical reasons since business software typically uses known technology. And if technical problems do arise, a solution is based on the ability to identify and isolate the problem so that technical assistance is effective.

Project planning is the point of the Life Cycle Process Model where the overall system is partitioned into independent subsystems for separate development and installation. When we do this partitioning, the first consideration is observing the structural dependencies identified on the DFD. The second consideration is ensuring that the subsystems identified are small enough to provide effective control. If a subsystem takes two years to analyze, design, and install, there is no progress reporting for the two years other than percent completion measurement. Thus we need to keep the following goals in mind when we start to partition the system.

- Allow qualitative progress reporting based on installation feedback.

- Allow an iterative development approach in which prototypes are developed and a working system is installed as quickly as possible, based on the initial definition of requirements.

- Provide the ability to evolve the first working version based on operational experience.

Breaking a total system into small projects based on a time standard and using this standard to control the course of a project is now being called *timebox management*. This approach was first pioneered at the Dupont Company as a way of gaining control over large projects. A time standard, such as three or four months, is used to partition a system into smaller projects. The goal then is to install a working version of the subsystem at the end of this time period.

If problems arise that interfere with achieving the goal of a working system at the end of the time period, the recommended solution is to cut back on the subsystem's functionality rather than expand the budget or time allowance. A new timebox can always be created to expand a subsystem's functionality, but lack of an initial working version delays gaining operational experience. Equally significant, it delays coming to grips with change management, frequently the most difficult part of the installation of any new business process.

RISK MANAGEMENT

If subsystems are to be installed in phases, a difficulty frequently arises because we are changing database structures that other systems still require. If we have observed structural dependencies and have already organized the complete data for the functional area, this problem is not significant. Bridge programs can be used to extract the needed information from the new database and to structure it according to the old file layouts. This is, however, an extra programming expense that might add 10 to 20 percent to the basic cost of the programming.

If we look at this expense from a risk management standpoint, this 10-to 20-percent additional cost is a good investment. If installation is done all at once at the end of the project, there is a major risk that at installation we will discover major problems, with the result that the system is not accepted. Studies have documented that major project failure is not an isolated incident and that it happens 15 to 20 percent of the time. Using game theory, we can evaluate the two alternatives of phased installation versus total installation at the end of the project. This evaluation is done using the following formula:

Cost = amount at risk x probability of incurring expense

To illustrate this evaluation, let's assume a $200,000 total project cost. A reasonable breakdown of this cost might be that programming represents 30 percent of the total project cost. Now assume a 20-percent increase in the programming cost in order to write bridge programs to support a phased installation. Also assume a 15-percent probability of failure of the whole project if we wait until the end of the complete project to start installation.

Using the formula, we can evaluate the two approaches as follows:

Option 1: Phased installation

Programming cost = \$200,000 x 30% = \$60,000

Amount at risk = \$60,000 x 20% = \$12,000

Probability of incurring expense = 100%

Cost = \$12,000 x 100% = \$12,000

Option 2: Total installation at end of project

Amount at risk = \$200,000 (total cost of project)

Probability of incurring expense = 15% (probability of incurring
expense because of the project failing)

Cost = \$200,000 x 15% = \$30,000

Thus prudent risk management tells us it is better to spend the \$12,000 for extra bridge programs than to run a 15-percent risk that the whole project might fail. For any one project, we might get lucky, but the laws of probability tell us that in the long run it is wise to take out insurance.

THE PARIETO PRINCIPLE

As DeGrace and Stahl point out, in defining requirements, we are lucky to get 90 percent of the most important requirements initially. The basic development approach we suggest is to focus on the initial requirements and then carry the project all the way through construction and installation. On an iterative basis, new timeboxes can be established to add to a system's functionality. Since we have traditionally attempted to get complete requirements, is this approach reasonable?

The *Parieto Principle,* more popularly known as the *80:20 rule,* states that a small proportion of the cause is responsible for a disproportionate portion of the results. This principle has had its greatest impact on manufacturing since it encourages a focus on the small number of processes that are responsible for the greatest number of defects.

This principle is also applicable to software development. As shown in Fig. 3.6, when we start to automate the various functions of a business process, automating 20 percent of the functionality will typically produce 80 percent of the benefits.

One example from my experience was developing an automatic pricing capability for order entry. As part of the functionality, we were asked to include the ability to handle a foreign currency. But because of the company's marketing focus, they only received ten foreign orders per year. This represented approximately 20 hours per year of manual exception processing. Automating this function would have added $10,000 (25 percent of the original) to the cost of the project but it would only have eliminated $400 per year of clerical effort. Contrast this saving of $400 with the primary objective of the project. Without dealing with foreign currencies, the basic system cost $40,000 and reduced clerical costs by $30,000 per year.

But when we initially focus on the primary 20 percent of the functionality of a business process that produces the greatest benefits, who is to decide what are the most important functionality? If the objective is to automate all the functionality of a business process, all we need to do is to discover it, the objective of the traditional requirements analysis. With an objective of cost effective automation, judgment is needed to identify the most important functions to be automated. This judgment can only be provided by the user, and to get it effectively, we need a new relationship and sense of participation. This new approach, *Joint Application Design* (JAD), is the subject of the next chapter.

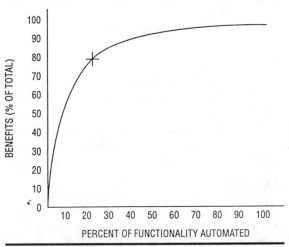

Figure 3.6 The Parieto Principle—automating the most critical 20 percent of the functionality of a business area provides 80 percent of the potential benefits of the automation effort.

REFERENCES

1. From a speech by Representative Newt Gingrich before the National Conference of State Legislatures, March 13, 1992.

2. Davenport and Short. "The New Industrial Engineering, Information Technology and Business Process Redesign," *Sloan Management Review*, Vol. 1, No. 4, Summer 1990.

3. Finklestein, Clive. *An Introduction to Information Engineering*. Addison-Wesley Publishing Co.: New York, 1989.

4. Martin, James. *Information Engineering, Book I. Prentice-Hall: Englewood Cliffs, N.J., 1989.*

5. Kerr, James M. *The IRM Imperative*. John Wiley & Sons, Inc.: New York, 1991.

6. Blanchard, Benjamin S. and Fabrycky, Wolter J. *Systems Engineering and Analysis*, 2nd ed. Prentice-Hall: Englewood Cliffs, N.J.

7. DeGrace, Peter and Stahl, Leslie Hulet. *Wicked Problems, Righteous Solution.*, Yourdon Press, Prentice-Hall: Englewood Cliffs, N.J., 1990.

4

Joint Application Design

In the house-building example, one of the homeowners' first requirements was that their daughter's bedroom be painted blue. The architect reacted to this request by explaining that the initial task was to
design the house's basic structure. Specifying a feature such as a
bedroom color should be deferred. After the house was built and just
before the room was to be painted, the daughter could select the color.
Now, whether the architect had heard of Just-In-Time planning or
whether his own experience made him aware of the volatility of teenage
fads, his suggestion was very sensible. The architect could have used
alternative approaches, however. Of course, he could have picked the
color himself and then asked whether the daughter liked the result.
On the other hand, at the beginning of the project, he could have spent
a great deal of time documenting all requirements in detail. The results
might have been a 200-page text specification of all the details. Page
one hundred might have identified the bedroom color. Then he could
have said that the responsibility to find the relevant page in order to
verify the color and make any changes was the daughter's. Certainly
the architect would have been justified in saying he had done his job

thoroughly, particularly if the homeowner had signed off on the specification.

Do the architect's two alternatives sound unworkable? If so, then perhaps we should look at the way we build complex software systems since we frequently rely on these two approaches. In some instances we make decisions on our own and then show the results to the user after the fact for verification. Some formal software development methodologies rely on elaborate text documentation prepared in advance that is difficult for the user to understand. As an illustration of the latter approach, listen to a story a friend recently told me. He described a problem his wife was having at work. She was given a two-inch-thick binder of specifications for a new software system that would probably change almost every function in her department. Since the IS department was under great pressure to start constructing the new system as soon as possible, the wife was asked to write up her comments and sign off on the system within two weeks. The specifications were complex, and she had not been trained in data processing. So she took a very straightforward approach: She signed off on the document without really understanding it. She justified not reading the specs with the idea that software could easily be changed later if it didn't work.

Returning to the story of the hypothetical house helps us focus on the next issue: identifying a new planning process that effectively brings together the IS professional's design and technical skills and the user's business process knowledge. IS traditionally relies on one-on-one or group interviews to collect data from users. Then, the design effort occurs off in a corner. This is not the approach we want. No doubt the traditional interview works satisfactorily if the automation target is an isolated process: such as a new payroll calculation or a specific report from an existing database. But if the objective is business process redesign, the fundamental redesign of the tasks required to accomplish a business objective (such as, process a customer order), a new partnership between user and designer is required. The traditional over-the-wall relationship between user and designer does not permit the fundamental redesign of business processes. And even if it did, the probability of the user accepting significant change without being a part of the planning is very small.

The alternative to the traditional approach to relationships between users and designers is team development. Instead of individuals with various areas of expertise and perspectives participating sequentially (and frequently as adversaries), people can come together at the same time to solve a problem, design a product, and so on. This approach has gained support in product design, where engineering, sales, manufacturing, accounting, and the like, come together in a team to design a new product.

JAD OVERVIEW

The techniques of team development have been formalized for IS professionals in a methodology known as JAD. (1) The basic idea of JAD is to select key end users and conduct workshops that progress through structured steps for planning and designing a system. (2) Participants are shut away in a workshop knowing they have a given task to accomplish by a given time, within the framework of a given agenda. JAD recognizes that users cannot design complex procedures without professional help. By the same token, IS professionals have trouble understanding the details of user requirements. Traditional methods of interviewing users and writing text specifications have proved inadequate. Fundamental changes in business processes require active user participation to gain acceptance of the software product. And if development resources are limited, the user must work to reconcile wants and needs.

IBM initially developed JAD as a methodology in Canada in 1977. Currently it is an IBM-sponsored methodology and a GUIDE (IBM users group) project, and it is being incorporated into several general methodologies such as James Martin's RAD (TM)—Rapid Application Development.

The basic tenants of JAD are:

1. Group dynamics to tackle a problem.

2. Visual aids to make a design tangible.

3. An organized, rational (top-down) process that relies on Just-In-Time planning to solve problems.

4. A WYSISWYG (what-you-see-is-what-you-get) documentation.

The JAD methodology described in this chapter is based on the availability of both upper and lower CASE tools:

- An upper CASE tool to automate the preparation of the graphic diagrams

- A lower CASE tool (a code generator or a fourth-generation language—4GL) to reduce program construction time and to facilitate an evolutionary approach to development.

An alternative to an upper CASE tool would be to use a plastic template to manually prepare the diagrams suggested later in this chapter. However, a satisfactory upper CASE tool to automate the preparation of these diagrams can be purchased for less than $1000. At such prices, it seems worthwhile to invest in a tool that can help prevent lost time. A great deal can be lost, for example, if JAD sessions rely on white boards since documentation will not be as clear and must be reworked after the development session is completed.

A lower CASE tool is an important enabler for an evolutionary development approach which is incorporated into the JAD methodology. Functionality can be added to the programs without producing the spaghetti code that makes future maintenance expensive. Lower CASE tools also typically include a prototyping capability that makes prototypes a very practical means of testing the look and feel of the system. Perhaps even more important, a lower CASE tool reduces the labor intensity of the construction process, bringing the user's specification effort and the benefits from installation closer together in time. The alternative to a lower CASE tool is to continue using a 3GL, such as RPG. If the 3GL is used, structured programming methods should be strongly emphasized to avoid the deterioration of the program structure that will create future maintenance problems.

To gain understanding of a JAD methodology, we need to look at objectives, participants and their roles, preparation for JAD, the JAD session, and deliverables and documentation.

JAD OBJECTIVES

The objective of JAD is to develop and obtain approval for a design and a development plan for a new system. This objective is achieved through the preparation of external design documents and a formal systems development plan.

The external design documents (the user's view) identify the scope and components of the proposed system, the data model, the look and feel of the system (to include screen and report formats), edit and business rules, and the like. The systems development plan includes project breakouts, schedule and staffing commitments, project milestones, equipment requirements, and other factors. WYSIWYG documentation must be complete and coherent enough to serve as the absolute control over physical construction and should not be departed from without going back through the JAD process for approval.

The identification of the JAD participants and the outlined set of tasks which we will discuss departs significantly from traditional JAD concepts. Design strategies of Information Engineering and Object Oriented Design are a significant change from the process orientation of early JAD methodology writeups. Specifics of the design and construction tools require technical support in order to establish a coherent development approach. Knowledge of available software components that can be purchased from vendors affect the economics of design options that are considered. In addition, much of business process reengineering is based on new Information Technology such as telecommunications, bar coding, electronic data interchange, and so on. As a consequence, an understanding of the enabling features of this new technology and planning for its use is an important part of the discussions in the JAD environment.

JAD PARTICIPANTS

A number of key roles must be filled to make the process of group development work. These roles are executive sponsor, user representatives (management and operating), session leader, analyst(s), IS representative, and scribe (CASE tool specialist). In some companies, the same individual might fill several roles.

The *executive sponsor,* who exercises ultimate responsibility and authority over the functional areas that the new system is to address, has responsibilities similar to the homeowners'. These responsibilities for a systems project include:

1. Leading the strategic planning effort that identifies the goals and objectives of the systems development effort.

2. Identifying and empowering user participants in the JAD sessions.

3. Imparting strategic insights to guide the development process.

4. Making decisions and commitments that are consistent with the organization's objectives.

5. Approving the JAD outputs.

Perhaps more critical than these specific duties, the executive sponsor must create the environment that permits business processes to be redesigned without regard to organizational boundaries. This environment includes a total quality emphasis, a focus on wants rather than needs, timebox management, and the users' early ownership of the system and corresponding responsibility for the success of the effort. These philosophies can be a significant departure from the existing company culture. And they typically involve change even before the point of installing the new system. The successful management of this change will determine the success of the attempt to benefit from advances in Information Technology.

The *user representatives* are the focus of the JAD workshop sessions. Their role is to examine the organization's information needs and to participate in preparing the external design (the user's view) and the system development plan for the proposed system. Both user management and users need to participate. Typically, senior user management first participates in the strategic planning to finalize the goals and objectives. Senior user management then identifies the business processes required to accomplish the business goals and objectives that are the focus of the development effort. This initial activity results in both a formal statement of project objectives and a Business Model that establish the proposed system's scope, major components, and structural dependencies of these components.

Senior user management then identifies the participants in the database design. The final role of senior user management is to participate in creating the development plan for the system. This planning activity uses the Business Model, which identifies the major components and structural dependencies, in order to partition the overall system into specific projects for detailed design and construction. As part of this task, it is necessary to identify the needed participants for the follow-up detailed design sessions that will be a part of each project.

Both user management and knowledgeable users then design each required subsystem as an individual project. This detailed design includes a review of the appropriate parts of the Data Model and the decomposition of the major processes in the Business Model that are part of the subsystem under development. It also includes a review of business and edit rules and the design of screen and report layouts.

The *session leader* fills many roles. The most important role is to help prepare for and then lead the JAD sessions through an organized, rational process for problem solving. This involves guiding the sessions through a top-down (from general requirements to specific solutions) series of tasks that emphasize Just-In-Time planning. The session leader also works with the executive sponsor to identify the JAD participants, prepares the agenda and the material for the sessions, and formalizes the JAD documents that record the results of a session.

The session leader is responsible for identifying and resolving *issues* and *considerations*. These terms have a formal meaning in the JAD methodology. An *issue* pertains to the session scope but cannot be resolved by the participants because they lack either the information or the authority. A *consideration* arises during a session but is outside the scope of the current session.

The most important role of the session leader is to harness the process of group dynamics to obtain the full contribution from each session participant. The session leader must lead the transition from a collection of individuals with personal interests and perspectives into a group that is effective in solving a shared problem. This involves establishing a sense of identity and common purpose and stimulating the interaction among the members of the group. The goal is for each member to contribute as much as possible and to reach a consensus.

The *analyst* assists the session leader in preparing the initial JAD documents and in formalizing the JAD deliverables that result from the sessions. The analyst is also responsible for producing prototypes and then serving as the lead person in the post-JAD construction activities.

In addition, the analyst investigates current systems that are within the proposed system's business process scope. This review identifies existing data files that will be redesigned as part of the new system. Once these old files are identified, the analyst prepares a conversion plan to reformat any data that needs to be saved. The analyst also prepares the specifications for any bridge programs needed to maintain data in old formats. An example of this conversion and bridging is a customer master. Data from an old file might need to be converted into a new file format used by order entry. Future customer additions or changes must also be brought to the old files since the old formats are still used by accounts receivable.

The *IS representative* provides strategic guidance and advice during the JAD sessions. This guidance is both technical and architectural. Technical guidance keeps the external design within the bounds of realistic solutions and optimizes the use of available technology and IS personnel and equipment resources. Architectural guidance ensures that system boundaries do not conflict with other project boundaries and that individual systems are consistent with long-term corporate information strategies.

The *CASE tool specialist* acts as scribe or secretary. This technician is skilled in using the upper CASE tool used to document the external design. When the JAD methodology was first developed in the late 1970s, the JAD deliverables were necessarily text-oriented documentation and a manually prepared flow chart known as a work flow diagram. Paperwork was circulated to the participants in advance, notes were taken of discussions, and copies of any diagrams prepared during the sessions were made.

Since the advent of Structured Analysis and Design, new graphic techniques, namely the Data Flow Diagram, Entity Relationship Diagram, Structure Charts, have replaced the work flow diagram. With the availability of PC-based upper CASE tools that automate the preparation of these diagrams and the use of a display panel, system diagrams can be displayed during a session and used as the basic working documents. A technician skilled in the use of the upper CASE tool can usually keep up with the JAD discussions and immediately update the diagrams or the database definition. Updated printouts of this documentation can then be available for confirmation before the participants leave the session.

Another critical role for the CASE tool specialist is to serve as the equivalent of a manufacturing engineer for the project. In industries such as automobiles and machine tools, the manufacturing engineer has several roles:

- Ensuring that the product as designed can actually be built based on the machine tools and other technology available.

- Ensuring that, from the perspective of the manufacturing process, the design specifications provide the detail to determine how to accomplish production.

- Incorporating standard internal components and commercially available parts into the design when this will reduce manufacturing costs.

A great deal of theoretical discussion about software reuse is occurring in IS. If reuse is to occur, it must be planned for during design rather than be left to programmers during construction. In addition, many lower CASE tool vendors are now providing software chips and program templates that can significantly reduce programming time and expense. The CASE tool specialist should be aware of these options and assist the design process in making the best use of internal and vendor-supplied components. Even if a lower CASE tool is not being used, the CASE tool specialist should still evaluate process designs to determine whether a routine is a candidate for reuse and should be programmed as a reusable module or subroutine.

PREPARING FOR JAD

The JAD sessions address two phases of the total application development life cycle: enterprise modeling and analysis and design. During these two phases, the external design documents are prepared. JAD also addresses part of the construction phase since it includes the verification of these designs through the use of prototypes.

For the results of JAD to be smoothly integrated into the total development process, session activities and deliverables should be customized to conform to the methods and tools available for analysis, design, and construction. The customization process starts by formalizing the life cycle, which identifies the major phases of software development. The major phases of the life cycle are then broken down into an ordered set of tasks (a methodology), some of which are to be accomplished through JAD. Once tasks are agreed to, methods must be established for accomplishing the tasks and notations agreed to for organizing and expressing ideas.

An example of this process is to identify a *task* such as "define and bound the system scope." A notation to express this scope bounding might be a data flow diagram. The *method* might specify that a one-page top-level diagram called a *context diagram* should identify external sources and dispositions of data and the actual data that flows to and from these external agents. The method might then specify that this initial diagram is to be decomposed into an essential functions diagram that identifies the major processes in the proposed system and the linkage of these processes to the data flows identified on the first level diagram.

The executive sponsor and the session leader organize the JAD team. An initial identification of the development effort's scope is used to identify user management and users who can contribute to the proposed effort. For example, once you determine what related departments, such as auditing and finance, are affected, you can assign individuals from both user and support departments.

Typically a cross-section group such as this has a varied skill set, so once the group is identified, an orientation is necessary. This orientation should cover:

Proposed objectives and constraints.

Proposed scope of the effort.

Concepts of information engineering.

The software development life cycle.

Process managements concepts such as:

Software triage.

Concurrent scheduling.

Structural dependencies.

Timebox management.

The Parieto Principle.

Concepts of data modeling.

Tasks, methods, and notations.

You can start with an initial overview. But when it comes to specifics, a Just-In-Time approach is suggested for explaining the concepts of data modeling and the tasks, methods, and notations to be used. If too much detail is presented initially, the users might be overwhelmed with new information whose relevancy to the task is not apparent. For this reason, it is best to deal with the details of the new information technology as they are needed. For example, a full understanding of data flow diagrams is needed for the business modeling. Action diagrams document a process's detail logic at a much later phase.

The session leader and the analyst prepare the material for a session. Using an upper CASE tool, material for the business modeling session might include the first several levels of a Data Flow Diagram. These diagrams provide a first cut at defining the boundaries, processes, and data for the proposed system. In subsequent sessions for defining the Data Model, prepared session material might include files from existing systems or fields from manual forms. These data elements might be preloaded into a reengineering tool (if available) to help define the details of the new Data Model.

THE JAD SESSION

The process of determining requirements and creating the external design occurs during the JAD sessions. Specific tasks to be accomplished during the sessions represent a subset of the total development methodology. Following is a suggested set of activities that elaborate on the Life Cycle Process Model discussed in Chap. 2. The uppercase items represent the life cycle phase or subphase; lowercase items represent the JAD tasks.

A. *Business Modeling*
1. Identify high-level goals, problems, critical success factors.

2. Define and bound the system scope (using the context-level Data Flow Diagram).

3. Identify system characteristics and requirements.

4. Expand the scope definition to identify major processes and data categories (using the essential-functions-level DFD).

5. Plan the JAD design activities (overall schedules, staffing levels, cost and benefit projections, and milestones).

6. Publish and obtain approval of the JAD planning documents from both the JAD participants and the executive sponsor.

B. Data Modeling

1. Using the general data types, such as *customer*, identified in the Business Model plan the design of the proposed database by specifying entities (files) and entity relationships (Entity Relationship Diagram).

2. Identify attributes (fields), derived fields, and so on, and organize the attributes by entity (file) according to the relational database rules for normalization.

   Note: Traditional software development strategies such as Structured Design and Information Engineering take a minimalist view of the definition of data. This means that during data modeling, the data definition only consists of such basics as the size of a field, type, and so on. The data modeling approach described in Chap. 10 incorporates an Object Oriented Design strategy. As a consequence, the data modeling phase is used not only to develop basic data descriptions, but also to document methods that operate on the data. In particular, it is suggested that the business rules and methods for editing the data should be established as part of this phase.

3. Publish and obtain approval for the JAD Data Model from the JAD participants.

C. Project Planning

1. Partition the overall system into projects (timeboxes) for detailed analysis, design, and construction.

2. Identify interfaces to related projects and existing systems.

3. Establish staffing for both the remaining JAD design activities and the construction phase to follow.

4. Establish schedules, budgets, milestones for each project.

5. Publish and obtain approval for the individual project plans from both the JAD participants and from IS since it represents a commitment of IS resources.

D. Process Modeling

1. Decompose high-level processes identified during the business modeling phase. This decomposition continues to an elementary process level where activities meaningful to the user (eventually represented as menu items) are identified.

2. Document additional processing logic and business rules for each elemental process identified in step one.

Note: In addition to text, a variety of documentation techniques is available. A partial list includes action diagrams, decision tables, and decision trees. For further information on this subject, see Chap. 12.

3. Verify the Data Model prepared during the *data modeling* phase. Determine any changes or additional editing rules.

Note: Any changes in the Data Model during detailed process modeling must be reviewed and approved before incorporation into the design. This typically involves reconvening the original JAD group that designed the Data Model. It is important to establish a policy that the database design does not belong to the individual projects and must be controlled and coordinated on an IS departmental level. Otherwise, individual development projects might go off on their own and the pieces of the system developed individually might not fit together.

4. Prepare program Structure Charts for any complex processes identified in step one.

E. Prototyping

1. Based on the Process Model prepared in phase D and the Data Model prepared in phase B, prepare and finalize screen and report formats.

2. Review processing logic and program structures in order to establish final specifications for the construction phase.

The JAD sessions are an iterative process, during which material originally prepared by the session leader is refined into a working system. The use of diagrams and prototypes that can be updated during the sessions provides the intermediate results the users need to make up their minds about the design and impact of the proposed system. And the users are key players in the decision if technical or resource constraints require compromises in the design of the proposed system.

DELIVERABLES AND DOCUMENTATION

When JAD was first evolving in 1977, structured techniques for analysis and design were in their infancy, CASE tools had not yet been developed, and relational database software and data-driven design were still in the future.

As a consequence, much of the JAD literature includes homespun documentation techniques (such as a work flow diagram) and relies on obsolete session techniques such as drawing diagrams on a blackboard and recording the results for later formalization).

With PC-based upper CASE tools and display panels that can project a PC monitor to an entire room, much of the documentation work of a JAD session can be automated. A technician skilled in the use of the upper CASE tool can typically keep up with the JAD discussions and produce intermediate and final results during the sessions. In addition, reengineering concepts and tools facilitate preloading data elements from existing files or forms so the JAD session can focus on creating a logical database design rather than on the initial discovery of attributes (data fields). In addition, lower CASE code generators with a prototyping facility mean that the screen and report formats formalized in the JAD sessions can be quickly evolved into a working program.

Because such tools are available, a JAD group development approach should use formal structured analysis and design techniques during the sessions. And with the availability of inexpensive PC-based upper CASE tools, even the smallest project can afford to automate the production of the diagrams for structured techniques. These diagrams include the following:

Data Flow Diagram: Establishes the scope of a system by identifying its components: processes and data.

Entity Relationship Diagram: Provides an architectural overview of the logical Data Model by identifying major data groupings (entities or files) and the relationship between these entities.

Program Structure Chart: Shows the structure of a complex elementary process by using a tree or hierarchical diagram to identify the tasks and the relationship among these tasks.

Action Diagram: Shows the details of any complex logic performed in the tasks identified on a program Structure Chart.

These diagrams document the accomplishment of each task and are prerequisite for starting the next task. For example, Fig. 4.1 shows the diagrams produced during the enterprise modeling phase.

The Data Flow Diagram, the first diagram produced, identifies on a high level the data the proposed system needs. This initial identification is the starting point for the data modeling phase. The first step in this phase is to take a high-level identification, such as *Customer*, and identify logical components or entities. These high-level logical entities

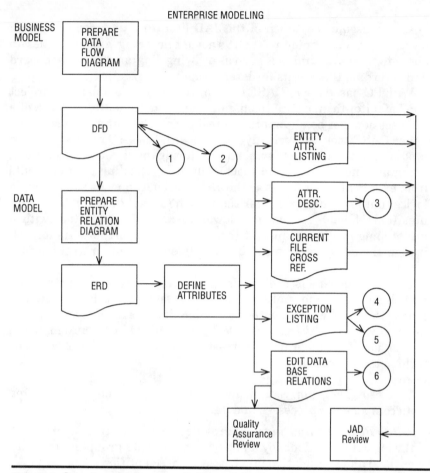

Figure 4.1 Overview of the major activities and the documents produced during the Enterprise Modeling phase of software development.

will eventually be physically implemented as files. For example, in a distribution application, *Customer* might be structured as Bill-To and Ship-To entities.

These entities are then documented on the Entity Relationship Diagram (ERD). The ERD is the starting point for the next task, attribute definition. Figure 4.2 shows the major processes and the diagrams produced during the analysis and design phase.

The DFD from the prior phase is first used to partition the system into small projects for detailed design and construction (timebox planning). The DFD is absolutely critical for this planning activity since it

APPLICATION ANALYSIS AND DESIGN

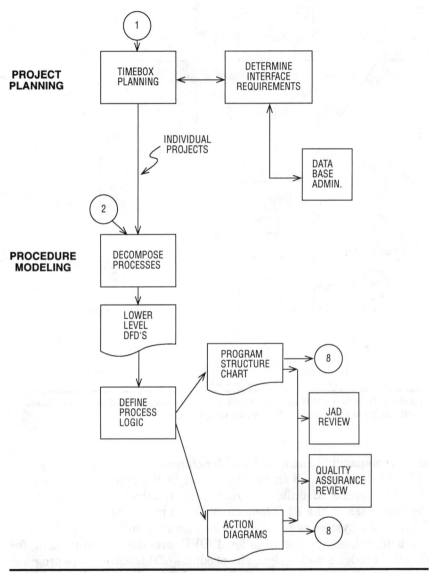

Figure 4.2 Overview of the major activities and the documents produced during the
Analysis and Design phase of software development.

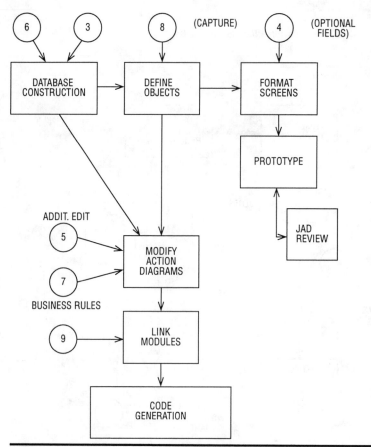

Figure 4.3 Overview of the linkage of various documents produced in earlier phases to specific steps in the contruction (programming) phase.

shows components and structural dependencies. When a major system is being developed, IS frequently is put in the same position as the architect asked to build the roof first. Illustrating the structural dependencies on the DFD helps avoid such problems.

Once the system is partitioned into smaller subsystems, the processes identified on the high-level DFD are the starting point for detailed analysis and design. The products of this activity are program Structure Charts and action diagrams that explain the detailed logic of the individual processes. Figure 4.3 shows the linkage of the Data Model definition and the process logic diagrams to various phases of construction.

In identifying these diagram linkages, it is important to remember that the approaches to construction vary significantly from one lower CASE tool to the next. As a consequence, the methods for preparing the diagrams vary significantly.

To gain a perspective on how construction techniques can influence the design process, let's return to the house example. It is possible to buy standard structural panels for a new house. An alternative to traditional stick-built construction, structural panels are simply dropped into place. These panels make it unnecessary for the architect to prepare part of the traditional detailed plans. Instead just the standard component is specified and the manufacturer's plans are used for the details.

Analogously, lower CASE tool vendors now provide software chips and program templates that can be customized and assembled to meet logical processing requirements. As a consequence, the design process should be customized to fit the construction environment, and the detailed design plans should recognize the degree to which software components can be used. We will discuss this problem in more detail in the next section of the book when we deal with the methods for accomplishing the specific tasks in the JAD methodology.

A PERSPECTIVE ON JAD

In his acceptance speech on winning the Malcolm Baldridge award for quality, John Grettenberger, general manager of Cadillac, identified the winning factor: Cadillac's emphasis on designing quality in from the start, rather than inspecting in or adding in quality later. A key technique for this accomplishment was getting together everyone with expertise as soon as the first working drawings for a new product were developed. GM management's emphasis on total quality means people are organized and empowered, and quality is the goal.

In light of GM's recent history, this approach is a radical departure. GM's former approach was based on the assumption that people caused quality problems, and $80 billion was invested in robots and other new tooling to replace people. This approach did not work, and Cadillac's recent award was based on recognition that people are the solution, not the problem. New approaches, including group development for product design and emphasis on doing things right the first time, resulted in the award.

Applying to software development the lessons learned throughout the manufacturing segment of our economy shows that consumer acceptance, which is the goal of total quality, cannot be obtained only through new methods and tools, such as structured analysis and design and CASE tools. Rather, these advances are enablers, and improved approaches to the people processes of developing systems are necessary to solve quality problems.

REFERENCES

1. August, Judy. *Joint Application Design.* Yourdon Press, Prentice-Hall: Englewood Cliffs, N.J., 1991.

2. Martin, James. *Rapid Application Development.* MacMillan: New York, 1991.

3. Ruud, Dennis. "JAD: A Better Way to Design Systems," *Information Management,* August 1991.

4. Porter, John. "Systems Development and CASE Tool Integration," *NEWS 3X/400,* April 1991.

Tips for Stimulating User Participation

1. Since the motivation level of users is typically based on management's interest level and management tends to be motivated by money, I typically initiate a discussion with management on the costs of traditional development approaches. Quantifying the cost of not doing it right the first time for a large project, say with a budget of $200,000, gives us dollar figures to use in discussions with management:

   a. *Cost of Failure:* large projects typically run a 15- to 20-percent risk of failure (never being installed). Using game theory to quantify this risk gives us the following: 15 percent x $200,000 = $30,000

   b. *Cost of Rework:* Assuming that the system is eventually installed, experience indicates that 20 to 50 percent of the system development cost will be spent on rework to make the system acceptable to the user. Quantifying this cost gives us: 40 percent x $200,000 = $80,000

2. An accepted definition of quality is *fitness for use* (J. M. Juran). I use his definition as the theme for an exercise by the users to evaluate information they receive from current systems. This invariably results in a full-participation session.

3. The goals for a project can vary significantly based on each user's level in the organization. Start the JAD exercise with a clean slate by having the group determine its goals before any attempt is made to reconcile them with senior management's objectives. This stimulates a sense of empowerment, which is needed for the group to succeed.

Software Development Overview

Chapter 2 suggested a Life Cycle Process Model that identified the major phases of software development. The chapter on JAD then decomposed the planning, analysis, and design phases into more specific tasks and deliverables for developing a software design. The next step is to discuss methods and notations for accomplishing each of the tasks identified as part of our JAD methodology. A *method* is the way to accomplish a task. A *notation* expresses the solution reached using a method.

The objective of both methods and notations is to design a software system fit for use. The chapters in this section discuss in detail the methods and notations appropriate for the development and expression of a software design.

Another example from outside software design can illustrate the significance of design for any complex product. General Motors lags behind its competitors in almost every measure of efficiency. In terms of how many workers it takes to assemble a car, GM is approximately 40 percent less productive than Ford. (1)

A study designed to explain this productivity gap compared GM's assembly plant at Fairfax, Kansas to Ford's assembly plant near Atlanta. (2) The study suggested that 48 percent of the productivity gap was due to plant practices: people and management issues such as the ones discussed in the first four chapters. To GM's surprise, 41 percent of the productivity gap was due to differences in the manufacturability of the GM and Ford designs.

For example, Ford's front bumper consists of only ten parts, whereas GM's totals 100. Also, the Ford parts fit together more easily than GM's. In addition, the study showed that the level of automation—much higher in the GM plant—did not resolve the productivity gap. This shows that the results produced by two technically capable design organizations can differ radically when they are evaluated with a quality criterion—fitness for use. In this instance, fitness for use applies not only to fitness for the consumer but also to fitness for the next step in the production process.

The moral of the story is that a software design that focuses only on the needs of the end user will be deficient. Software design must address manufacturability (programming) and maintenance (future enhancement and modification). In software design, programming and ease of upgrading are based largely on the design of the system's database. Data modeling identifies and organizes the data the system needs into a logical structure that improves the individual programs' access to information.

From the beginning, computer science has put great theoretical effort into discovering the most efficient manner of storing data in files and retrieving the data. Researchers pursued two objectives. The first was to develop system software called database management systems (DBMS) that relieved the programmer of the housekeeping tasks of managing files. The second was to establish concepts that identified how to design files. For the AS/400 developer, the system software research led to a relational database management system (RDBMS) that is a basic part of the AS/400 operating system. The second led to the concepts of relational database theory which provides a theoretical basis for designing databases.

The first step in developing a formal design approach to software development is to understand the basic concepts of relational database design and normalization rules, that is, empirical rules for organizing data. (Chapter 6 will discuss both issues.) These concepts help determine whether the files which are part of an old system should be redesigned for use by a new system. The basic criteria for this evaluation is the same as in the Ford/GM example. Is the basic functionality which is the objective of the design provided by ten parts, or does the design incorporate 100 parts, many of which could be eliminated. In the AS/400 arena, file designs are frequently based on system software and concepts that originate in the days of the S/34 and S/36. Updating these old database designs to eliminate unneeded parts becomes a critical factor in improving software development and maintenance productivity.

The other chapters in this section discuss methods and notations which bring a structured or engineering approach to software development. Three software design strategies serve as the basis for the methods and notations which are discussed in these chapters.

Structured Design provides the conceptual basis for the discussion of the graphics used to define the scope of a system which is to be developed and a high level identification of the components of the proposed system. The approaches suggested are based on the work of Ed Yourdon, Chris Gane, Tom DeMarco, and others in the late 1970s and early 1980s. Their methods were first formalized under the generic term, structured systems engineering (SSE). (3) (Chapter 7 will discuss methods and notations developed as part of Structured Design.) Early proprietary methodologies based on these methods were STRADIS (structured analysis design and implementation of information systems) marketed by McDonald Douglas and LSDM (LBMS structured development methodology) marketed by Learmonth, Burchett Management Systems.

Information Engineering represents a departure from the process orientation of these early methodologies. Theoretical advances and pragmatic insights have resulted in the abandonment of this process orientation in favor of a focus on data as the structural foundation for a software system. So once the scope of a system is established and the major components identified using the methods and notations of Structured Design, the emphasis changes from the process orientation of Structured Design to the data orientation of Information Engineering. With this change of emphasis, the issue becomes one of developing a structure for the data—a database design. Graphic techniques to provide a high level view of the database design, specifically the Entity Relationship Diagram, which were first popularized as an Information Engineering design notation, are discussed in Chap. 8.

Object Oriented Design is the newest design strategy which is emerging as a guide for software design. It suggests a different approach to the organization and documentation of business rules and process descriptions, and provides a new approach to designing the structural solution for complex business processes. In Chap. 9, we will examine the concepts of Object Oriented Design (OOD), and contrast them with the earlier principles of Structured Design. In Chap. 10, basic ideas from OOD are then incorporated into a method for establishing the details of a database design. The final two chapters in this section are devoted to methods and notations for designing solutions for complex business processes, and for documenting complex processing logic.

For the sake of a coherent design approach, methods and design detail deliverables which are discussed in this section should be customized once tools are decided upon. Because of the diversity of lower CASE tools, design coherence is a very complex issue. For example, consider editing an account number defined as a field in an order header. The account number is a foreign key and identifies the customer master record related to this order.To ensure that the account number represents a valid customer when an order is entered into the system, several lower CASE tools automatically generate referential integrity validation code and make account number validation an unnecessary procedural specification. In other tools and in 3GLs, however, this validation positively must be included in the program code. Otherwise, it is left to the discretion of the programmer whether an edit check is performed.

REFERENCES

1. "Can GM Remodel Itself?" *Fortune,* January 31, 1992, p. 26.

2. Womack, James. Jones, Daniel. and Roos, Daniel. *The Machine That Changed the World, The MIT International Motor Vehicle Program.* Harper Collins: New York, 1990. pp. 96-97.

3. Gane, Chris. M *Computer-Aided Software Engineering.* Prentice-Hall: Englewood Cliffs, N.J., 1990.

4. Martin, James. *Rapid Application Development.* MacMillan Publishing Co.: New York, 1991.

Relational Database Concepts

ORIGIN OF THE RELATIONAL DATABASE

Relational Database Management Systems (RDBMS) were developed to permit data to be stored in a manner which allows for easy data retrieval, while at the same time avoiding the redundant storage of information. Relational databases are based on the concept of relations, which are expressed as *tables*. RDBMSs implement these tables as flat (conventional) files. The benefits of RDBMSs come with the use of keys. With keys, an RDBMS can combine individual tables to produce very complex and sophisticated views of the data. In 1970, IBM's Edgar F. Codd published "A Relational Model of Data for Large Shared Data Banks." (1) This paper provides the conceptual underpinnings for RDBMSs and the theoretical foundation for the database management system underlying the AS/400 operating system. (2) Within the framework of set theory and first order logic, Codd suggested organizing data into individual *tables* (also called entity types, entities, or files) made up of rows and columns as shown in Fig. 6.1.

A *row* (also called an entity occurrence or a record) represents a relationship among a table's *columns*. Each column (also called an

Order Header
Columns

Customer #	Name	Address	Status	Terms

R
o
w
s

Figure 6.1   The basic table format that is used in the design of a relational database.

attribute or a field) represents a fact for that row. In each table, one column uniquely identifies the row and is called the *primary key*. If a column represents a primary key in another table, it is called a *foreign key*. This foreign key establishes a relationship between the facts in the row of one table and the facts for a specific row in another.

As you realize from the brief discussion above, several distinct sets of terms have evolved when relational database concepts and designs are discussed. The first set of terms is used by the mathematical *theorists,* and includes such terms as table and tuple. Database designers have evolved a different set of terms, primarily to distinguish a *logical* structure for the data in an organization from the physical structure of the implemented design which considers the hardware such as a computer disk drive or a tape file. The third terminology set is used by the programmer (construction professional), and includes terms associated with *physical* implementation such as file, record, and field. Figure 6.2 lists the terms commonly used in relational database (RDB) theory and their equivalents in logical database (LDB) and physical database design (PDB).

The following terms are relevant for us since they are typically used by an upper CASE tool to express the logical design of database, and by the lower CASE or 3GL programmers when the physical database is being implemented.

Entity	implemented as a	File
Entity Occurrence	implemented as a	Record
Attribute	implemented as a	Field

Relational database	Logical database	Physical database	Description	Example
Relation or table	Entity type	File	A table with rows and columns	Customer
Tuple	Entity, occurrence, row	Record	A row from one of the tables	John Smith's data
Column or attribute	Attribute (a property of an entity)	Field	A column from one of the tables	Tel. #
Candidate key	Candidate key	Field	An attribute (or set of attributes) that uniquely identify each entity of tuple (usually one candidate key exists)	Account #
Primary key	Primary key	Key field(s)	Where only one candidate key exists, it is the primary key. Where more than one key exists, it is the most important key.	Account #
Alternate key	Alternate key	Alternate key field	Where more than one candidate key exists, those that are not primary are alternate.	Last name
Relationship link	Foreign key	Foreign key field	An attribute (or set of attributes) in one relation that forms a candidate key in another relation.	State code

Figure 6.2 Equivalent terms used by mathematicians, software designers, and programmers when a relational database is being discussed.

Using these terms, each occurrence of an entity describes a particular set of facts. An attribute describes one fact for an entity. The table format of relational theory with its unique definition of each column (attribute or field) is a departure from the design approach used in many early computer systems. In the early systems, a file stored on a device such as a tape drive would frequently contain multiple record formats so that the processing was simplified. Programs were written to check a code field at the beginning of a record to identify the format of the specific record that was being processed. The basic file format was then internally redefined within the program to properly identify the fields in the record being processed. Newer systems such as the AS/400 with its object oriented file definition strategy have abandoned such file design practices. The goal of the new object strategy is to permit the definition of a database design which is independent of the logic defined within the internals of a specific program.

DOMAIN INTEGRITY

As we just briefly discussed, relational database design theory specifically provides that each column (attribute or field) in a table has a unique significance. This concept is also expressed by saying that each attribute has a *domain.*The domain is the allowable values (such as length, editing characteristics, and validation rules) of that attribute. Specifying allowable values for an attribute ensures *domain integrity.* For example, a product code might be defined as alphanumeric, six characters in length, and the first character must be A, B, or C. Domain integrity requires that a given attribute has only one semantic meaning, that must be specifiable as part of the database design.

REFERENTIAL INTEGRITY

An attribute of a table which is identified as a foreign key is the primary key of another table. *Referential integrity* refers to the fact that any data value that serves as a foreign key must have a matching primary key value in another table.

NORMALIZATION

The process of organizing data in the simplest form which eliminates redundancy (duplication) is called *normalization.* Following the structure of interrelated columns and rows, data items are evaluated, duplicates of the same items are eliminated, and then the unique data elements are organized into a table format so that they can be physically stored in the database. The process of organizing this data in its simplest form is accomplished in steps, called first, second, third normal forms, and so on. When each attribute relates to its own entity and is not mixed up with attributes relating to other entities, *third normal form* is achieved. The processes (programs) that create and update data can then be designed so that a simple structure handles one normalized record at a time. This process of normalization creates a structure that is more stable and capable of accommodating change.

This is an example of how to normalize a record:

```
Original Record =   Order #
                    Account #
                    Account Name
                    Product One Code
                    Product One Desc.
                    Product One Quantity
                    Product One Price
                    Product One Extended Value
                    Product Two Code
                    Product Two Desc.
                    Product Two Quantity
                    Product Two Price
                    Product Two Extended Value
```

First normal form is obtained by eliminating repeating groups. This creates two record formats:

```
Order Header =    Order #
                  Account #
                  Account Name

Order Detail =    Order #
                  Line #
                  Product
                  Product Desc.
                  Price
                  Extended value
```

Second normal form is obtained by eliminating all nonkey attributes that are not fully dependent on the primary key. In our example above, the primary keys for the Order Header and the Order Detail are the Order # and the line # respectively. When we examine the formats of the first normal form, neither the Account Name or the Product Desc. are based on the primary keys of their respective formats. So these attributes are organized into separate records. This procedure elimi-nates Account Name and Product Desc. from the original record for-mats and creates two new records:

Customer Master = Account #
                  Account Name

Product Master = Product Code
                  Product Name

The order header and the order detail now include:

Order Header =   Order #
                  Account #

Order Detail =   Order #
                  Line #
                  Product Code
                  Price
                  Quantity
                  Extended Value

Third normal form is obtained by eliminating any nonkey attribute that is functionally dependent on another nonkey attribute. Since Extended Value is functionally dependent on Price and Quantity, this attribute is eliminated from Order Detail. Order Detail now looks like this:

Order detail =   Order #
                  Line #
                  Product Code
                  Price
                  Quantity

VIRTUAL AND DERIVED FIELDS

The normalization example above established a relationship between two tables (entity types or files) by using a foreign key in one of the tables. Figure 6.3 illustrates this relationship.

When a foreign key in the primary entity relates two entities, the AS/400 DBMS permits creation of joined logical record displays. In a relational database, these logical records or *joins* relate two or more files. A join is the merging of records from two or more files, using keys as links. This permits a single view of data from two or more files. What distinguishes a relational database management system from a con-ventional system is that the work of preparing the single view is done by the DBMS, not by program code.

Order Detail
Order #
Line #
Product Code
Price
Quantity
Foreign Key
Product Master
Product Code
Product Description
Primary Key

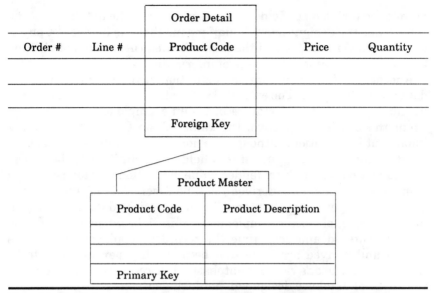

Figure 6.3 The linkage of tables (entities or files) through the use of a foreign key.

Figure 6.4 illustrates a joined logical record display that calls fields from a related file that are to be added to the view of a primary file. These fields that are added to the format of the original record are called *virtual fields*. The primary file is Order Detail. A virtual field has been added to this file from Product Master. Virtual fields

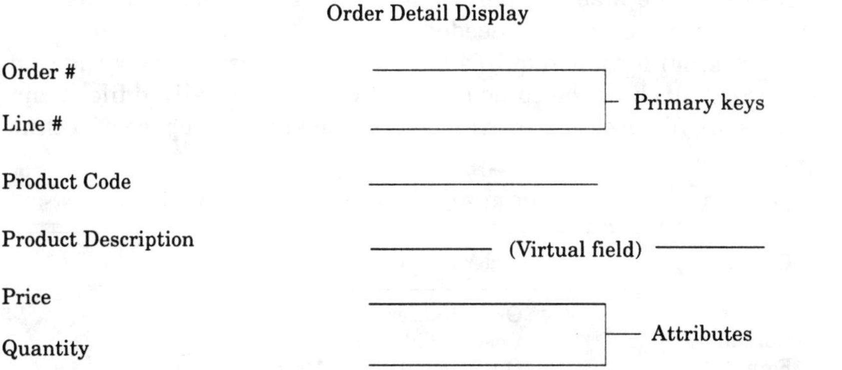

Order Detail Display
Order #
Line #
Primary keys
Product Code
Product Description
(Virtual field)
Price
Quantity
Attributes

Figure 6.4 A view of the database called a "Joined Logical." The database management system combines data stored in separate files to present the appearance of a single file.

permit the inclusion of fields in the user's view of the database. At the same time, the designation "virtual" means that the field is not physically included in the file and the normalization rules were not violated by specifying redundant storage of information.

Another useful concept for the definition of the user's view of the data is a *derived field*. The extended value shown as part of the original definition of the Order Detail record is an example of a derived field. From the user's perspective, the value of the Order Detail line is important information. Although the normalization process (reaching third normal form) eliminated this field, the definition of the logical database can include the extended value. A relational database design identifies this field as a derived field, however. This means that the value is not permanently stored in the physical database. Rather, program code physically implements this field when the order is initially entered and each time the record is displayed. The terms virtual and derived are important because they permit fields to be included in the user's view of a database while recognizing the fact that the physical database design will not include them.

DESIGN FOR MANUFACTURABILITY AND MAINTAINABILITY

File normalization is frequently a compromise between computer performance and software flexibility. The original order record in the example of record format normalization provides the best computer performance. Third normal form, on the other hand, avoids redundancy and provides long-term flexibility. Figure 6.5 illustrates that the difference in the machine performance for the two formats based on the number of file accesses needed.

The original format requires only one file access to show the complete order. To show the same information, the normalized file format requires six file accesses. Nevertheless, the enormous pace of techno-

FORMAT	RECORDS TO BE READ	# OF ACCESSES
Original	Order Record	1
3rd Normal Form	Order Header Customer Master Order Detail Product Master	1 1 2 2

Figure 6.5 A comparison of the file accesses involved in retrieving a sample "flat" file design versus a "normalized" file design.

logical development in computing suggests that optimizing programming productivity should have priority over improving machine performance. The more flexible the database design, the easier initial development and, more significant, future maintenance will be. But when the trends in price/performance of the hardware versus the trends in the productivity of the programmers who develop the software is suggested as a primary design consideration, traditionalists who grew up in the field might voice strong objections. But when we consider the rate at which the hardware price performance productivity is increasing, a new perspective is in order. T. Forester provides an interesting perspective on the improvement in computer performance:

> . . . if the automobile and airplane businesses had developed like the computer business, a Rolls Royce would cost $2.75 and run for three million miles on one gallon of gas. And a Boeing 767 would cost just $500 and would circle the globe in 20 minutes on five gallons of gas. (3)

To illustrate the improvement in maintenance programmer productivity when normalized file formats are used, let's return to the file formats which we used in our discussion on file normalization. Suppose that the nature of the business changes and the database has to provide for two more products on an order, a total of four instead of two. This would have increased the number of fields in the original order format from 13 to 23. The normalized format, on the other hand, would still only contain 11 fields, and the additional requirements would be handled by additional detail records in the same format. Thus using the original format, adding two more products would be a significant program maintenance change, and adds to the number of fields that are defined in our record format. The example from General Motors shows that the more parts in the bumper assembly, the more labor it takes to assemble it. Analogously, the more fields a database definition contains, the more lines of code and greater program complexity are needed to deal with them. As a final note on relational database design, please consider the following:

> Domain integrity and referential integrity carry the quality concepts of do-it-right-the-first-time into software development. Data should be thoroughly validated when it first enters the system so there is no need for inspection and rework down the line.

DEFINING THE DATABASE

The graphic notation that presents an overview of a database design is the *Entity Relationship Diagram* (ERD). It is based on the table structure of a relational database and the need to express relationships

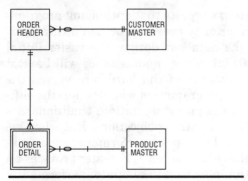

Figure 6.6 Sample Entity Relationship Diagram.

among tables. Figure 6.6 is an example of an ERD. The methods and notations associated with this diagram are presented in Chap. 8.

But before we discuss the methods and notations for defining the details of a database, let's first return to the first step of our life cycle model—business modeling. As you will recall, this subphase is used to define the scope of the system to be built, and to identify the major components of the new system. The suggested notation used in conjunction with this subphase is the Data Flow Diagram, the subject of our next chapter.

REFERENCES

1. Codd, E.F. "A Relational Model for Large Shared Data Banks," *Communications of the ACM,* 13(6) pp. 377-387, June 1970.

2. Codd,E.F. "Further Normalization of The Database Relational Model," *Rapid Application Development,* ed., James Martin. MacMillan: New York, 1991.

3. Forester, T. *The Story of the Information Technology Revolution.* MIT Press: Cambridge, Mass., 1987.

Defining the System— Data Flow Diagrams

The chapter on Life Cycle Process Models identified business modeling as the first formal phase in software development. The purpose of this phase is to establish the boundaries and major components of a proposed system. The notation to express this overview of a system is a Data flow Diagram (DFD). And an approved DFD is one of the first deliverables from JAD sessions. This chapter will look at a method for preparing DFDs. To illustrate the process, let's return to the building of a house. The architect's rendering and the floor plan diagrams can serve as a guide for preparing a DFD:

1. The initial design diagrams for any large building project provide a communication vehicle between the designer and the user (customer) and between the designer and the individuals responsible for detailed design and construction. DFD's serve the same purpose.

2. The initial architectural drawings focus on logical design rather than on physical implementation. Construction details, such as brick versus wood or electric versus oil heating are not included since these details detract from the focus of the drawings. In the

same way, a DFD is not concerned with implementation details, such as which processes are to be computerized, or types of data storage devices.

3. The basic design approach to house building and software development is top-down: The first step identifies the scope of the proposed system, and subsequent steps identify in greater and greater detail the components the system needs to accomplish its objective. The structure of the DFD reflects this approach.

4. A key function for the initial design drawings of a house and a system is to provide a basis for partitioning the system into small, detailed design and construction projects. The diagrams should also identify any structural dependencies within a system. These dependencies determine the sequence in which individual projects are to be carried out.

The DFD was first developed before World War I by industrial engineers as a paper-flow analysis tool. Subsequently, it was popularized as a computer-related systems analysis notation by Gane/Sarson (G/S) and Yourdon/DeMarco (Y/DeM) in the late 1970s and early 1980s. (1&2) These two proponents of the DFD suggested it as the first step in structured systems design to show processes and the flow of data among these processes. And they emphasized the use of a DFD to show the flow of information rather than the flow of control, which would be portrayed by a flow chart. Although G/S and Y/DeM agreed on some basic concepts, they had a number of differences. Chris Gane's comparison (3) of the differences between the Gane/Sarson and Yourdon/DeMarco approaches provides an overall perspective on the method advocated here for preparing a DFD. The comments are this author's.

Symbols.   Figure 7.1 shows the symbol sets suggested by G/S and Y/DeM, respectively.

Comment: The G/S notation is becoming the standard, but your selection is probably an issue of what symbols your CASE tool supports.

External environment.   G/S place much more emphasis on a positive definition of the environment that is outside the boundaries of the proposed system than do Y/DeM. G/S use a symbol for objects (organizations, systems, and so on) that are the source or destination of information the system uses or provides. While Y/DeM provide a symbol, they place little emphasis on its use to identify these External Agents positively. Instead Y/DeM tend to start a DFD by showing the data coming into or exiting a system.

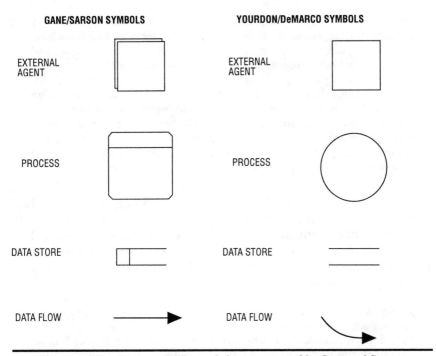

Figure 7.1 Data Flow Diagram (DFD) symbol sets suggested by Gane and Sarson versus Yourdon and DeMarco.

Comment: A major problem in any systems definition effort is the specification of the system's limits or boundaries. The positive identification of what is outside the system's boundaries provides a clearer picture of the system's scope. In addition, identifying External Agents permits documentation of other computer systems that will be interfaced with, as well as identification of departments or functions of the organization that should participate in JAD teams.

Structuring. Y/DeM recommend a scheme for documenting a system by using successive levels of diagrams, each level expanding on the details of the higher level. Y/DeM also suggest that this explosion process continue until primitive processes are identified. And a primitive process is defined as one that can be documented by a page or less of Structured English or some other technique. G/S recommend that a DFD contain as few explosion levels as possible and that a single process need not be exploded if it can be documented by 5 to 10 pages of logic.

Comment: A structuring or organization scheme is necessary to document most large systems. A later section of this chapter, dealing with *leveling,* discusses the Y/DeM approach in detail as the suggested way to organize diagrams. As to how far to go in decomposing high level processes, both the G/S and the Y/DeM approaches were developed when the primary programming approach was a monolithic program developed using a 3GL, such as COBOL. With the advent of lower CASE tools for the midrange and the evolution of object oriented design (OOD), these earlier guidelines have become inappropriate. In my view, the decomposition should occur to a level where a process is identified that is a candidate for computerization. When this level is reached, other planning and design techniques are more appropriate. These alternative techniques will be discussed in Chaps. 11 and 12.

Current system modeling. Both Y/DeM and G/S suggest using a DFD to document the current system or business process. Y/DeM strongly recommend documenting the current system, whereas G/S make it an option. G/S suggest that a more efficient alternative might be to start from scratch and start modeling the future system based on the real needs of the business.

Comment: Most businesses are looking for quantum gain in productivity, not small evolutionary improvements through the computer. To spend much time documenting a current system that probably had its origins in the past before computers were invented probably will not be very productive. Documenting a current system in detail also is inconsistent with the basic team concept of JAD. With effective user participation, it isn't necessary for the systems analyst to learn the nuances of the current system. And it is typically the user representatives on the JAD team who would be responsible for assessing the before and after effects of any proposed system.

Note: In his latest book, Ed Yourdon has radically changed his initial position on current system modeling. Following is an excerpt from his book:

... they promulgate the "old" structured analysis approach of building a "current physical" model and a "current logical" model before beginning to model the user's new system. But only bozos build current physical models today because it takes too long and involves too much wasted work. (4)

Data definition. Both Y/DeM and G/S suggest conventions for documenting the data structures identified on a DFD.

Comment: Early conventions for documenting data structures have been superseded by new notations developed to document a relational database. These notations will be discussed in more detail in Chaps. 8, 9, and 10.

SYMBOLS

As a first step in gaining a more detailed understanding of DFDs, let's look at the symbols used. The symbols used for this explanation and for developing sample diagrams are Gane and Sarson's.

The symbols used on a DFD are as follows:

External Agent or Entity: Logical classes or specific sources or destinations of transactions, such as customers, A/P department, A/R system. By designating something or some system as an external agent, you explicitly state that it is outside the boundaries of the system being considered.

Figure 7.2

Data flow : A Data flow is like a pipe, down which parcels of data are sent. It represents the transfer of data between objects on a DFD, such as between two processes or between an external agent and a process. An electronic data interchange transmission of an order from a customer to a processing routine is an example. The retrieval of order information by the process that prepares work orders is another.

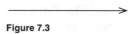

Figure 7.3

Process: A process is an event that transforms or stores data. Data is accepted as input, some transformation occurs, and the result is output to some other object on the DFD. It is important that this processing can be either manual or computerized. At this stage in the development of a logical design, whether or not the process is automated is not a consideration. A process name is an imperative verb plus an object (such as Edit Order).

Figure 7.4

Data Store: A data store indicates where data is at rest for a time. This occurs between processes, when information must be stored since it is not to be acted upon immediately by the next process. This storage can occur using disk storage, a printed report on a desk, or another storage device.

Figure 7.5

In addition to the standard symbols, several upper CASE tools also use the following symbols.

Context Junction: This symbol automatically appears on lower-level DFDs created to decompose a high-level. It represents the entrances or exits of data flows to or from the process on the high-level DFD being functionally decomposed. These data flows on the high-level DFD must be linked to the decomposed processes on the lower-level DFD.

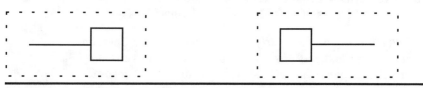

Figure 7.6   Figure 7.7

Junction:. This symbol helps organize and clarify diagrams. Divergent junctions split data into two or more outputs. Convergent junctions combine two or more inputs into one flow. Linear junctions produce one output from one input.

O

Figure 7.8

PREPARING A DATA FLOW DIAGRAM

The preparation of a DFD starts with identifying the business objectives that are the purpose of the proposed system. In the example used in the discussion of enterprise modeling in Chap. 3, the business objective was "process a customer order." The system information that we know about concerning the initial activities involved in meeting this objective are as follows. The process is triggered by a physical order received from a customer (the initial stimulus). This is also called an "event" in some texts on object oriented design. (6) The initial order is edited, and then it is stored for use in subsequent processing. A notice is sent to Production Planning to initiate production. Figure 7.9 shows how these initial facts might be expressed in a DFD.

The customer is identified as the external agent outside the bounds of the system and is the source of information for the system. The order is expressed as a data flow that is the transfer of information between the external agent and the process, Edit Orders, which will first operate on this information. Once the order has been initially processed, a notice is sent to Production Planning (an external agent) that a work order should be prepared. This notice is shown as a data flow , New Requirements. And since the order will not be acted upon immediately by all the processes that

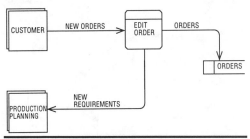

Figure 7.9 Initial Data Flow Diagram showing initial "facts" known about a proposed system.

use the order information, the order information is shown being added to a data store, Orders. To complete the first cut of the DFD for Process Customer Order, let's expand the diagram to include the initial processes discussed in the enterprise modeling section of Chap. 3. The initial processes identified also included *Plan Production,* Post Production, and *Process Shipments.* The system's scope also included three other processes: *Maintain Customer Master, Update Product,* and *Prepare Invoices.*

Also, the new system had to provide information to two related systems outside the scope of the design effort. These two related systems were Accounts Receivable and Sales Analysis. Adding these components and environment entities results in Fig. 7.10.

Figure 7.10 shows that we identified several processes, such as Maintain Customer Master and Post Production, that transpose or process data. But we didn't identify the data being processed or the source of the data. So, a number of data flows, as well as the external agents that are the source of this data, have been added to the diagram. These added components include:

External Agents:
   Customer service department
   Engineering department
   Production department
   Production
   Shipping department

Data flows:
   Customer updates
   Product information
   Production information
   Shipping authorizations

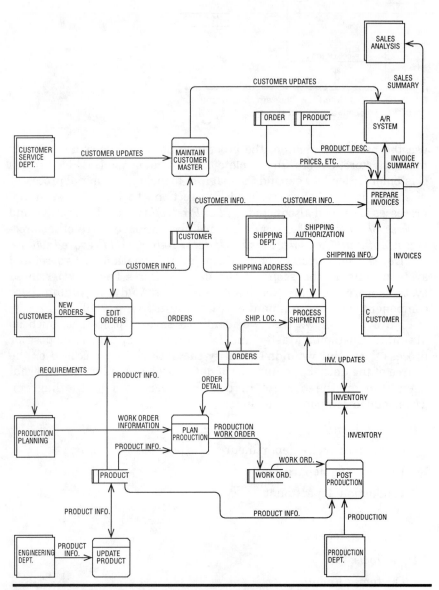

Figure 7.10 Expanded Data Flow Diagram showing the additional processes, data stores, and interfaces to external organizations and applications that are involved in the complete system.

To avoid tangled data flow s, several data stores, Order and Product, are also duplicated. The G/S convention for indicating a duplicate data flow is to precede the symbol with /2, which indicates this is a second use of the data store. The external agent, Customer, is also duplicated. This duplication is indicated by adding D2 to the label. Most upper CASE tools permit different symbol sizes, so a smaller size can also be used to indicate the duplication. Using the smaller symbol size is typically easier than attempting to conform to the G/S convention.

If the diagram in Fig. 7.10 were used in a JAD session, the participants might want to add the following information to reflect the system requirements fully:

New Data flows:

_Order revisions and cancellations

_Order acknowledgments

_Available to ship

_Order exceptions to management

_Bookings report

_Shipping exceptions

_Shipping advice to customer

_Shipping report

Adding this new information to Fig. 7.10, creates a very crowded chart. So first, let's examine a concept called *leveling,* a means of structuring the chart.

LEVELING

When a system is too large to show its DFD on a single page, an organization scheme is needed so that readable documents can be produced. The basic approach creating this scheme is decomposition, and in the context of a DFD, this approach is called *leveling.* Following is Yourdon/DeMarco's suggested set of DFDs for leveling and guidelines that might be helpful in their production. The linkage of these diagrams is shown in Fig. 7.11.

1. *The Context Diagram:* The Context Diagram provides an overview of the system to be developed and identifies the system interfaces to the external environment. This diagram contains on one page an identification of the sources and destinations (external agents) of

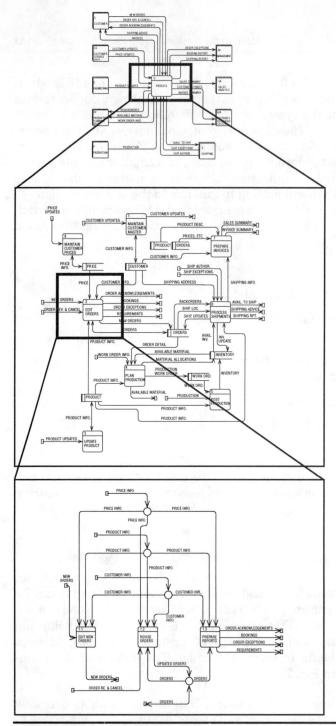

Figure 7.11 The linkage of Data Flow Diagrams (DFD) as a high-level "process" is decomposed to show greater detail.

data and the net inputs and outputs of data. This diagram defines what the system must produce, who is to receive these products, and what data resources are necessary to produce them. In this diagram, external agents and meaningfully labeled data flows are identified. A process is indicated on the chart, but it has no definable significance and is used as a link to the next lower level for functional decomposition.

2. *Essential Functions Diagram* (also called the Level 0 Diagram): This diagram is a decomposition of *Process* in the Context Diagram. It identifies the major processing functions in the system under study. A guideline in determining the degree of functionality to be shown on the essential functions and lower-level diagrams is seven +/–two functions. With more than nine functions, the diagram becomes difficult to understand. Fewer than five functions make it necessary to carry the diagram to excessive levels.

3. *First-/second-/third-, etc., level diagrams:* These diagrams represent further decomposition of the functions on the previous level. This decomposition is carried to a level at which meaningful processes that can be converted to computer programs can be identified. While no objective standards are established, the goal is to identify unitary person/machine tasks or cohesive machine transforms of data. Below this functionally primitive level, program structure charts accomplish further decomposition of complex processes. Such charts identify program modules and subroutines. Action diagrams (which show both the overall structure of a program and detailed logic), is another technique for decomposing a process.

Other helpful guidelines in the leveling of diagrams are as follows:

1. Numbering conventions provide a way to assign each process a numeric value for identification. On the Essential Functions Diagram, each process is given a number. Then a process on a lower-level diagram receives the number of the related process on the parent diagram plus a suffix. For example, the Essential Functions Diagram might identify a process, Edit Orders. This process is numbered 1.0. On the lower-level diagram, Edit Orders is decomposed into two processes, Create New Orders and Update Orders. These processes on the lower-level diagram would be numbered 1.1 and 1.2 respectively.

2. Data stores are shown on the first level where they serve as an interface between two processes or as the interface between a process and a system external to the boundaries of the system being

considered (an external agent). On the first level where the data store is shown, all references (data flows to and from the data store) to a data store should be shown. It might also be helpful to repeat the data stores on the lowest decomposition level (such as level 1 or 2) where the programmable processes are identified. This repetition is useful in planning the program structure for the process.

Note: With some CASE tools, repeating a data store can complicate the automatic analysis.

3. *Context-level DFD.* Start the preparation of a context-level DFD by drawing the external agents around the periphery of the diagram. If possible, draw sources of data to the left and the disposition of data to the right.

Figures 7.12 and 7.13 are updated DFDs that include the additional JAD feedback. In Fig. 7.12, the Context Level Diagram, we now have

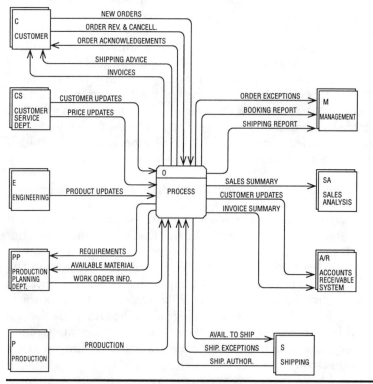

Figure 7.12 Sample "Context" level of a Data Flow Diagram (DFD) that identifies the boundaries of the system and the interfaces between the environment and the system.

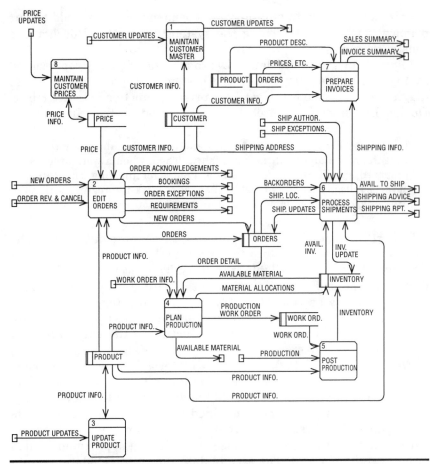

Figure 7.13 Sample "Essential Functions" level of a Data Flow Diagram (DFD). This diagram decomposes the component "Process" shown on the "Context" level DFD.

the bounding of the system. This identifies external functions or computer applications which are outside of the scope of our new system and the organizational entities that deal with the new system.

The organizational identification also tells which critical representations are needed on the JAD team. The data flows from and to these external agents relate the new system to these organizations. The Essential Functions Diagram, Fig. 7.13, now provides an overview of the proposed system. Major processing functions are identified on a high-level, and the data stores that will serve as the starting point for the database design effort are also shown. Equally significant, we are able to determine data and process dependencies that should be our primary guide in partitioning the system into detailed design and construction projects.

Figure 7.13 shows the data flows that were originally represented in Fig. 7.10. The company whose system is represented in these diagrams is a textile finisher whose primary function is to dye fabric. During JAD sessions, user participants pointed out the following.

> During the Production Planning process, it is important to know the Inventory availability of the basic fabric. Then, when a work order is prepared, specific rolls of fabric are designated for finishing. The status of these rolls in Inventory must be changed to work-in-progress so they are not shown as available for assignment to another order.

This requirement was met by adding three more data flows. The first was from the data store Inventory to the process Plan Production, which showed available inventory. The second data flow was from the process Plan Production to the data store Inventory. This data flow contains the status updates to Inventory necessary to reflect the material assignments to work in process. The third data flow was from the process Plan Production to the external agent Production Planning.

Note: To add the data flow Available Material between Plan Production and the external agent Production Planning, I first went back to update the Context Diagram to add the data flow at that level.

Several data flows were also added between Process Shipments and Orders. The first, Back Orders, is used to make a comparison with available inventory to advise the shipping department which orders can be shipped. The second data flow, Ship Updates, represents the updating of open orders once a shipment has been made. Note that the original data flow, Inv. Updates, which was a bidirectional data link between Inventory and Process Shipments in the original diagram, has now been split into two unidirectional data flows, Available Inventory and Inventory Updates. A general rule is that data flows should be unidirectional, but if it is as straightforward as the data flow showing updates to the data store Customer, the dual directional linkage is acceptable. This is typically done when the primary function of the related process is the creation and maintenance of master information.

Figure 7.14 represents the next lower level of decomposition for the system. This level 1 diagram decomposes the process Edit Orders from our Essential Functions Diagram. At this level, we are close to identifying candidate processes for computerization.

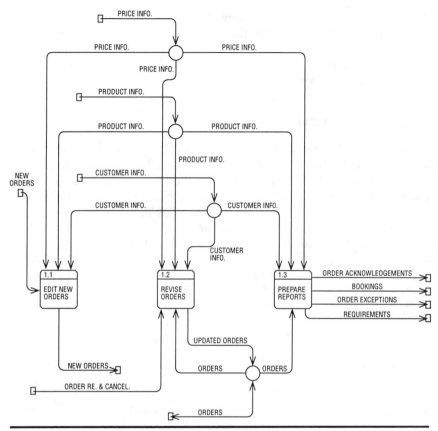

Figure 7.14 Sample "1st"-level DFD, which shows the decomposition of the process "Edit Orders" on the Essential Functions DFD.

BALANCING

When DFDs must be decomposed into multiple levels because of their complexity, you need to ensure that no data flows have been lost or added to the parent process in the progression from the top level to bottom. This verification is called balancing. The three types of balancing are visual, graphic, and data dictionary balancing.

1. Visual balancing is sight checking to ensure that the data flows entering and leaving the child diagram are the same as those entering and leaving the parent process.

2. Graphic balancing is when the child diagram is automatically populated with the Data flows entering or leaving the parent process.

3. Data dictionary balancing occurs when the data dictionary contains a definition of every data flow and data store identified on the diagrams and the processes to which they are linked. Balancing is accomplished by verifying that data flows linked to a process on the parent diagram are included on the child diagram.

USING A DATA FLOW DIAGRAM

The Essential Functions Diagram used as an example provides a first look at a system to process a customer order. This diagram is similar to a floor plan an architect prepares, in that it provides an overview of the system we want to build. It identifies the major components and the dependencies among these components. So, let's review how this information can be used to plan the development of the system.

First, we have identified a number of data stores and processes that tell the types of information that will be part of the database and the general processing that occurs using this data. These components include:

Data Stores	Processes
Customer	Maintain Customer Master
Product	Maintain Product Master
Order	Edit Orders
Work Order	Plan Production
Inventory	Post Production
	Process Shipments
	Prepare Invoices

The diagram also tells that we need to interface with two other systems outside the scope of the new system. These two systems are Accounts Receivable and Sales Analysis. Several interfaces are needed from the new system to these two old systems. First, the process that will maintain the new customer master must also update the old customer master that these two legacy systems use. Second, the new invoicing process must provide invoice summaries and sales summaries in formats these old systems will accept.

To establish a schedule for developing the system, let's return to the Life Cycle Process Model developed in Chap. 2 and review the major phases for developing a software system. The first step was business modeling to define the scope of the proposed system and its major components. This is the step just accomplished by preparing the DFD.

The next step is data modeling, designing a logical database for the system that covers the data stores and data flows identified on the DFD. The next step after database design is project planning, partitioning the overall system into a series of discrete subsystems that can be installed on a stand alone basis. Once these subsystems are identified, they can be organized into projects that then go through the traditional steps of analysis, design, construction, and installation.

Following is a suggested way of partitioning the sample system into specific projects and the suggested development sequence.

Project 1 = Maintain Customer Master

Project 2 = Update Product

Project 3 = Edit Orders

Project 4 = Plan Production

Post Production

Project 5 = Process Shipments

Project 6 = Prepare Invoices

A major goal of partitioning a system and establishing a sequence for developing a software system is to set up a schedule that minimizes time to market. One way to accomplish this is to use the scheduling technique of concurrent development. With this technique, life cycle phases overlap to the degree possible, and the overall system is broken down into subsystems to be developed and installed independently. Figure 7.15 represents a suggested schedule for developing the system.

This schedule includes no times. The point to be explored is the dependencies discussed in Chap. 3, which are constraints for this type of scheduling. Three types of dependencies are significant in planning a software development effort:

Structural dependency: The reliance of one subsystem on information created or maintained by a prior process.

Phase dependency: The reliance of one phase in the Life Cycle Process Model on the completion and the deliverables from a previous phase.

Task dependency: The reliance of one task or project within a life cycle phase on the completion of another task within that phase.

These dependencies affect the schedule. First, structural dependencies determine the sequence of the subsystem projects. Each subsys-

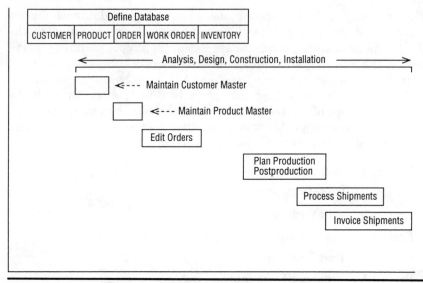

Figure 7.15 Project schedule in which the start of individual projects is based on the structural and phase dependencies first identified on the DFD.

tem is scheduled after any other subsystem that creates or maintains needed data. For example, the Edit Orders project is scheduled after the Maintain Customer Master and the Maintain Product Master projects since the Edit Orders subsystem needs these databases. Second, phase and task dependencies determine the possible start date of the individual projects. For example, as soon as the customer part of the Data Model is defined, project 1 can start. This subsystem deals with the process to maintain the customer master. Completion of other parts of the Data Model provides the signal that an equivalent part of the process modeling phase can start.

In scheduling the projects dealing with Process Shipments and Prepare Invoices, an additional consideration arises. This consideration is task dependencies. To install the Process Shipments subsystem, Inventory information produced by Post Production is needed. So the start of the Process Shipments project is delayed because it might not be practical to test the Process Shipments subsystem until Inventory information is available. And definitely the Process Shipments subsystem cannot be installed until the Inventory information from Post Production is available. The same relationship exists between the Process Shipments and Prepare Invoices subsystems, so the invoicing project is also delayed until the Shipping Info. Data flow is available.

For a concluding perspective on the importance of a DFD, let's look at what the diagram tells us if the user wants to schedule the Process Shipments project first. As the diagram shows, this process needs the following information that is produced by prior systems:

The ship-to location, and so on, from the order

The ship-to address from the Customer Master and product information from the Product Master

Inventory information from the inventory file

In the integrated system with shared data files shown on this DFD, all this information is provided by prior subsystems. If the shipping process were to be automated first as a stand alone system, however, this information would not be available in a computerized format. Instead this information would have to be entered directly into Process Shipments. As a result, additional data entry screens and editing procedures would be needed to accomplish the functions of the prior processes shown on the DFD. In addition, if Process Shipments is part of an integrated system, important functions to be accomplished by this process would be to update the back-order balance in the order file and to relieve Inventory. Neither function can be accomplished if the files to be created by the prior processes are not available. A reasonable estimate is that if Process Shipments were first done on a stand alone basis and then redone so the process is integrated into a total system, 50 percent would be added to the usual software development costs for this process.

REFERENCES

1. DeMarco, Tom. *Structured Analysis and System Specification*. Prentice-Hall: Englewood Cliffs, N.J., 1979.

2. Gane, Chris, and Sarson, Trish. *Structured Systems Analysis: Tools and Techniques*. Prentice-Hall: Englewood Cliffs, N.J.

3. Gane, Chris. *Computer-Aided Software Engineering*. Prentice-Hall: Englewood Cliffs, N.J.: 1990.

4. Yourdon, Ed. *The Decline and Fall of The American Programmer*. Yourdon Press, Prentice-Hall: Englewood Cliffs, N.J., 1992, p. 325.

5. For an overall explanation of CASE tools, the following is suggested: Martin, James. and McClure, Carma. *Structure Techniques—The Basis for CASE*. Prentice-Hall: Englewood Cliffs, N.J.

6. Martin, James. *Principles of Object Oriented Analysis and Design*. Prentice-Hall: Englewood-Cliffs, N.J., 1993.

Developing a Data Model Overview—Entity Relationship Diagrams

Data Modeling is a systematic method for defining the data items identified in the Business Model as data stores and data flows. The primary emphasis in data modeling is on decomposing the data stores since they will be implemented as physical files when the system is constructed. Data flows, on the other hand, usually need be defined in detail only when they represent interfaces to other systems. The reason is that other data flows in a system are usually a subset of the information covered by one of the data stores. So the purpose at this stage of system development—to establish the architectural structure for the system—can be accomplished by decomposing and defining the data stores. Data modeling identifies the details of all data the system needs, organizes this data in its simplest form, and establishes edit rules for each element of data. This simplest form for data consists of the table structure described in our chapter on relational database design. Using this table structure, each instance of a data type (a row or record) is identified by its unique key, and the facts (columns or fields) about the data instance are related to this instance by the unique key.

Creating a Data Model for an enterprise is an iterative process in which a logical design for each data store is created. The first step is to nominate entities for each data store that most likely conform to the basic table format. Then you determine the relationship among these entities and identify the details (attributes) for each nominated entity. The final step is to optimize the entity/attribute grouping through normalization. With entities nominated and a preliminary determination made of the relationship among these entities, the next step is to express the results graphically. The notation used is an Entity Relationship Diagram (ERD). This diagram can then be used in a process of refinement to identify attributes, check the rules of normalization, and fine tune the initial diagrams. An approved diagram and attribute definitions then become additional deliverables from the JAD sessions.

This chapter will discuss methods for decomposing the data stores on data flow diagrams to prepare an ERD. But first let's define an ERD in more detail.

> An ERD is a systems design tool that shows how information retained by a system is organized and how the organizational elements (entities) relate to each other.

An *entity* is something real or imagined, about which we store data. Examples are CUSTOMER, EMPLOYEE, CONTRACT, and so on. An entity can be decomposed into *attributes* that define the entity's characteristics, such as street address, size, price, and the like. The terms entity and attribute are logical design terms that in the AS/400 physical environment equate to file and field.

ERD COMPONENTS

Three basic components, entity, relationship, and cardinality, are used in an ERD. The icons that represent these components are as follows:

Entity: A class of people, things, and so on, with characteristics in common, about which data is stored.

Figure 8.1 Entity.

Weak Entity: An entity that can only exist when connected to (related to) another entity. An example is order detail, which cannot exist if there is no Order Header.

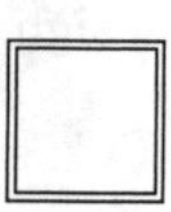

Figure 8.2 Weak Entity.

Associative Entity: A secondary-use symbol provided to show interrelationships among entities. It resolves a many-to-many relationship by creating one-to-one or one-to-many relationships.

Figure 8.3 Associative Entity.

Relationship: A relationship between two entities is expressed by a line drawn between the two entities. This line can be labeled to express the nature of the relationship.

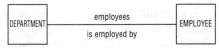

Figure 8.4 Relationship between two entities.

Cardinality: Identifies the nature of the relationship between two entities by specifying the number of instances of a relationship that may occur between two related entities. For example, in the example of the normalization process that was discussed in Chap. 6, we established two entities, Order Header and Customer, that are related. The nature of this relationship is that a given order can relate to only one customer, but a given customer can relate to many orders. Standard symbols to express cardinality are shown below. It should be noted, however, that these symbols can vary from one CASE tool to another. The symbol set shown is the Martin notation.

0 equals optional, | equals one, —< equals many

Following are examples of the use of these symbols.

A is associated with one B.

Figure 8.5 ?-to-one relationship.

For a given instance of A, there can only be one B. An example of this relationship might be that for a given Customer Order, there can only be one customer.

B is associated with many As.

Figure 8.6 ?-to-many relationship.

For a given instance of A, there can be many Bs. An example of this relationship might be that for a given Customer Order Header, there can be many Customer Order Details, one for each product being ordered.

A is associated with zero, one, or many Bs.

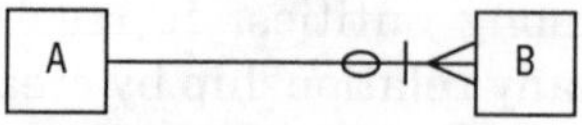

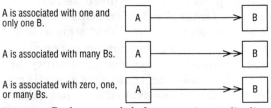

Figure 8.7 ?-to-zero, -one, or -many relationship.

For a given instance of A, there can be zero, one, or many Bs. An example of this relationship might be that for a given product, there might be zero, one, or many customer orders.

An alternative set of symbols to express the same relationships is the Bachman notation. This notation does not have a way to express an optional relationship.

A is associated with one and only one B.

A is associated with many Bs.

A is associated with zero, one, or many Bs.

Figure 8.8 Backman symbols for expressing cardinality.

EXTENDED RELATIONSHIPS

In addition to the standard relationships discussed above, there are relationships called extended relationships. Following are examples of the extended relationships that can exist in a relational database structure.

Recursive relationship: A recursive relationship is one in which an entity type might have a relationship with itself. This type of relationship is often called a hierarchy or bill-of-material structure. Recursive relationships are always named. The name describes the one-to-many relationship. The relationship must be identified as optional on both sides in order to stop a loop.

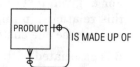

Figure 8.9 Recursive relationship—an entity has a relationship with itself.

In the example above, an entity called *product* is shown to have a relationship with itself. This indicates that a specific instance of the entity type can be related to other instances of the same entity type in order to identify parents. And going in the other direction, the relationship and the cardinality indicate that a given instance of the entity can be the parent for zero, one, or more children.

Chasm Traps: The presence of a many-to-many relationship is called a Chasm Trap. This type of relationship is not permitted in a relational database management system. The Chasm Trap is resolved through the addition of an Associative Entity through which one-to-many relationships can be established. An example of this type of relationship might be on the product offerings of distributors. For any given product, it can be supplied by many vendors. And a given vendor can supply many products. Thus we have a many-to-many relationship between products and vendors. By establishing an associative entity called Product Source we can resolve the many-to-many relationship. This new entity has as its key a concatenated key which is made up of the keys for both the product entity and the vendor entity. For each instance where a specific product is supplied by a specific vendor, an entry is made in this file. This resolves the initial many-to-many relationship, and identifies which products are supplied by which vendors.

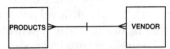

Figure 8.10   Chasm Trap—a many-to-many relationship between two entities. This type of relationship cannot be physically implemented using a Relationship Database Management

Transitive relationship: A transitive relationship exists if there is more than one path between entities. The direct link is frequently redundant, but it is allowed.

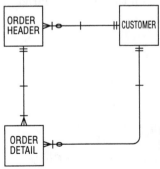

Figure 8.11   Transitive relationship—alternate paths exist between entities.

PREPARING AN ENTITY RELATIONSHIP
DIAGRAM

The suggested process for creating an ERD is essentially the reverse of the leveling or decomposition approach used to produce a Data Flow Diagram. The leveling approach first creates a high-level or overview process. This high-level process is then decomposed through successive levels of detail until a primitive functional process is identified that can be implemented as a computer program. In the assembling process to create an ERD, the low-level entities that can be implemented as files are identified first. This is done by decomposing the data stores identified on a DFD. As part of this initial decomposition, the relationship among the entities for a given data store are defined. Composite views of these low-level entities are then created to develop a process and a system-wide perspective. As these high-level views are created, additional relationships can be added to gain a full picture of the structure of the database.

This approach assumes that a system DFD has already been prepared. You are then using an ERD to structurally decompose each instance of one type of component, the data store, shown on this DFD. As part of this decomposition for each data store, you show the entities and the relationships among entities within the boundaries of a given data store. But there are also relationships across the boundaries of the individual data stores in a system. For example, the information contained in the data store Order is related to the data store Customer. To show this relationship, you need to prepare high-level views of the initial ERDs. These high-level ERDs show on one diagram the entity breakdowns for multiple data stores and the relationship among all these entities.

As a first step in preparing a sample ERD, let's nominate entities for each of the following data stores identified on the DFD prepared in Chap. 7:

Customer

Product

Orders

Work Orders

Inventory

Figure 8.12 represents a first cut at a table structure for the Customer data store.

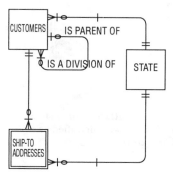

Figure 8.12 Sample Entity Relationship Diagram (ERD) for a data structure "Customer" which was identified as a component on a DFD.

The Customer data store has two nominated entities, Customer and Ship-to Addresses. The relationship and cardinality symbols indicate that for a given customer, there can be zero, one, or many Ship-to Addresses. But a given Ship-to Address is related to only one specific customer. The Ship-to Address is also identified as a Weak Entity. This means there can only be a Ship-to Address if there is a regular customer entity that the address relates to. The customer also has a recursive relationship. This relationship indicates that a given customer might be a division of a larger company. By establishing the relationship with a parent, a future sales reporting system will be able to consolidate bookings and sales by the parent company as well as by the individual division.

The sample ERD for Customer also included State as a nominated entity. State is an appropriate entity only if there will be significant information, such as a sales tax rate, in the system. However, if this table represents only a simple table of state codes and the full state name, it would be unnecessary to represent it on the ERD. The typical database contains hundreds of these simple tables. If you attempt to show them on an ERD, the resulting diagram might be so cluttered that it is unreadable. A more appropriate approach is that when you are defining the attributes for an entity, an attribute such as state code should be identified as having a discrete domain. This means that the attributes have specific allowed values that will be organized either as an external table or as part of the value definition for a field (using, for example, the VALUES keyword of the Data Definition Specification—DDS). The decision as to whether a value or an external table is the more appropriate technique will be based on whether there is only a list of allowed values (such as, O, or C, for a status field) or whether the allowed values have a meaning used by the system (such as, CT = Connecticut).

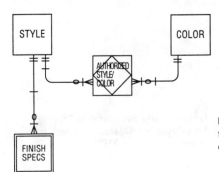

Figure 8.13 Sample ERD for a data structure "Product" which was identified as a component on a DFD.

The nominated entities shown in Fig. 8.13 represent the logical structure for the data store Product.

The example used for the DFD was from the textile industry. In this industry, a product code often contains an embedded structure as follows.

Product code = Style Number + Finish Code + Color Code

An option used in many manufacturing software packages is to assign a unique code to each combination of style, finish, and color. This approach requires only one entity or table to contain the facts about the product. But suppose the company deals with 100 styles, an average of five finishes per style, and each style/finish combination is dyed in 10 different colors on average. This would mean that the physical solution would be 5000 (100 x 5 x 10) large records. Information such as a basic description of one style would then be duplicated in 50 records.

The alternative to the one-table format is the structure shown in Fig. 8.13. Three primary entities are identified: Style, Finish Specs, and Color. Finish Specs is shown as a weak entity, which means the entity instances relate to specific styles. This is also shown by the cardinality of the relationship: an entity instance can relate to zero, one, or many finish specifications, but a finish spec relates to a maximum of one and a minimum of one entity occurrence. The cardinality of the relationship between the Style and the Color entities is many-to-many. This relationship is a Chasm Trap. There is no way to implement this relationship in a relational database. Therefore, the relationship must be resolved into one-to-many relationships. In the example, this was accomplished by adding an Associative Entity. With the addition of this entity, the relationships are now one-to-many.

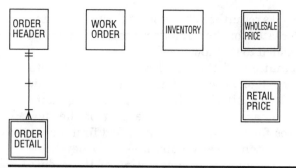

Figure 8.14   Sample ERD's for the data structures Order, Work Order, Inventory, and Price, which were identified as

Figure 8.14 represents the nominated entities for the remaining data stores on the original DFD.

Once the data stores are decomposed into an entity structure, attributes for each entity can be determined and organized. Attributes are the facts that are significant to the database, such as the customer name and address. But this is only part of the information needed to build a database. The other information necessary to take advantage of the relational database capability is the relationships across the boundaries of the individual data stores. These relationships can be determined by developing process and system views of the ERD.

A PROCESS AND A SYSTEMS VIEW OF THE DATABASE

To obtain a view of the relationships among the set of entities defined for each data store, a combining approach is used. A process view should be developed first to show the relationship among all the entities defined for the data stores a given process uses. Additional views can then be prepared as needed to show any additional relationships among entities that are not identified on the individual process views.

The combining approach can be accomplished in two ways:

A merging approach is the method of several basic CASE tools. The process view is obtained by first selecting an ERD created for one of the data stores. Then an ERD for another data store associated with the process is selected and merged with the first ERD to create a new view. Next, new relationships are established as required. The process is then repeated until all the ERDs created for the data stores associated with a process have been added to the new view.

Automatic combination of the individual views of data stores is used if the tool automatically will create a new diagram which includes all the ERD components of data stores on a DFD that are identified to be part of the new diagram. Data stores for a process are identified first on the DFD. Then the tool automatically populates on a new view the entities that represent the decomposition of these data stores. All that needs to be done to complete the view is to establish the additional relationships among the entities.

Figure 8.15 is a view of the data stores for the process Edit Orders. In this view of the database, several new relationships have been established. For example, a given order is related to one and only one

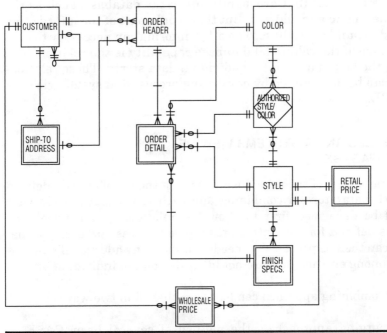

Figure 8.15 A "process" view of the various entities that were nominated to provide the structure for the data stores used by the process Edit Orders. This diagram shows additional relationships among the various entities initially nominated for each data store.

customer. But a given customer can have zero, one, or many orders. The relationship between the Order Header and a Ship-to Address is comparable. For a given order, there might be a special Ship-to Address, an optional relationship. For a given ship-to, there can be zero, one, or many orders. Incidentally, the ship-to order relationship could be used to consolidate shipments to a given address.

In the Order Detail to Product relationship, the embedded structure of the product code is used to establish several relationships. Each component of the product code has been used to establish a one-and-only-one relationship between the order detail and the corresponding entity, the product. In addition, there is a relationship between the order detail and the Associative Entity—Authorized Style/Color. The primary key for Authorized Style/Color is made up of the two data elements, Color and Style.

When a key consists of two or more data elements, it is called a *concatenated key*. The significance of this concatenated key becomes apparent when we eventually specify referential integrity validation for the system. We need to ensure that the elements of the embedded structure of product are valid individually. But in this instance, the style/color combination must also be valid.

When the relationship among the data stores for the process Edit Orders is established, the next process that uses new data stores is Plan Production. This process uses or creates two new data stores: Work Order and Inventory. Figure 8.16 shows a new process view of the database that includes these new elements.

Both Work Order and the Inventory entities have a relationship with the various components of the original data store: Product. In addition, there is a zero/one relationship between Inventory and a Work Order. This relationship indicates that a given lot of raw material Inventory can be in open stock or can be assigned to a specific Work Order for processing. The zero, one, or many relationship between the Work Order and Inventory means that a given Work Order might have zero, one, or many lots assigned to it for processing. When the Work Order is first created, no material is assigned to it. Then one or more lots might be assigned at a later time.

Figure 8.16 also shows that there is a relationship between the Work Order and the Customer Order. Initially there was a many-to-many relationship between the Work Order and the Customer Order. This had to be resolved by adding an associative entity and changing the relationship to one to many. The relationship (zero, one or many) now shown means that a given Work Order might be for stock—the zero relation-

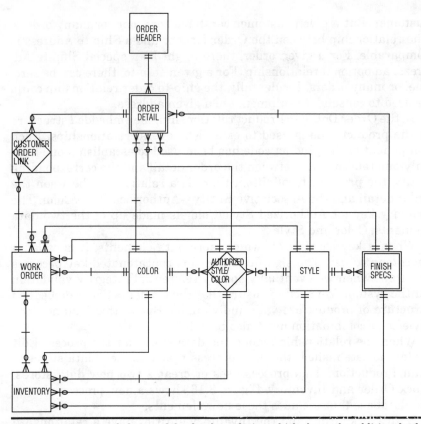

Figure 8.16   An expanded view of the database design which shows the additional relationships that are identified when data stores used by the process—Plan Production—are considered.

ship—or it might be used to cover one or more Customer Orders. It also means that a given customer's order might be satisfied by stock or by the production from one or more Work Orders.

The final process view of the ERD series is for the process Post Production. In this view, shown in Fig. 8.17, no new data stores are involved, but several new relationships have been added. When finished Inventory is posted, the Work Order that initially authorized the production is identified. This relationship is established so that at a future date, a report can be prepared that identifies all raw material lots assigned to the Work Order and all finished lots produced against the Work Order: the yield of the Work Order. In addition, a relationship is established between the new production of finished goods and the Customer Order to which the goods are assigned.

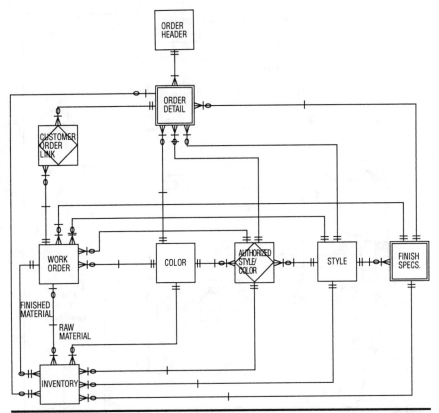

Figure 8.17 An expanded view of the database design showing the additional relationships identified when the requirements for the process—Post Production—are considered.

This permits a shipping procedure to call up the specific lots of goods produced for the order when a shipment is to be made.

A final combined view of the system is shown in Fig. 8.18. At this point, all the original data stores shown in the original DFD have been decomposed into entities, and all major relationships have been identified. We now have the basis for the next steps in defining the database, establishing the keys and foreign keys for each entity, using an ERD.

IDENTIFYING KEYS

Each table (entity or file) generally has one column or group of columns that uniquely identifies each instance (row or record) of that table. For example, the customer number column uniquely identifies the row that contains all the

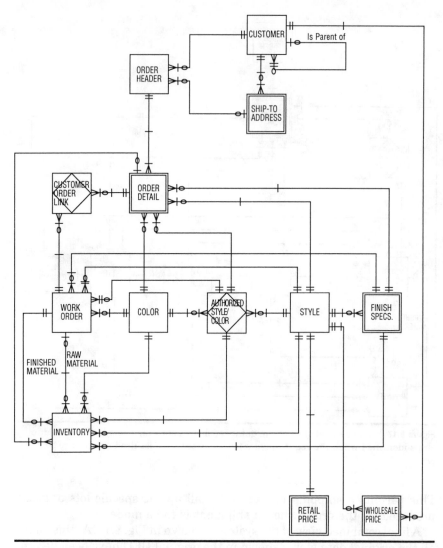

Figure 8.18 A "system" view of the database design showing the additional relationships identified when the full system is considered.

facts concerning that customer. This column or field is the primary key for the entity. If one column or fact concerning an entity is the primary key for another table, this column is a foreign key. The foreign key in one table establishes a relationship with the other table and lets the relational database management system provide a single view of data from the two tables. So the next steps in defining the database are to establish primary keys and foreign keys for each of the entities identified in Fig. 8.16.

Entity	Entity type	Primary key
Customer	E	Customer Code
Ship-to Address	WE	Customer Code
		Ship-to Code
Style	E	Style Number
Finish Specs	WE	Style Number
		Finish Code
Color	E	Color Code
Authorized Style/Color	AE	Style Number
		Color Code
Order Header	E	Order Number
Order Detail	WE	Order Number
		Line Number
Work Order	E	Work Order Number
Customer Order Link	AE	Work Order Number
		Order Number
		Line Number
Inventory	E	Lot Number
Retail Price	WE	Style Number
Wholesale Price	WE	Style Number
		Customer Code

In the table, a unique key identifies each primary entity (type E). The suggested key for the weak entities (entity type WE) consists of the primary key(s) of the entity upon which the Weak Entity depends, as well as an additional code to provide a unique key. Using the key from the primary entity as part of the Weak Entity's key establishes the relationship between the two tables and facilitates validity checking during maintenance. This check prevents the primary table entry from being deleted when a Weak Entity exists. The relationship between the primary table and a Weak Entity could also be established by including the primary entity's key as a foreign key within the Weak Entity. This approach would not demonstrate the dependency as well, however.

The suggested key for an Associative Entity (type AE) is a concatenated key. This key is made up of the primary keys of the two entities that originally had the many-to-many relationship.

IDENTIFYING FOREIGN KEYS

Once the primary key for each entity is identified, the next step is to express the relationship among entities by adding foreign keys to the appropriate entities. A common relationship among entities is one-to-many. In this relationship, A is related to many Bs, and B is related to only one A. This relationship is expressed by including the primary key for A as a foreign key within the table definition for B. Let's complete the first cut for the table definition of each entity by adding foreign keys as required.

Entity	Foreign keys	Relates to
Order Header	Customer Code	Customer
	Customer Code* Ship-to Code	Ship-to
Order Detail	Style Number	Style
	Color Code	Color
	Style Number* Finish Code	Finish Specs.
	Style Number* Color Code*	Authorized Style/Color
Customer/Order Link	Order Number Line Number	Order Detail
	Work Order Number	Work Order
Inventory	Style Number	Style
	Color Code	Color
	Style Number* Finish Code	Finish Specs.
	Style Number* Color Code	Authorized Style/Color
	Work Order Number**	Work Order Assigned to
	Work Order Number**	Work Order Produced Against

In the first example, a relationship exists among the Order Header and the Customer entities. This relationship is implemented on a table level by including the key for the Customer entity in the table for the Order Header entity. The other relationships shown on the ERD are implemented in a similar fashion. It is worth noting that the relationship of a weak entity to its parent entity is implemented by including the key of the parent as part of the key for the weak entity. A similar approach is taken to implement the relationship of an associative entity to the original two entities that had the many-to-many relationship.

In the foreign key structure presented above, several fields are marked with an asterisk. These fields are required as part of a key and are duplicate entries of this field in the table. My suggestion is to permit this duplication at this stage since it is a reminder on a file specification level that a relationship exists with another file. Closer to a physical file specification, this duplication will be eliminated when we specify the referential integrity edit. The double asterisks next to Work Order Number indicate an intentional duplication of this field. While both instances of this field refer to the same file, the reference is for two different purposes. By establishing separate fields, we know not only the file being referred to but also the purpose or context of this referral.

A DATA MODELING LANGUAGE

The first diagram discussed, the DFD, lets us portray a proposed system at a high-level of abstraction. The next diagram, the ERD, lets us take one component from the DFD, the data store, and graphically portray a structure for each instance of a data store on the DFD. The structures portrayed on the ERDs are a set of relational database tables that can eventually be implemented as physical files on the AS/400.

The next step in defining the database was to identify the primary key(s) for each table shown on the ERD. And as a final step, we identified for each table the foreign keys needed in a relational database system to implement the relations between tables.

Primary keys, foreign keys, and attributes can also be added to the ERD to enhance the graphic portrayal. Figure 8.19 shows the symbols used to indicate a primary key and foreign keys for an entity. Figure 8.20 shows the use of these two additional symbols to define part of the table structure for the entity Inventory.

When we reach the level of detail where we are starting to identify keys for a table, foreign keys, and so on, reliance on graphic technique can result in diagrams that are so cluttered that they are unreadable. Just as an architect starts to rely on parts lists to identify the detailed material requirements of a building, an appropriate technique for us would be to use lists for the details. When we switch to the use of lists, we can use a Structured English format that not only identifies the

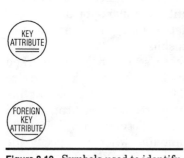

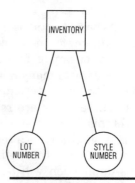

Figure 8.19 Symbols used to identify keys and foreign keys for an entity.

Figure 8.20 Diagram showing the use of graphic symbols to identify a key and a foreign key for the entire "Inventory."

part, but also tells us something about the role that this part plays in the database design.

Structured English was initially developed to express the detailed logic of a process. A variation of this original process-oriented language was developed by the Synon Corporation as a way of developing specifications for a relational database. Synon uses Structured English to permit relational database specifications to be entered into their CASE tool. The English structure consists of a specific set of verbs used to label the relationship between an entity and its primary key or the relationship between two entities. These verbs are:

Known By

Owned By

Refers To

The *Known By* label expresses the relationship between an entity and its primary key(s). The *Owned By* label expresses the relationship between a Weak Entity and its parent entity or between an Associative Entity and the original two entities that had the many-to-many relationship. The *Refers To* labels the many-to-one relationship between two entities.

When we use the *Known By, Owned By,* and *Refers To* verbs, we should attach a construction significance to them. In effect, these verbs tell us the primary and foreign keys. They also serve as a shorthand which tells us the editing that is to occur. From a physical implementation standpoint, these verbs have the following meaning:

Known By identifies the primary key field(s) for a record. This identifies a physical field to be included in the record and the primary access path to be created over this record.

Owned By results in the primary keys of the parent entity being included as part of the primary key of the child entity.

Refers To results in the primary keys of the related entity being included as foreign keys in the referring entity. The *Refers To* verb should also be interpreted so that referential integrity code is included in the program. Thus the physical implementation of *Refers To* results in the inclusion of required foreign keys in the record format and the addition of procedure code in the program to check referential integrity.

In addition to the verb to express a relationship between two entities, we might also need to qualify or explain the relationship. In the example used above, there are two relationships between the Inventory entity and the Work Order entity. Using a qualifier, these two relationships might be expressed as follows:

INVENTORY *Refers To* WORK ORDER for finishing

INVENTORY *Refers To* WORK ORDER for produced by

The first qualifier explains that this relationship identifies the Work Order to which a lot of Inventory has been assigned for processing. The qualifier that is part of the second relationship records the Work Order that authorized the processing of a new lot of material. A qualifier should also be used to define the recursive relationship that an entity can have with itself. In the customer entity example, the relationship between a specific instance of a customer and its parent would be expressed as:

CUSTOMER *Refers To* CUSTOMER for parent

A third type of qualifier handles the situation where the implementation of a relationship will add duplicate foreign keys to a table. An example of this situation occurred when we defined the foreign keys to implement the relationships for the order detail entity. The foreign keys were:

Entity	Foreign Keys	Relates To
Order Detail	Style Number	Style
	Style Number*	Finish Specs
	Finish Code	

*Duplicate Foreign Key.

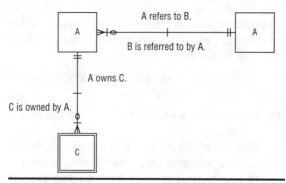

Figure 8.21 The use of "Structured English" verbs to label the relationships among entities.

These relationship can be expressed as follows:

ORDER DETAIL *Refers To* STYLE

ORDER DETAIL *Refers To* FINISH SPECS *Sharing* Style Number

Adding the *Sharing* qualifier means that when the relationship is implemented in the physical database design, a second Style Number does not need to be included because of the second relationship.

To visualize how these verbs and qualifiers label the relationships between entities, let's look at a sample ERD with labels added (Fig. 8.21). As a convention for the placement of labels, the following is suggested:

A label is written on the top when the relationship goes from left to right.

A label is written on the right when the relationship goes from top to bottom.

But instead of going back and labeling all the relationships on the sample ERD, let's now convert to Structured English and express what we have defined so far in this new format. The reason for converting to a new format at this point in the database definition is that the next step involves that addition of a great deal of information, the attributes that need to be defined for an entity. The table format used with Structured English is more conducive to handling this amount of detail than an ERD. Figure 8.22 is an example of a Structured English presentation of the information developed so far concerning the sample system.

Entity	Relationship	Entity or attribute	Extension
Customer	Known By	Customer Code	
	Refers To	CUSTOMER	For Parent
Ship-to Address	Owned by	CUSTOMER	
	Known By	Ship-to Code	Sharing Customer Code
Style	Known By	Style Number	
	Owned By	STYLE	
Finish Specs	Known By	Finish Code	
Color	Known By	Color Code	
Authorized Style/Color	Owned By	STYLE	
	Owned By	COLOR	
Order Header	Known By	Order Number	
	Refers To	CUSTOMER	
	Refers To	SHIP-TO ADDRESS	Sharing Customer Code
Order Detail	Owned By	ORDER HEADER	
	Known By	Line Number	
	Refers To	STYLE	
	Refers To	COLOR	
	Refers To	FINISH SPECS	Sharing Style Number
	Refers To	AUTH STYLE/COLOR	Sharing Style/Color Numbers
Work Order	Known By	Word Order Number	
	Refers To	STYLE	
	Refers To	COLOR	
	Refers To	FINISH SPECS	Sharing Style Number
	Refers To	AUTH STYLE/COLOR	Sharing Style Number Color Code
Customer Order Link	Owned By	WORK ORDER	
	Owned By	ORDER DETAIL	
Inventory	Known By	Lot Number	
	Refers To	STYLE	
	Refers To	COLOR	
	Refers To	Finish Specs	Sharing Style Number
	Refers To	WORK ORDER	For Finish
	Refers To	WORK ORDER	For Prod. from
Retail Price	Owned By	STYLE	
Wholesale Price	Owned By	STYLE	
	Owned By	CUSTOMER	

Figure 8.22 Sample of the listing format used to show a relational database design using Structured English. Special verbs identify the primary keys for entities and express the relationship between entities.

This new format identifies all entities, relationships, and primary keys. It also specifies whether a relationship is optional and expresses any qualifiers that apply to the relationships. To complete the database definition, we now need to add attributes to the individual tables and to specify the editing that applies. Methods for accomplishing these tasks, which are needed to finish the definition of the database, are the subjects of the next two chapters.

A Choice of
Design Strategies

The last chapter discussed a method and a notation for defining the architectural structure of a database. This method started with the high-level identifications of data called data stores defined on a DFD. A proposed structure for each data store was then established using an ERD. This diagram identified entities and the relationships among them. Once this database structure was created, the next step was to identify the primary keys for each entity and the foreign keys needed to implement the relationship between entities expressed on the ERD. At the point where keys and foreign keys were being documented, a form of Structured English was suggested as a more appropriate method for documenting the additional details of the database design rather than continuing to rely on a graphical technique. The next step in the process of designing the system is to determine the additional information (the attributes) for each entity. Attributes (or fields, to use physical database terminology) are the detailed information needed in the database for the system to accomplish its goals. But at this point in the software development process, developing fairly detailed design

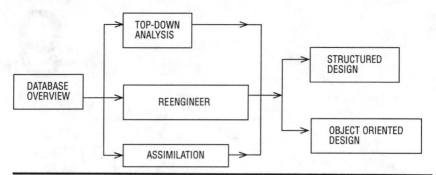

Figure 9.1 Strategy options that are available to guide the development of detailed database specifications.

specifications, several development strategy options are available. Figure 9.1 shows an overview of some choices. Let's examine these choices before proceeding any further.

TOP-DOWN ANALYSIS

A top-down Data Analysis starts with the question, "What information is necessary to capture for an entity?" This is answered in a formal JAD session or through informal interviews, a review of existing documents, and investigations by an analyst. For example, starting with the customer entity identified on the ERD, a JAD session might determine that we need to capture the following information:

Address—Type—Credit Status—Date Created—Status

Once we determine these significant attributes for the customer, the attributes are recorded manually or entered into the CASE tool.

However, there are several problems with a top-down approach.

- The completeness of the attribute identification cannot be controlled. It depends on the thoroughness of the JAD participants or the analyst since there is no firm starting point.

- Minor, and frequently arbitrary, differences between the existing data structure of the organization and the proposed new data structure are difficult to spot.

- Conversion of old data to the new format is not considered.

There are also several other problems with many of the available upper CASE tools that use this top-down approach.

- Many available upper CASE tools serve primarily as a notebook to record the results of the analysis. These tools do not actively aid in the iterative process usually needed to define the new database.

- Available tools generally do not conform to the AS/400 DDS format. As result, there is not a convenient way to store edit specifications with the data that will eventually be implemented through the DDS. Instead this information tends to get stored as a process specification, and might be overlooked when the DDS is being created. Generally, many of the tools provide for a *text* name and permit the specification of data type and field size. They do not permit the documentation of extended DDS edit rules such as allowed values, range and greater than/less than editing, check digit verification, and so on.

- As part of the database documentation, they do not provide a convenient place to record the process-oriented business rules used to validate and create data. As a result, you cannot obtain a full understanding of a field in the database and the changes that can be made to it without looking at procedural specifications.

REENGINEERING

In the mainframe arena, an alternative to top-down analysis has been evolving for several years. This alternative was developed because many organizations with millions of lines of old COBOL code needed to upgrade both to new hardware and new database management systems such as DB2. In response to this need, new CASE software was developed to assist organizations that are unwilling to abandon old legacy systems and start from scratch. And as part of this new CASE software, two new concepts have been developed, *reverse engineering* and *forward engineering.*

Reverse engineering consists of taking existing applications (databases and programs) and putting them into both a format and a tool which facilitates upgrading to both new software technology and to new hardware.

Forward engineering is taking the old system that has been put into a working format through reverse engineering and producing a new software system that uses the advanced technology of the new data processing environment.

The Bachman/Reengineering Product Set is a well-known mainframe CASE tool developed to address the problem of legacy systems. But unfortunately reengineering tools are platform, software, and language specific. The needs of the IBM midrange have not received the same focused attention from tool vendors as the mainframe has. To the degree that the issue has been addressed for the AS/400, it has been by lower CASE tools vendors, such as Synon and SSA (the vendor for AS/SET).

Synon, for example, has a capability called *assimilation* that lets you bring existing files into the tool, modify the file formats, and then use the restructured files to generate new programs. AS/SET also lets you use existing file definitions and provides a facility to take existing procedural code and convert it into the 4GL part of AS/SET. But both Synon and AS/SET were developed primarily as an aid for the construction phase of a system life cycle. They do not support the analysis and design phases to the degree that is desirable, and their early use in the life cycle to facilitate reengineering tends to change the project focus from planning to construction.

So, rather than use a top-down design tool or adapt to the capabilities of existing construction tools, let's see what kind of a tool might help overcome the problems associated with top-down Data Analysis discussed above. But before we do, let's also examine the other options identified in Fig. 9.1, Structured Design and Object Oriented Design (OOD). A choice between these two options influences not only the type of tool you choose but also the point in the analysis/design process where you perform certain tasks.

ORIGINS OF STRUCTURED DESIGN

One of the first attempts to introduce order into the process of programming was the top-down design method. This method starts with identifying a process and a set of tasks to be accomplished as part of this process. These tasks are then functionally decomposed into smaller and smaller tasks, and the results are eventually arranged into blocks as a hierarchy chart.

The initial top-down design methods were later refined into a set of techniques, strategies, and methods called Structured Design. Three significant concepts were formulated to better design a program:

1. Design strategies called *transform analysis* and *transaction analysis* provide a formal approach to decomposing and structuring the tasks needed as part of a process.

2. Measures called *coupling* and *cohesion* provide guidance during the functional decomposition and provide a means of developing a modular solution.

3. A graphical structure chart aids the design process and provides a way to express the solution effectively.

TRANSFORM ANALYSIS

Transform analysis is a formal method for functional decomposition of a process that identifies the primary functional components and the high-level inputs and outputs for these components. This approach starts with a process identified on a DFD. The first step of transform analysis is to divide the process into three parts: inputs, logical processing, and outputs.

The input part is called the *afferent* branch and includes the processes that read data (such as, from a terminal, disk, and so on) and transform the data from physical (a character from a terminal) to logical form (an internal table). The afferent branch includes the data validation routines, preparation of error messages, and so forth. A DFD may have more than one afferent branch for a given process.

The output part is called the *efferent* branch and includes the processes that write data (such as to a disk or to a printer) and transform data from its internal form to physical form (for example, report print line or error message).

The *central transform* is the linking process between the afferent (input) and efferent (output) branches. It is furthest removed from the processing associated with the input and output of data. It is used to perform tabulations, summaries, and other functions of the data before the output process.

Once you have identified the three major parts of a process, you can prepare a structure chart by drawing a component for the central transform and for the afferent and efferent branches. Figure 9.2 is an

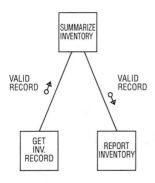

Figure 9.2 Structure Chart developed using the Transform Analysis guidelines of Structured Design. Three parts of a process are identified: the Input part (the afferent branch), the Output part (the efferent branch), and the Central Transform.

example of a structure chart for an inventory summary report. In this chart, the central transform is at the top level. This function serves as the root segment that controls the other two branches. The role of the root segment could also be accomplished by defining an independent function and placing it at the top of the chart.

TRANSACTION ANALYSIS

For a complex process, such as Edit Customer Order, the basic input, transform, and output structure needs to be expanded to handle the various types of data involved. For example, a typical customer order involves an order header, one or more detail lines, and frequently a special ship-to address. Each of these types of data is a transaction, and the basic structure chart can be expanded to include a transaction center function. The transaction center function is placed at the top of the chart, and a function for each transaction is placed below it. Each transaction function is then decomposed to show the subfunctions for input, central transform, and output. Figure 9.3 is an example of a structure chart for the transactions involved in Edit Customer Order.

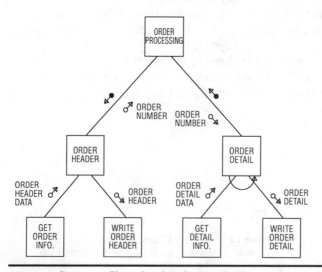

Figure 9.3 Structure Chart developed using the Transaction Analysis guidelines of Structured Design. First the transactions involved in a process are identified, and a transaction center function is established. Then each transaction is broken down into its afferent, central transform, and efferent branches.

MODULARIZATION

Once the functions for a process have been identified using functional decomposition, the question then becomes whether to write one multi-function program to accomplish the goals of the process or to break up the total functionality into a number of discrete modules.

But before answering this question, let's briefly review the concept of a module as it applies to the AS/400. A *module* can be defined as a named collection of contiguous program statements that can be referenced by other parts of the system through use of the module name. (3) This broad definition includes routines that are compiled independently and referenced at run time with a CALL operation (external subroutines) and subroutines that are referenced at compile time with a COPY facility (RPG) or with the COPY statement (COBOL) (internal subroutines). In our discussion, the term *module* is used to refer to independently compiled programs, and *subroutine* refers to subprograms copied into the program at compile time.

Both Structured Design concepts and performance considerations on the AS/400 support the use of modular program design. The advantages of modular programming are as follows.

- It is easier to deal with a complex process in small pieces that can be defined, programmed, and tested independently.

- Future maintenance is facilitated if various parts of a process solution are isolated into separate pieces so that changes to one part can be made without affecting the other parts.

- Reuse is encouraged by encapsulating program statements (both modules and subroutines) that have an identifiable function.

From a performance standpoint, small independent modules typically improve system performance. This improvement comes from better memory utilization, which is obtained by the AS/400's ability to share application code [see References for a discussion of performance considerations (4 and 5)].

COUPLING

If a decision is made to use a modular approach to the design of a process solution, you need a basis for identifying and organizing the module. Structured Design provides several guidelines for arriving at a solution and judging results. The first guideline of structured programming is that a module should have a single entry and exit point.

In effect, the internal mechanics of a module are hidden, and any process solution that incorporates the services of a module should enter and exit the module in the same way. As to the actual contents of a module, two other concepts are significant, coupling and cohesion.

Coupling measures the degree of independence between modules. The most desirable relationship between modules is a simple call for execution in which the calling module does not need to provide any information for the called module to do its job. In practice, search arguments or data parameters typically need to be passed, and there might be other forms of interdependence that bind modules together. An example would be the passing of a format code to a date routine to indicate which edit routine within the module to use. The nature of this interdependence is called coupling, which consists of the following categories.

Data coupling: This represents the most desirable form of coupling next to the simple call for execution. Only data in the form of parameters is passed between two modules. The data is used only for processing, not for program control.

Stamp coupling: Two modules are stamp coupled if they communicate through a composite data item (such as a record). The composite data item may contain pieces of data that a module does not use even though they are passed to it.

Control coupling: Two modules are control coupled if the information passed includes both data and control elements. The control elements then direct the order of instruction execution in the called module. An example of this type of coupling is the date format code previously described.

Common coupling: Two modules are common coupled if they share the same global data areas. This occurs on the AS/400 if we define a module as an *Internal* subroutine rather than as a called module.

Content coupling: Two modules are content coupled if one module uses data or control information contained within another module or changes the internals of another module. As with common coupling, on the AS/400 this is an issue for subroutines rather than for independently compiled modules.

COHESION

While coupling looks at the relationship among modules to evaluate the degree of interdependence, cohesion looks within the module. Cohesion measures how strongly the elements within a module are logically related. Ideally, a module contains only those elements needed to accomplish a single unique purpose. This permits the module to be readily understood when a future need for maintenance arises. Following are the types of cohesion for a module:

Functional cohesion: The most desirable type of cohesion occurs when each element of a module is necessary for the module to accomplish its unique task.

Sequential cohesion: The next most desirable type of cohesion occurs when the elements of a module are related by the fact that the output of one step in the series becomes the input for the next. This typically occurs when a series of mathematical formulas is needed to determine a final result.

Communicational cohesion: This type of cohesion occurs when the elements of a module all operate on the same data (such as the edit routines that validate the various fields of a terminal input).

Procedural cohesion: This occurs when the elements of a module are part of a sequence of steps that have to be performed in a certain fixed order (such as when a module contains an iterative loop that dictates a sequence of steps before the loop can be repeated).

Temporal cohesion: The elements of a procedure are related by time but not necessarily by function (such as initialization or reset routines).

Logical cohesion: The elements of a module perform a related class of operations instead of a single function. Control elements are needed to decide which operation to perform.

Coincidental cohesion: There is little or no relationship between the elements of a module.

OBJECT ORIENTED DESIGN (OOD)

The functional decomposition and Structured Design philosophies previously discussed evolved in the 1970s before relational database concepts emphasizing the structure of data evolved. The focus was on defining procedure logic, and when data was considered, a minimalist approach was taken. This means that once data associated with a process was identified, little about this data was defined other than the basics such as size and type. Editing was considered a procedural issue, and the details of editing were buried within the specifications for process logic. As a consequence, once the high-level view of the database is established by identifying files and fields as we did in Chap. 8, the focus switches to the process.

OOD is an alternate design strategy that emphasizes the structure of the data as the basis for developing a modular solution for a business process. As a result it changes the way we document requirements associated with creating, retrieving, and updating data. OOD establishes a much stronger link between data and processing. The key word in this design philosophy is *encapsulation*. This term denotes the bundling of related data and procedures. The basic encapsulation unit is the *object*, which includes both a specific instance of data and the processes that operate on this data.

OOD segments systems into a set of objects capable of interacting with each other to accomplish the system objectives. The individual objects are independent and can be used in a variety of process solutions.

Several new terms have come out of OOD. Familiarity with these terms will show how the concepts of OOD might affect AS/400 design strategy.

OBJECTS / CLASSES / INSTANCES

OOD begins with the identification of an object. An object consists of a collection of related data elements and the procedures that operate on this data. Many individual objects can have the same methods and data characteristics, and the term *class* is then used to identify a group of objects of the same general type. The individual occurrences of objects are then identified as instances of the class. In AS/400 programming terminology, for example, an object might be a record for an individual customer plus the modules or subroutines that process this record. But since all records in the customer file are typically handled the same, the customer master file plus all related modules that operate on this file can be considered a class.

METHOD / MESSAGE

A *method* is a procedure that operates on the data that is part of an object. An important OOD concept relating to a method is that the processing is absolutely restricted to the data in the object of which it is a part. This means that a module would have no access to data outside its object definition. If, as part of order-header processing, it was necessary to validate the account number, a separate object, Customer, would be necessary. The order header object would send a validation request, and the Customer object would return a response. The communications medium between objects is called *messages*. A message consists of the name of a receiving object with the name of one of its methods. On the AS/400, this would be the equivalent of a program call plus any parameters passed at run time.

POLYMORPHISM

Polymorphism is the ability of two or more classes of objects to respond to the same message, each in its own way. This means that an object does not need to know to whom it is sending a message. It just needs to know that when a message is sent, appropriate objects will receive it and act accordingly. An example of the use of this type of message might be a scheduling argument. When an accounting period close notice is posted, appropriate reporting programs use this message to trigger their reporting cycle.

INHERITANCE

Although each class is fully defined separately, a class can also be defined as a special case of another class. In this instance, a class is considered a subclass, and through a process of *inheritance,* the subclass can use the methods and variables of its class. In addition, the subclass can have other methods unique to itself.

COMPOSITE OBJECTS

If an object is made up of not only data and methods but also includes other objects, it is called a *composite object.* This amounts to a nesting procedure in which an assembly, an object in its own right, can include other objects and also other composite objects. For example, an *order* can be a composite object made up of an order header object and an order detail object.

FRAMEWORKS

Frameworks are skeleton structures of programs that must be fleshed out to build a complete application. (6) On the AS/400, Synon provides a notable example of the concept of a framework. Synon has a variety of program shells called *device functions.* An example of one of these skeleton structures would be a shell called "Display Record." When this shell is linked to a specific file specification, a complete program can be generated which permits the retrieval and display of a specific record in the designated file.

OBJECT ORIENTED DESIGN—AN EVOLUTIONARY STEP

Ideas such as encapsulation, objects, and composite objects used as the basis for designing a system in many ways follow in the footsteps of other design disciplines. OOD terms (such as composite object, object, and instance) are similar to the terms assembly, part, and piece used by mechanical design engineers. The approach of OOD is also similar to the planning methods used by many engineering disciplines. The encapsulation of data and methods, which is advocated by OOD, is the organizational technique that a manufacturing engineer uses to prepare the production or assembly specifications for a part or an assembly.

A pulley and a pulley assembly can demonstrate how OOD comes close to the way engineers organize specification information prior to production. In OOD, the pulley assembly would be a composite object, and the pulley—a components of the assembly—would be an object.

When design and manufacturing specifications for the pulley and the pulley assembly are being prepared, two different approaches might be used.

Figure 9.4 represents one possible way of preparing the specifications for the pulley and the pulley assembly. One of the first problems apparent in Fig. 9.4 is that the design specification for the pulley

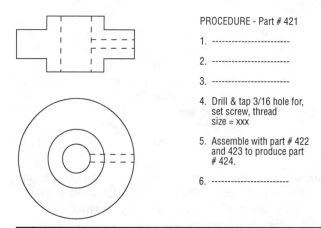

PROCEDURE - Part # 421

1. -----------------------

2. -----------------------

3. -----------------------

4. Drill & tap 3/16 hole for, set screw, thread size = xxx

5. Assemble with part # 422 and 423 to produce part # 424.

6. -----------------------

Figure 9.4 Sample *craft*-type manufacturing instruction in which specifications describing the characteristics of the part are commingled with the manufacturing instructions telling how the part is to be produced.

contains a minimum amount of information. For example, the dimensions of the pulley and the size of the set screw hole are not included.

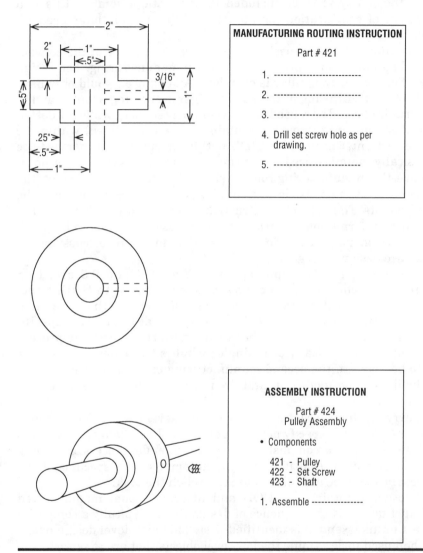

Figure 9.5 Modern manufacturing instructions in which *what* is to be produced, *how* it is to be produced, and *how* it is to be *used* are described in three separate documents.

Instead, dimensions such as the size of the set screw hole are included as part of the machining instructions. Also, the final instruction shows that the pulley is to be included in a specific assembly; this is a problem of specification maintenance if this part is later used for another assembly.

The alternative approach in Fig. 9.5 is an example of the conventional specification approach now used in manufacturing. The design specification for the pulley is complete. An engineer would only have to look at the drawing of the part to learn everything about it and to determine if could be reused for another purpose. Also, while the design specifications are completely contained (or encapsulated) within the one document, this document tells nothing about how the part is to be physically manufactured. Production information is in another document—the manufacturing routing sheet. And the final document, the assembly instructions, is organized around the assembly, not the components. The assembly instructions also omit any design or manufacturing information concerning the parts used in the assembly. Such an omission is called *information hiding* in many discussions on software design.

Comparing the two approaches in Figs. 9.4 and 9.5 are, to a degree, also comparing functional decomposition with OOD. Functional decomposition takes a minimalist view of the data in a system, and typically you would have to look at the process specifications to fully understand the editing performed. And the process decomposition typically commingles what is to be done with how it is to be done. In the second manufacturing example above, what is to be done is defined first, and then how it is to be done is defined separately.

Carrying this concept over to software development, for example, the first step is to specify detailed edit rules. Later, you specify if this editing was to be accomplished as part of a manual process or if it was to be automated. And if it is to be automated, the specifics of the program would be established to accomplish the task.

Another point in both OOD and in conventional manufactured product design is the sequence of design tasks. Typically a composite object or an assembly is identified first. This high-level design object is then used to determine the low-level objects that are to serve as the basis for detailed design. Then, the details of these low-level objects are designed. In a separate step, the manufacturing process for each object (part) is established. The final step prepares an assembly specification and describes how the components of the composite object or the assembly are to be put together.

A PERSPECTIVE ON DESIGN STRATEGIES

To a significant degree, both a design strategy and a design tool set are strongly influenced by the intended downstream construction environment. Structured Design evolved primarily in the mainframe arena during the 1970s. At that time, the construction option was effectively limited to procedural languages such as COBOL. And as one author explained, "If you write in COBOL, everything is a procedure." (7) For example, if you compare the information content of a COBOL picture clause to the specifications for data which are part of DDS, you can see a reason for the process orientation of the time. Edit checks, such as range validation and check digit verification, would all have had to be specified as process requirements since they could not be specified as part of the COBOL picture clause. These types of checks would also have had to be implemented by procedure code rather than by including them in the screen DDS as we would on the AS/400.

OOD, on the other hand, had its origins primarily in the PC world. The PC platform has object-oriented programming languages such as Smalltalk and C++. These languages include features such as inheritance that facilitate many of the concepts of OOD. On the AS/400, we have a variety of construction options that include procedural languages such as RPG and COBOL, 4GLs such as those associated with AS/SET's or COGNOS's CASE tools, or framework technology such as Synon's. What we don't have is a mature language with inheritance capabilities or some of the construction specifics associated with object-oriented programming. As a consequence, we would not want to use as a guide to the size of a method the three to five Smalltalk statements mentioned in one book on OOD. (8) It also does not seem practical that the concept of encapsulation should be carried to the degree advocated in OOD. This would mean, for example, that if a referential integrity check was needed on a field such as an account number in an order header, it would be accomplished by a call to a separate module rather than by chaining to the customer file.

What is appropriate for us from the evolving concepts of OOD is the basic idea of encapsulating both data and its associated methods. When we adopt a strategy of encapsulation, it leads to the idea that a solution for a complex process is obtained by assembling a group of independent objects. This approach facilitates a number of design objectives. First, it reinforces the idea of modularity we first discussed as part of Structured Design. It also fosters reuse since the starting point for a complex process solution is a determination of what objects should be assembled. Thus, we start by looking to identify objects first rather than attempt to modularize a hierarchy solution as the last design step.

This approach also suggests methods for dealing with the varied construction environments we face on the AS/400. These methods will be discussed in the next several chapters.

The OOD approach also leads us away from the minimalist approach to the database design in which we only define basic domain integrity rules as part of the database specification. The traditional structured analysis approach typically leaves the task of defining in detail the editing of the data until the process definition phase. As a consequence, this approach intermingles the determination of what is to be done with how it is to be done. Traditional engineering has provided the example that there should be one self-contained design document that identifies the what (the design specification) and another document that identifies the how (the manufacturing specification or routing sheet). This permits an evaluation of reuse by only looking at the design specification without the need to review a process or program specification.

As a final comment on the design methodology introspection, I definitely favor a reengineering approach to a top-down approach when we are identifying the attributes (fields) that are part of an entity (file). When we are developing a new system, we are usually replacing a prior automation effort. By analyzing old file formats in the context of the new relational file structure, we have a firmer starting point and we are also addressing data conversion problems at an early date. This should reduce the number of data surprises at implementation time. I do not place the same emphasis on process reengineering, however. When we analyze old systems, it is frequently difficult to tell what procedural elements reflect an underlying business requirement and what part is a physical solution based on the technology available when the system was developed. In addition many old systems evolved as a piecemeal automation of the business processes in effect when the system was being automated. These old business practices and task structures typically need to be completely restructured if we are to obtain the full benefits of newer technology.

With this brief review of design strategies completed, let's now go on to the next step of the process for software development—completing the Data Model.

REFERENCES

1. Stevens, W. Myers, G. Constantine, L. "Structured Design," *IBM Systems Journal,* 13, 1974.

2. Yourdon, E. and Constantine, L. *Structured Design.* Prentice-Hall: Englewood Cliffs, N.J., 1979.

1. Stevens, W. Myers, G. Constantine, L. "Structured Design," *IBM Systems Journal,* 13, 1974.

2. Yourdon, E. and Constantine, L. *Structured Design.* Prentice-Hall: Englewood Cliffs, N.J., 1979.

3. Conte, Paul. and Jones, Roger J. "The Sum of the Parts: An Introduction to Modular Programming," *NEWS/34-38,* April 1987.

4. Conte, Paul. "The Monolithic Myth," *NEWS/34-38,* April 1987.

5. Barsa, Albert S. Jr., "RPG–The Next Generation," *Systems 3X/400,* October 1992.

6. Wirfs-Brock, Rebecca, Wilkerson, Brian, Wiener, Lauren. *Designing Object-Oriented Software.* Prentice-Hall: Englewood Cliffs, N.J., p. 13.

7. Dixon, Robert L. *Winning with CASE,* McGraw-Hill: New York, 1992, p. 45.

8. Yourdon, Edward. *Object-Oriented Design,* Yourdon Press Computing Series, Prentice-Hall: Englewood Cliffs, N.J., 1991.

10

Completing the
Data Model

The review of design strategy options was intended first to show that most software development approaches are based on a specific construction environment. The detailed tasks and methods to accomplish these tasks reflect this environment. The environment that influences both the tasks and the methods includes the programming language, features of the systems software, and the database management system. As a consequence, any process for developing a software system for the AS/400 that relies on a historical approach usually must be customized for the AS/400.

The second point of the review was to point out significant advances in software design strategies since the early days of structured design. Two notable examples of these advances are reengineering and OOD. The next phase of the application development life cycle demonstrates how these development options influence the choice of methods and tools.

PLANNING FOR REENGINEERING

The first option, reengineering of existing software, involves both existing data and existing programs. Of these two, data is the more fruitful object for reengineering. The underlying information required to run an organization tends not to change unless the objectives of the organization change radically. The computer programs, on the other hand, frequently represent both transitory needs of the users and a physical solution to processing requirements based on the technology available at the time the programs were written.

Database reengineering starts with the data structures from existing manual or computerized applications. Reverse engineering of the existing data structures converts them into a format that can be used to create a system that incorporates present-day knowledge. In practical terms, this frequently means taking flat files from a legacy S/34 or S/36 and putting them into a work file. This work file facilitates the conversion of the old file layouts into the third normal form of a relational database design.

An important part of the reengineering process is to maintain an audit trail as old data structures are redesigned. This audit trail first lists changes to existing field definitions as well as any additions or deletions to existing forms or files. This permits arbitrary field definition changes, such as the size, to be highlighted, so that they can be reviewed in a JAD session. The second purpose of this audit trail is to provide a map for data conversion purposes that shows the source and destination of historical information that is to be retained.

PLANNING FOR OBJECT ORIENTED DESIGN

The basic concept of OOD is the encapsulation of data and the methods that operate on this data. What does this concept mean from a practical standpoint during the development of a detailed database design? Should all methods that will operate on the data be considered, or is a limited approach more appropriate?

A limited approach would initially focus on the methods for editing data when it is created or when it is modified. A comprehensive approach would also determine how the data is to be used and identify the methods for permitting this use.

Again, data in an organization tends to be very stable while the uses of data tend to be very volatile. So, a focus on data and the methods for editing this data can produce a relatively stable design document that has long-term design value. Extending the methods identification and definition beyond the point of creating and modifying the data involves the most unpredictable aspects of a system. Since the primary goal at this point is to establish an architectural overview, a comprehensive identification of the uses of the data should be deferred to a later life cycle phase.

TOOL SELECTION

Identifying a tool for completing the details of the Data Model must begin by defining the tool's desirable features and characteristics. The discussion of reengineering and OOD suggests that the following features are needed:

1. A work file for loading existing data structures (manual forms or computerized file layouts) to provide a starting point for reengineering.

2. An audit trail capability to compare old and new database designs. The ability to highlight changes in field definitions and to provide a conversion map between the old and new file structures is crucial.

3. A field definition capability that conforms to the AS/400 DDS structure.

4. An expanded file and field definition capability to capture all editing information consistent with the adoption of an OOD philosophy.

5. Compatibility with the related tools used in construction phase of the life cycle.

A homegrown tool that contains the necessary features provides a perspective on how to meet these requirements. Later, Chap. 15 will look at an established upper CASE tool that performs these tasks and, in the process, maintains an integrated system repository that contains both a high-level Business Model and a detailed Data Model.

Figure 10.1 represents an example of a customized form for capturing information for the detailed analysis and design phases of Data Modeling. This form is comparable to the data element description form and the edit and validation form that were part of the original deliverables from a JAD session. This new form departs from traditional documentation because it conforms to the specification content of DDS and permits two of the tasks identified earlier, reengineering data and encapsulating editing methods.

Note: I automated this form and associated reports by using SYMANTEC's Q&A. Q&A is a PC-based file server that permits the rapid definition of a database and any reports that are needed from this

```
                            DATA BASE DEFINITION
********************************************************************************
                       1. Present File/Document Definition
       Original System    :
       Orig. File/Form #  :              Orig. File/Form Name       :
       Field Name         :              Type (Data) :     Length :
       Field Text Name    :                                Start  :
********************************************************************************
                       2. New Entity/Attribute Definition
       New Entity (File) #                :
       New Entity Name (File)             :
       New Attribute Name (or Ref. Obj)   :
       Function           :     (Key,Attr,For Key,Virt,Der)
       Field Type (Global) :              Attr/Rel Optional Y/b :
       Field Seq.         :              New Length             :
       Type (Data)        :
       Range         From :              To                     :
********************************************************************************
                       6. Structured English Definition
       Relation (Verb) :              Qualifier :
********************************************************************************
```

```
                           3. Field Conditions

           Condition 1    :                    Value  :
           Condition 2    :                    Value  :
           Condition 3    :                    Value  :
           Condition 4    :                    Value  :
           Condition 5    :                    Value  :

********************************************************************************
                           4. Business Rules

   1 :
   2. :
   3. :
   4. :
   5. :
   6 :
   7. :
   8. :
```

```
********************************************************************************
                       5. Object Cross Reference

   1. :
   2. :
   3 :
   4. :
   5. :
   6. :
   7. :
   8. :
```

Figure 10.1 Sample form for developing detailed specifications for a database using the concepts of database reengineering and object oriented design (OOD). Separate sections of the form permit you to document the details of an existing database (manual forms or computerized records), revise the initial field definitions, and document additional specifications such as allowed values, relevant business rules, and related objects (independent processing routines).

database. The cost of Q&A is under $500, and I have found that automating the form facilitates the iterative process of defining a database. I used a PC rather than prepare a similar analysis system on the AS/400 to stay with the PC as the platform for analysis and design. This consistency simplifies the equipment setup up for the JAD sessions.

The form shown as Fig. 10.1 serves as a repository for all the information concerning an entity and its attributes. It has also been expanded so that it can be used to print a listing of the database in a Structured English format. This listing is comparable to the data modeling format Synon uses. If Synon is the intended target, preparing this listing in advance facilitates a quality assurance review before conversion to the construction environment of the lower CASE tool. Regardless of the intended CASE construction target, however, this listing is useful. It permits the preparation of a summary report that provides a quick overview of the database architecture.

The database definition form is divided into six sections as follows:

1. Present File/Document Definition

2. New Entity/Attribute Definition

3. Attribute Allowed Values (Field Conditions)

4. Business Rules

5. Object Cross-Reference

6. Structured English Data Definition

Let's take a brief look at each section on the form, and then examine some of the specifics as well as the reports to be produced from this database.

PRESENT FILE / DOCUMENT DEFINITION

The first section (Present File/Document Definition) stores the definition of any existing database design or any manual forms to be evaluated during detailed database design for the new system. If there is an existing DDS, this might be down-loaded from the primary computer system through PC Support/400 or another AS/400 PC interface. If the starting point is manual forms or verbal definitions from users, this section would be entered manually.

This section permits a data reengineering approach in which individual fields and files can be redefined and restructured according to the guidelines for relational database design. This is the controlled starting point discussed earlier. Completing this section also permits the preparation of a report that is a cross-reference between the old file formats and the new file design. This report is the planning basis for the conversion if data from the old system is to be brought forward to the new system.

NEW ENTITY DEFINITION

The second section (New Entity Definition) establishes the attributes for each entity identified on the ERD. The starting point for completing this section is an analysis of an old field from the original file or form. This original field was recorded in the first section of the form. The original field is then reassigned to a New Entity according to third normal form. The entity structure used as the basis of this normalization is the entities and relationships previously identified on the Entity Relationship Diagram. During this process of restructuring the details of an old database or defining a new one from scratch, the original ERD is being updated. Designing the new database is an iterative process, and it is important to keep the database design details and the ERD in synch.

This section also permits addition of New Attributes (fields) and redefinition and renaming of fields. Provision is made to include some additional information concerning the attribute, such as whether it is a key, attribute, or foreign key. Whether the attribute is optional can also be recorded. Provision is also made to indicate the sequence in which the attribute is to appear on the related reports.

ALLOWED VALUES

The third section (Allowed Values) stores any Allowed Values for an attribute that have been identified during the analysis. This section is implemented using the VALUES keyword of the screen DDS if the programming language is RPG, COBOL, or CL. If construction is to be accomplished by one of the code generators, there typically is a special specifications screen for entering definitions of this type.

BUSINESS RULES

The fourth section (Business Rules) stores additional validation rules that govern the creation or updating of the individual field. Examples of appropriate entries are as follows:

Ship date must be later than the Order Date.

When inventory is assigned to a customer, change the stock status indicator from O (open) to A (allocated).

Traditionally the description of such editing rules has been left to the process definition phase of a project. Inclusion of these rules at this point has a number of advantages.

The first advantage is that the resulting document is a complete design specification. It tells the *what* in the same manner that an engineer's blueprints describe a product or part to be manufactured. As a consequence, when we reach the phase of defining processes to create or maintain data, the focus needs to be only on the *how*—the program design. What the program needs to accomplish will already be specified.

This document separation of the *what* and the *how* also provides a good focus for a JAD session. The determination of edit rules is no longer mingled with the task of designing a program through the transform or transaction analysis approach of Structured Design. As a consequence, users do not get involved in programming considerations in which they have little interest or expertise.

Another advantage of capturing complete edit specifications at this point is that it is consistent with the OOD philosophy of encapsulating data and the methods that operate on it. This evolution in design philosophy will come in handy as object-oriented tools and languages become more readily available on the AS/400.

A final advantage of this approach is that it provides great flexibility in the options available for program construction. Depending on the construction tools to be used downstream, there might not be any need for an elaborate process definition activity for many programs required in a system. If the OOD framework technology is used, many basic programs to create or maintain files can be generated automatically from the data specifications. The Business Rules then serve as the basis for specific enhancements to these generated programs rather than as part of the specifications for a complete new program.

As a cautionary note on this section, some of the data editing in a system might involve logic that is too complex to adequately describe using text oriented Business Rules. As a consequence, a better notation might be a decision tree or table or an action diagram. These alternative notations are described in detail in Chap. 12. If these are used, it is very important to cross-reference these documents to the Business Rules. It is also helpful to organize these logic design supplements on as low an AS/400 object level as possible. On the AS/400, an individual field is an object entry in the field reference file. In the same way, a physical file is also an object. The individual field, rather than the complete file, would be the preferred basis for any supplemental document, such as an action diagram. This way, if a field is reassigned to a different file based on performance considerations, for example, there is no need to change or reorganize underlying specification documents.

OBJECT CROSS-REFERENCE

During definition of the Business Rules governing the editing of data, a basic issue is the boundaries for any specific documentation effort. For example, a price field in an Order Detail record might have several relevant Business Rules:

Capture the price quoted to the customer as part of the order. Base all subsequent processing on the Order Price rather than on the price book.

Get approval from sales management for quoted prices that are not covered by the price book or that vary by more than 10 percent from the price book in response to competitive situations.

Verify prices quoted prior to the printing of the order confirmation.

A boundary question arises from the second business rule. Looking at this business rule closely shows that there are two parts:

1. Determining the correct price from the price book.

2. Comparing the correct price to the price entered with the order.

The boundary question is whether the rules for determining the correct price should be documented as part of the edit details for the Order Price entered with the order. Putting the issue very simply, should we document "determining the correct price" as if this procedure were a basic part of the processing of the Order Price, or is an alternative documentation approach preferable?

The traditional Structured Design technique, transform analysis, groups all editing rules into the afferent branch. This grouping then serves as the basis for partitioning a process into modules that can be programmed and tested independently. So, following Structured Design, determining the correct price as well as price verification are documented as part of the edit criteria for the Order Price. This procedure is then included in the same module as the other editing procedures for the Order Detail record. And if the criteria of coupling and cohesion are applied to this modularization scheme, it becomes apparent that this module has the most desirable type of cohesion—functional cohesion—since the price editing is necessary for the module to accomplish its unique task.

Thus the concepts of Structured Design lead to an initial decision to document both the determination of the correct price and the price verification as part of the edit rules for Order Price . This decision then leads to a natural follow on decision to include both elements of the processing as part of an Order Detail processing module.

However, with OOD, the determination of a correct price is more appropriately considered a method that should be encapsulated as part of the Price object. As a result, a separate price determination module would be organized around the price files. This separate module would then be documented separately and cross-referenced by the basic edit documentation for Order Price.

With a separate module for price determination, the appropriate parameters are passed to this module to determine the book price. In turn, this module returns a message that includes the book price. The Order Detail module then performs the comparison of book price and Order Price and handles any error condition. And instead of documenting price determination as business rules for Order Price, cross-referencing a Price object that performs this function completes the documentation.

The choice between Structured Design and OOD will be based on many factors. For example, if a framework code generator is to be used for construction, there might be little choice since the basic program shells are organized around the files that will be used. This means that a basic price retrieval program module would be generated for the price file. This module would be linked by a program call to the primary module that edits the order data.

Even with the flexibility of a 4GL or a conventional 3GL for construction, issues of complexity and reuse might suggest the encapsulation of the data and the procedures that operate on the data.

Considering such distinctly different design strategies as structured design or OOD at this point in the life cycle raises the question of whether this is a relevant issue. When the Data Model is being defined, the primary focus is on working with users to determine the logical requirements rather than the physical programming solutions. But how well the logical requirements are organized can have a significant impact on the productivity level during construction. The partitioning of the system into separate segments for construction should be consistent with the documentation structure produced by the analysis and design phases. Otherwise the first task of a construction person (the programmer) would of necessity be to read all system specification documents to find the relevant parts.

STRUCTURED ENGLISH RELATIONSHIP

This section permits a Structured English presentation of the basic Data Model. This format is a way of identifying the key fields for a file and of expressing the relationship between files. We use this section of the form to identify the verb and the qualifier of the Structured English sentence.

As we discussed earlier, several verbs express the relationship within a relational table or between tables. The verbs that express these relationships are as follows:

Known By identifies the primary key(s) of a file.

Owned By expresses a parent/child relationship between files. This relationship is physically implemented by including the primary keys of the parent as part of the primary keys of the child.

Refers To expresses a relationship between files. This relationship is physically implemented by including the primary keys of the *Referred To* file as foreign keys in the *referring* file.

In addition to the use of verbs, Structured English also includes the qualifiers *for* and *sharing*. The *for* qualifier permits multiple relationships among the same files and explanation of these relationships. The *sharing* qualifier indicates when a relationship between files is to be implemented by including a foreign key in the record; the foreign key does not have to be duplicated if it is already in the record format for some other purpose.

To define the structure of the database model fully, three additional verbs are needed. These verbs are *Has, Displays,* and *Contains.*

The *Has* verb establishes the existence of an attribute for an entity. An example is

ORDER HEADER *Has* ORDER DATE

Order Date is an attribute of the entity Order Header and will be physically implemented as a field in the Order Header file.

The *Displays* verb is used with a virtual or a derived field. In effect, virtual or derived fields are not physically present in the record that will implement the Data Model definition. But from the perspective of users in a JAD session, it is frequently desirable to acknowledge a derived field, such as order value or a field from a related file (a virtual field) that would be included as part of a screen display. This permits the user to obtain a more complete understanding of all the information that would typically be included when an entity is displayed. Examples of the use of the *Display* verb are as follows

ORDER HEADER *Displays* CUSTOMER NAME

ORDER DETAIL *Displays* EXTENDED VALUE

In the first example, the statement expresses that for a screen display of Order Header, Customer Name from the Customer Master is displayed in addition to Account Number. The second example expresses that for an Order Detail line, the screen display includes a field identified as a *derived* field that is the result of the calculation—order quantity times price.

The *Contains* verb identifies the foreign keys needed to implement any file-to file relationship identified on the ERD. An example of this use is:

ORDER HEADER *Contains* CUSTOMER CODE

SOME DETAILS OF THE DATA MODEL DEFINITION

Most fields on the data specification form are self-explanatory. However, several fields should be commented on in more detail.

New entity: This field identifies the new entity that will eventually be implemented as a file in the new relational database file design. This new entity was first identified on the ERD when the data stores from the DFD were decomposed.

New attribute or referenced object: This field has several uses. It can store the revised name of a field first identified as part of the old database design. It can also identify a New Attribute (field) to be added to the database. This field also identifies the related object or entity (file) when Structured English is used to express the relationship between two files. An example of this latter use is as follows:

New Entity or Referenced Object—Order Header

New Attribute or Referenced Object—Customer Master

These two fields plus the verb *Refers To,* which would be entered in the Structured English relationship section of the form, give us the sentence

ORDER HEADER *Refers To* CUSTOMER MASTER

Field Type: Several CASE tools use the concept of a field type or a global data type to predefine default attributes and edit procedures for a field. A data class is established that uses the OOD concept of inheritance. Both attributes and procedures are then defined for this class. Subsequently, specific subclasses are established that inherit the attributes and procedures of this class. An example of a class is a date (DTE). A specific subclass, such as Order Date, is then identified as an attribute for the Order Header entity (file). Identifying Order Date as field type DTE lets this field inherit the attributes and edit procedures of the DTE class.

Function: This field identifies the purpose of an entry in the database definition. Suggested codes for identification include:

K = key field

F = foreign key field

A = attribute

V = virtual field*

D = derived field*

*Derived and virtual fields are not part of the physical file layout. They are implemented as screen fields and are shown as part of the Data Model to help the user visualize data that will be available for a screen display in the implemented system.

Attribute/Relationship Optional: A "Y" in this field indicates that the attribute (field) or the file-to- file relationship is optional. The fact that the entry of an attribute or a foreign key is optional does not imply that the editing of any data that has been entered is also optional. A key concept that permits a shared data design approach is that any program using data can assume the validity of the data. As a consequence, a downstream program does not have to include its own validation procedures. If data is entered, it must be valid.

REPORTS PRODUCED FROM THE METAMODEL

The information collected about a system's database design is called a meta model, which means a model of a model. The purpose of this metamodel is to collect in one spot all relevant information concerning

OR FL	File	Name	Field text name	Length
1	ORDREC	ORDNUM	Order Number	6.00
	ORDREC	ACTNUM	Account #	6.00
	ORDREC	ACTNAM	Account Name	25.00
	ORDREC	PONECD	Product One Code	. 6.00
	ORDREC	PONEDE	Product One Description	. 25.00
	ORDREC	PONEQT	Product One Quantity	6.00
	ORDREC	PONEPR	Product One Price	8.00
	ORDREC	PONEVA	Product One Ext. Value	8.00
	ORDREC	PTWOCD	Product Two Code	6.00
	ORDREC	PTWODE	Product Two Desc.	25.00
	ORDREC	PTWOQT	Product Two Quantity	6.00
	ORDREC	PTWOPR	Product Two Price	8.00
	ORDREC	PTWOEV	Product Two Ext. Value	8.00

Figure 10.2 Sample listing of the details of an existing database design that have been captured in a reengineering tool as the first step in designing a new database structure.

the database design for a proposed system. Specialized reports can then be produced to meet the needs of the JAD participants, the database programmer preparing the DDS, the application programmer developing application code, and the conversion team responsible for bringing files across from the old system.

Following are examples of reports that can be produced from the homegrown Data Modeling tool described earlier. It should be noted that these reports are first used as part of the iterative process in the JAD sessions and as JAD deliverables.

Original File Listing

Original File Cross-Reference

The first sample report is a listing of a legacy file that is the starting point for database reengineering. (See Fig. 10.2.)

The second report (see Fig. 10.3) provides an accounting for all the fields in the original database that served as the basis for reengineering. This report is also the basis for developing a conversion system to bring data from an old system into the new database.

In Fig. 10.3, it should be noted that the repeating group for the product ordering information has been assigned to a new file called ELIM. BY NORM. This new file is a trash bucket established to account for any fields in the original file layout that are eliminated in the new design.

Orig F	Field name	New file	New field
1	Order Number	ORDER HEADER	Order Number
	Account #	ORDER HEADER	Account #
	Account Name	CUSTOMER MASTER	Account Name
	Product One Code	ORDER DETAIL	Product Code
	Product One Desc.	PRODUCT MASTER	Product Desc.
	Product One Quantity	ORDER DETAIL	Ord. Quantity
	Product One Price	ORDER DETAIL	Price
	Product One Ext. Value	ORDER DETAIL	Extended Value
	Product Two Code	ELIM. BY NORMAL.	
	Product Two Desc.	ELIM. BY NORMAL.	
	Product Two Quantity	ELIM. BY NORMAL.	
	Product Two Price	ELIM. BY NORMAL.	
	Product Two Ext. Value	ELIM. BY NORMAL.	

Figure 10.3 Sample listing of an existing database that has been redesigned using the normalization techniques associated with relational database design. Fields eliminated in the new design are identified, as well as new names, etc.This listing servies as the basis for developing data conversion programs and as a quality assurance document.

New Entity Listing

This report lists the entries and attributes of the new database design. (See Fig. 10.4.) The report also identifies the function and source of the attributes (fields) in the new design. Several of these fields are identified as virtual fields for which no source is identified. These fields are

#	New entity	New attribute	Func.	Source field
101	ORDER HEADER	Order Number	K	Order Number
		Account #	F	Account #
		Account Name	V	
102	ORDER DETAIL	Order Number	K	
		Line Number	K	
		Product Code	F	Product One Code
		Product Desc.	V	
		Ord. Quantity	A	Product One Quantity
		Price	A	Product One Price
		Extended Value	D	Product One Ext. Value
103	CUSTOMER MASTER	Account #	K	
		Account Name	A	Account Name
104	PRODUCT MASTER	Product Code	K	
		Product Desc.	A	Product One Desc.

Figure 10.4 Sample listing of the fields that are part of a new database design. Derived fields (identified with a D) and virtual fields (identified with a V), that are not physically implemented as part of a record layout, are included in this listing.

added to the listing to provide the JAD participants with a better perspective on the user's view of a file. They will be implemented as screen display fields but not physically included in the file layout.

A derived field—extended value—is also included in the listing. This field was part of the original file layout, but when third normal form was reached for the new file design, the field was eliminated from the new physical layout. This was done according to the third normal form guideline—eliminate any nonkey field that is functionally dependent on another nonkey attribute. In this case extended value is functionally dependent on price and quantity. From the user's perspective, however, the extended value is important information. By showing the field as a derived field, it will be calculated and shown as a screen display field without being included in the physical layout.

Data Model Listing

This report in a Structured English format list the attributes and relationships of the new database design. The use of Structured English format permits the metamodel to express the entity relationships shown on the ERD. In Fig. 10.5, the *Owned By* in the Order Detail expresses the parent/child relationship between the Order Header and the Order Detail. Several *Refers To* verbs express relationships between files that require referential integrity validation. These relationships also permit the use of joined logicals to facilitate the display of information from multiple files.

Object	Relation (verb)	Referenced Object	Qualifier
ORDER HEADER	Known By	Order Number	
	Refers To	Customer Master	
	Contains	Account #	
	Displays	Account Name	
ORDER DETAIL	Owned By	ORDER HEADER	
	Contains	Order Number	
	Known By	Line Number	
	Refers To	PRODUCT MASTER	
	Contains	Product Code	
	Displays	Product Desc.	
	Has	Ord. Quantity	
	Has	Price	
	Displays	Extended Value	
CUSTOMER MASTER	Known By	Account #	
	Has	Account Name	
PRODUCT MASTER	Known By	Product Code	
	Has	Product Desc.	

Figure 10.5 Sample listing of the new database design using a Structured English format.

Field name	FLD type	Length	Data Type
Account #	CDE	6.00	A
Account Name	TXT	25.00	A
Extended Value	VAL	11.20	N
Line Number	NUM	3.00	N
Ord. Quantity	QTY	5.00	N
Order Number	CDE	6.00	A
Price	PRC	7.20	N
Product Code	CDE	6.00	A
Product Desc.	TXT	25.00	A

Figure 10.6 Sample field reference file listing showing the individual fields in the new database.

Field Reference File Listing

This report presents the base definition for each field in the new database design.

A COMMENT ON THE DATA ANALYSIS TOOL

A characteristic of business processes and organizational structures is that they evolved before computers. As a consequence, an application software design effort should include an examination of the underlying business processes before any attempt to automate. This examination is necessary if the advances in technology are to be fully incorporated into the new system design.

This same type of examination of the process used for software development is also necessary. Given the programming languages of the 1970s, the first formal software development process, Structured Design, took a minimalist approach to the data and included most system specifications as part of the process definition. For the AS/400, the introduction of a field reference file to provide a base definition of each data element has significantly changed the original boundaries between a process and a data specification. The mechanics of several lower CASE tools have changed this boundary even more.

The tool discussed in this section was developed as part of a process in which Synon was the intended code generator. When it was being developed, existing upper CASE tools for defining a database did not fit either the AS/400 or Synon. In addition, the existing tools did not facilitate newer design strategies, such as reengineering, or the data and methods encapsulation associated with OOD.

So the choices were to let existing tools dictate the process, to revert to manual documentation methods, or to develop a new tool to support the planned methodology. In most large software development efforts, an investment in tools will have a significant productivity payback. But if existing tools don't fit, the suggested approach is to investigate the development of the needed tools rather than attempt to accommodate the process to existing tools or to revert to manual methods.

The tool described is fairly basic. It facilitates the basic job: defining the details of the database. It does not address many issues that will improve the productivity of the design process. The first is the automatic population of the tool with the old file layouts. The second is an electronic interface with the downstream construction tool. Without this downstream interface, the new database design must be entered manually into the construction tool. And there are no reverse links, so changes made to the database design with the lower CASE tool are not automatically reflected in the repository (work file) of the design tool.

Tool linkages definitely save effort. But the first criterion in tool selection should be its ability to support the basic design process. The degree of automation is a secondary consideration.

11

Defining the Process

In the first phase of the life cycle process, we produced a DFD as the starting point for designing a new application software system. This diagram established the scope of the proposed system and identified the major data and process components.

The next phase in the life cycle process focused on one type of component, the data, and presented methods and notations for developing detailed specifications for this component type. The resulting specification for the data components included:

A database design with domain and referential integrity definitions.

A high-level definition of the business rules that govern the additional editing of this data.

A cross-reference to related stand alone procedural elements also to be used in the data validation.

Thus, developing the database model has resulted in a specification that will be implemented through two different facilities on the AS/400: DDS to define fields and physical and logical views of the files, and procedural code.

In this phase, the focus changes from the data to the process (procedural) components of the system. Within this focus, several system design goals are to be accomplished:

1. Establish the *how* for the physical processes to create data according to the *what* specifications of the database definition.

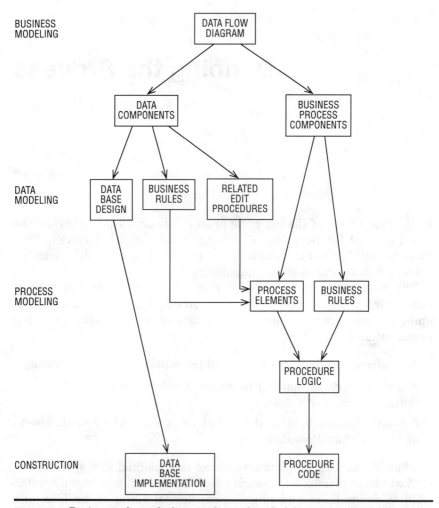

Figure 11.1 Business rules and edit procedures identified during detailed database design, as well as low-level business processes identified during business modeling, serve as the starting point for the detailed design of the procedure logic required in the new system.

2. Define the *how* for the other high-level business processes that modify or use the data captured in the system.

Figure 11.1 shows two starting points for the process modeling phase. One is the business process components identified on the DFD. The DFD decomposes the essential functions of a business system to a level of discrete business activities. There are no absolute criteria to determine how far to decompose the high-level functions on the DFD. However, the basic goal is to identify menu tasks with a recognizable starting and stopping point for the user. Thus, for example, an essential functions-level process, such as process orders, was decomposed to enter a New Order, Update an Order, Cancel an order, and so on.

The second starting point for the process modeling phase is the related edit procedures (identified during data modeling) that are candidates for design as independent program functions. The first type of candidate was an edit process, such as Determine Book Price where OOD guidelines suggest a separated method. This method is to be encapsulated with the data used, the price files. The second type of candidate identified during data modeling was a method associated with a field type or global data type. For example, Date might be identified as a field type, and Order Date as a specific subclass. For all subclasses of Date to use (inherit) a common date verification routine, such a routine must be designed and constructed as an independent program function.

Starting from the low-level processes identified on the DFD and from the candidate independent functions identified during data modeling, the task is now to specify structural and procedural logic that permits construction of physical programs. The follow-on construction methods available for generating these physical programs varies from frame technology code generators (such as Synon), to procedural 4GL code generators (such as AS/SET), and to 3GLs (such as RPG or COBOL). This variety complicates the choice of methods and notations.

METHODS AND NOTATIONS OVERVIEW

The methods and notations described in this chapter are primarily for the JAD team to use in developing the detailed plans for the subsystem they are working on. At this stage, an overall system has been broken down into subsystems for detailed design and construction. The goal now is to design a program structure for every program in the subsystem and to define in detail the logic for every program or program component.

This first step includes deciding about the modular structure of programs and incorporating reusable modules or subroutines into a program solution. Although this design function is beyond the expertise or interest of most business participants on the JAD team, the suggested JAD team does include technical specialists. From a practical standpoint, the team includes the programmers responsible for constructing specific subsystems as well as a technician who has an overall system or IS department perspective and can deal with the issue of program reuse.

This approach blurs the traditional distinction that many formal methodologies make between a logical design and a physical design. These traditional methodologies suggest that a business-oriented team develop a set of requirements and then pass these requirements on to another team for program design and implementation. Issues of technical practicality, system performance, and cost are resolved in separate meetings between the two teams.

Unfortunately, when separate teams are used for design and construction, members frequently approach resolution meetings as factional representatives. This frequently results in the need for third-party mediation by senior management. To prevent a false sense of progress, it is necessary to specify that the JAD is expected to deliver one set of specifications for a buildable system that meets business, technical, and cost requirements, and all interested parties must agree. Also, necessary compromises can be made before positions are set in stone.

The next two chapters describe three formal graphic notations for defining the structure of a process solution and the logic of individual program modules and routines. The first step in the JAD session might also include preparation of a text-oriented process overview to record process requirements. However, this initial process overview is only a transitory document, a wish list, to get the JAD sessions started. The JAD must evaluate the requirements in this list, delete frivolous items, and then reorganize the list so that requirements are included to serve as the starting point for the design process. The graphic notations are then used to formalize the design and to identify subcomponents of the design solution.

These formal notations used to document a process design solution are:

Structure charts: Identify independent subcomponents involved in the design solution for a business process and the linkage among these subcomponents.

Action diagrams: A form of Structured English or pseudocode to define the detailed logic of a complete business process or independent subcomponents.

Decision trees: A special form of graphical notation to express the logic involved in a multiple-decision situation.

The available construction tools determine whether this process-modeling phase also includes the development of screens and report formats. Many of the lower CASE tools, for example, permit the rapid development of screen prototypes that can quickly evolve into a working system. As a result, it may be more practical to address the look and feel of the system after the transition to the construction phase is made than to use design tools which do not permit automatic generation of working programs from a prototype. If a code generator is not available, screen and report formats should be included as part of the deliverables for this phase.

STRUCTURE CHARTS

A *structure chart* is a hierarchical diagram that breaks a program solution down into its constituent parts. It differs from the conventional hierarchical chart because it not only shows decomposition but also the type of control flowing between the elements of a program solution. Thus, this diagram shows that control is passed between segments and also whether data is passed in the form of parameters.

Structure charts first appeared as a notation used with Structured Design. Chapter 9 discussed that the original approach to Structured Design envisioned a monolithic program divided into program subsections and used transform or transaction analysis. In this chapter, the emphasis is on how to use a structure chart with an OOD method that results in independent modules and subroutines.

In adapting a structure chart to the concepts of OOD, the basic symbols for a module, subroutine, and so on, remain the same. So before we look at the methods for OOD, let's first review the symbols used to express the design solution for a complex business process. Several icons are used to represent the structure of a programming solution for a business process.

Figure 11.2 Notations used on a Structure Chart to express the design solution for a business process.

Module: Independently compilable program invoked by a CALL instruction (External Subroutine).

Function or Subroutine: A named group of procedural instructions organized as an internal subroutine. This type of routine can be included in a 3GL program module by a COPY from a reuse library. This symbol would also identify any processing to be added to a default program generated by a code generator. Typically the code generator will create a basic working program, but any special editing, linking of modules, and the like, must be added to the basic program through some type of 4GL instruction provided by the vendor of the code generator. Using this symbol to indicate the presence of supplemental logic implemented through the 4GL enhances the structural overview of the process solution, and it also provides a notice to construction that this additional logic must be added to the basic program module prepared by the code generator.

Control Couple: Indicates that control is passed to a new module, subroutine, or additional 4GL routine without passing data.

Data Couple: Indicates that data in the form of parameters and controls are passed to a new module, and so on.

OBJECT ANALYSIS

The traditional Structured Design method perceives the design of a process as task decomposition. Using transform analysis, a general process is structured as input tasks, central transform tasks, and output tasks. These tasks are in turn decomposed to a level that allows their implementation with procedural code. For a complex process, this basic approach can be enhanced by identifying the transactions in the process as separate high-level tasks. Once the transactions are identified, transform analysis then further decomposes the tasks associated with each transaction.

This method is geared to the design of a monolithic program that uses procedural code and implements lower-level tasks as individual paragraphs. It does not take into consideration issues like code reuse, modularization of programs, and the peculiarities of some AS/400 code generators.

The concept of encapsulation from OOD offers a fresh look at how to prepare a structure chart that considers some of these additional issues. Developing a structure chart starts with the data involved in a process. The organizational task is to identify the methods associated with this data. Next, these methods are organized into modules and subroutines for eventual construction.

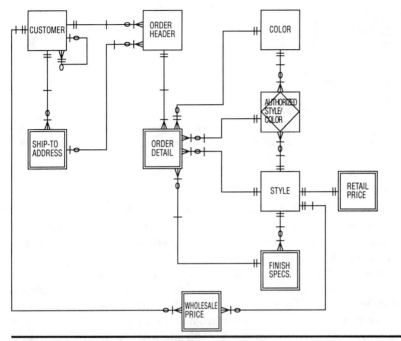

Figure 11.3 An Entity Relationship Diagram provides the starting point for designing a process solution. It identifies the data structures that are the basis for designing the modular structure of the process solution.

The sample ERDs prepared in Chap. 8 show the starting point for such a method. Figure 11.3 represents a process view of the entities (files) involved in the process, Enter Orders.

An analysis of the database in this process view shows that the files can be categorized into three groups:

Category 1: Records in the Order Header and the Order Detail files are created as part of this process.

Category 2: The Product Master files and Customer Master files that are used to validate the referential integrity of the foreign keys in the order header and the order detail.

Category 3: The Price file determines the standard price that is used to validate the price entered with the order.

A first cut at a structure chart that encapsulates data and its associated methods looks like the one shown in Fig. 11.4.

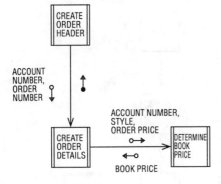

Figure 11.4 A first cut at developing a Structure Chart that encapsulates the data used by a process with the methods that operate on the data.

This first version establishes separate modules for order header and order detail records. In addition, a separate module performs the book price determination, which appeared as a separate method first during the data modeling phase.

The preceding illustration does not show verification of the foreign keys, that is, the account number and the product codes, as separate modules. While a purist approach to OOD would show these verifications as separate methods encapsulated with the customer or product files, performance realities of the AS/400 suggest a different approach. For example, the command Set Lower Limits (Foreign Key ..SETLL .. File) will perform this check with none of the system overhead associated with calling in a separate module. In addition, several code generators automatically produce code to perform this edit. So, identifying referential integrity validations as separate methods (modules) is not consistent with the most practical physical approaches to construction.

Once the base modules are identified, the structure chart for these modules must be expanded to account for the additional edits identified as business rules during the data modeling phase. However, the nature of these rules is also determined by practicality. A minor edit, such as verifying that the Ship Date of an order is equal to or greater than the Order Date, need not be identified on the structure chart. The programmer can account for this edit during the construction phase by reviewing the detailed database specifications. A major edit, such as a credit verification, should be identified, however. The reason is both to highlight it to make it subject of a JAD review and to provide a link to a lower level of documentation, such as an action diagram or decision tree that spells out the details of the edit.

At this point, any code reusable as part of the process solution (the routines needed to produce derived fields, perform special processing,

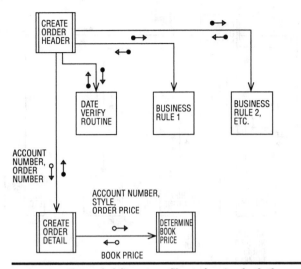

Figure 11.5 Expanded Structure Chart showing both the program modules and the subroutines involved in the design solution for a business process.

and the like) are also identified. Including these additional processing tasks expands the basic chart, as shown in Fig. 11.5.

In the JAD discussion, several additional process requirements might be discussed:

Provide the ability to display the customer master through a name search to assist the operator who does not know the account number.

Let the operator select a customer from the display and record the account number with the order.

Provide a display of all ship-to's for a given account and let the operator select one ship-to for the order.

Provide the ability to enter a special ship-to for this order.

Determine the extended value for each order line and the total value for the order.

Including these additional requirements expands the structure chart (Fig. 11.6).

The first cut structure chart illustrated in Fig. 11.6 shows the major subcomponents of a process solution. The emphasis is on identifying:

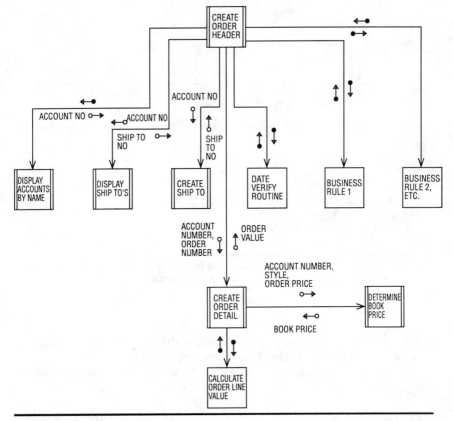

Figure 11.6 Representative Structure Chart showing the complete high-level design for a business process such as "Enter Orders."

- Independent modules.
- Routines to perform additional editing or to accomplish specific functional requirements.
- Subroutines from the reusable code library.
- Parameters that are data elements or structures passed between independent program modules.

Specific programming tasks (such as opening files, reads and writes, error message processing) are not shown at this point. If a code generator, such as Synon, is used, 3GL code to handle these tasks is automatically generated as part of the program shell. If construction is based on a 3GL, such as RPG, these tasks can be added to the original chart during the construction phase. In a 3GL environment, this addition offers a more complete blueprint for the program solution. It should also be noted that the placement of modules and subroutines across the page has no necessary relationship to the sequence in which they will be invoked. For the chart to be more meaningful, however, it should be organized so it can be read from top to bottom and from left to right. The module on the top level is the *root* and identifies the program module called from the menu. Below this root are subroutines included in the root program module and other program modules that the root calls. This hierarchy continues downward until all modules and subroutines are identified.

AN EXAMPLE OF MODULAR PROGRAM CONSTRUCTION

The use of OOD may require radical adjustments for many IS practitioners. But looking at this strategy from the perspective of one code generator, Synon, takes OOD out of the realm of theoretical recommendation and into the world of practicality. OOD strategy and the use of Synon as the construction tool provide a very good fit. With a 3GL or with many 4GL-oriented lower CASE tools, the use of OOD is optional. With Synon, OOD is the optimal approach.

Figure 11.7 shows that the starting point for constructing a program with Synon is an entity (file) definition using Structured English.

The following order header is an example of Structured English.

ORDER HEADER *Known By* Order Number

ORDER HEADER *Refers To* CUSTOMER MASTER

ORDER HEADER *Has* Order Date

ORDER HEADER *Has* Status Code

ORDER HEADER *Has* Status Date

Once the Data Model definition is entered into Synon's construction repository, a program framework or shell has to be selected from Synon's library. After this selection is made, the code generator combines the Data Model definition for a specific entity (file) with the program framework to produce a complete working program. This working program includes a default screen layout and all necessary procedural code to handle I/O, domain and referential integrity verification, error message handling, and so on.

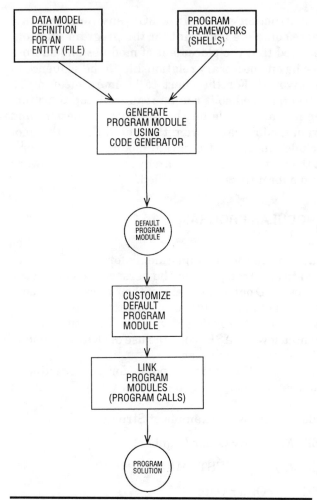

Figure 11.7 Overview of the process for constructing a program using the lower CASE tool—Synon.

The next step customizes the default screen layout and enhances the initially generated code to handle any additional editing and any functional requirements. An example of the latter is the automatic numbering of orders. The final step links this module with similarly generated modules for the other files used by the process to arrive at a complete process solution. These other modules might include:

- An order detail module.

- A module to determine the standard price.
- A module to retrieve and display customer masters by name.
- A module to display possible ship-to's.
- A module to create a new ship-to.

COMPOSITE OBJECTS

In the enter orders example, part of the process solution consisted of two independent modules that create the order header and the order detail records. Each of these independent modules contains an input screen and the complete procedural logic to perform program initiation, I/O, and editing for their respective files. But for a relatively simple order format, the JAD participants might suggest that the more efficient solution from the operator's perspective would be one input screen rather than separate screens for the order header and the order detail. This one screen would contain order header and order details information. How would this design solution be handled within the concept of data and methods encapsulation of the OOD?

One of the concepts of OOD is a *composite object*. A composite object is not only made up of its own data and methods but also includes other objects. So, a possible means of providing a single screen that preserves the original identification of the order header and the order detail as objects might be to create a composite object. This composite object would not only be made up of its own data and methods but would also include two other objects, the order header object and the order detail object.

Figure 11.8 shows part of the original process.

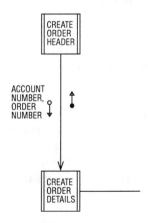

Figure 11.8 Structure Chart showing part of the structure of the design solution for the process "Enter Orders."

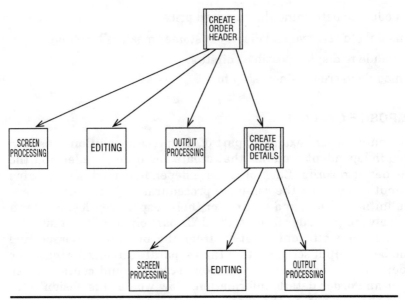

Figure 11.9 Expanded view of the design solution for the process "Enter Orders."

A look under the covers of this original solution reveals that each of the original modules has three major internal routines: input processing, editing, and output processing. This methods breakdown for each object is shown as Fig. 11.9.

The switch from an object to a composite object solution is a task of rearranging erector set parts instead of one of designing a fundamentally new solution. The methods for editing the data and updating the files remain the same. This means most of the initial design solution for the original two objects, the order header and the order detail, is retained. The composite object (Orders) requires only a new method of handling the input of the screen and the program housekeeping details. The new solution for the composite object is shown as Fig. 11.10.

Figure 11.10 demonstrates that the process solution consists of a new composite object that has its own methods for input processing. In addition, the composite object includes two other objects, the order header object and the order detail object. The remaining methods shown for these two objects are exactly the same internal routines shown in the first process solution (assuming there is no technical change, such as record versus subfile processing).

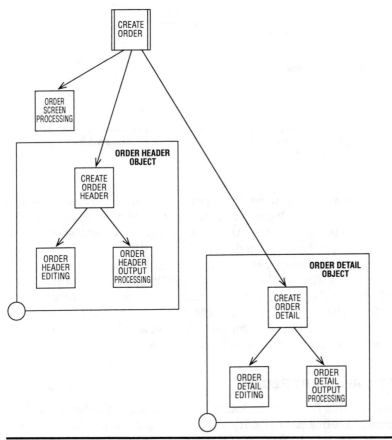

Figure 11.10 A "Composite Object" solution represents a rearrangement of an initial design solution—more than a fundamental redesign.

INHERITANCE

One of the basic concepts of OOD is the idea of inheritance. Related data elements can be defined as a unique class or as a special case of another class. In the latter case, they are a subclass and, through a process of inheritance, the subclass can use the methods of the class of which it is a part.

Previously, the concept of class and inheritance was used to define the details of the Data Model. For example, Order Date was identified as a specific instance of the class Date. Associated with Date might be a Date verification routine organized as a method (a reusable routine).

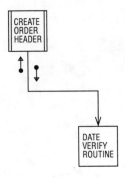

Figure 11.11 Graphic method for showing the inclusion of a reusable subroutine as part of a process solution.

If a code generator is used for construction, the Date routine might automatically be included in the procedural code generated. If a 3GL is used for construction, or if the lower CASE tool selected does not provide for this type of methods inheritance, it is up to the structure chart to positively identify this instance of code reuse.

Since an inherited method associated with a class is organized as a reusable internal subroutine rather than as an independently compilable module, the appropriate symbol for use on a structure chart is that of a lower-level function. Figure 11.11 is an example of how to include a Date routine into a business process solution.

STRUCTURE CHART RECAP

Progression from Structured Design to OOD changes the function of the structure chart dramatically. Its original role was to provide a graphic notation to support the process of decomposing a business process. In its new role, it supports the process of identifying components and shows how these components are to be assembled to arrive at a solution for the business process. The structure chart also used facilitates code reuse by making this a design decision rather than a construction option.

The composite object example also shows that an object approach provides significantly increased flexibility. When the initial solution structure of Process Orders was changed, the new design primarily involved a reorganization of methods associated with objects rather than a fundamental redesign. And since the basic specifications would have been organized on an object basis rather than on a business-process basis, documentation would have followed along to support the new solution. The limitation of a structure chart is that it does not clearly show the sequence of invocation, iterations, logic alternatives, and detailed logic. Methods and notations to deal with these issues are the subject of the next chapter.

12

Defining Process Logic

DOCUMENTATION HIERARCHIES

From the various phases of the application development cycle, a hierarchy of documentation notations arises that permits increasingly detailed system designs and definitions (see Fig. 12.1).

The final level of documentation is used to define the detailed logic of various parts of a process solution. This chapter discusses two notations that are useful for expressing detailed logic, *Action Diagrams* and *Decision Trees*. Up to this point in our narrative, the notations discussed on diagrams such as a Data Flow Diagram or Structure Chart identified the existence of a component part of a system or complex process, but they could not tell us too much about the details of the processing logic involved. Also in a number of instances provisions were made to record business rules that govern editing, updating and so on, in a text format. In many instances, the high-level identification of a component or the text description of a business rule does not tie down logic details, and a pseudocode level explanation is needed to avoid ambiguity.

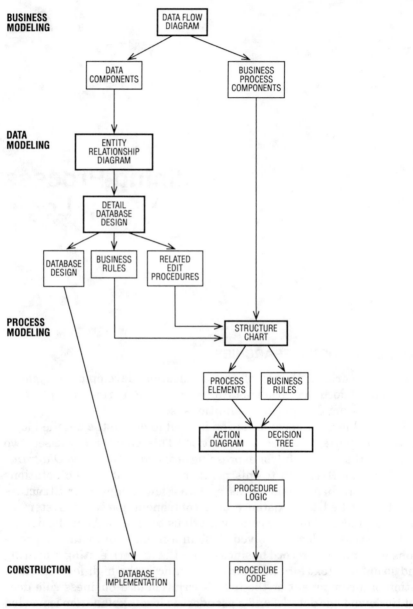

Figure 12.1 The hierarchy of documentation techniques used to express the design for a commercial software system.

Of the two notations to be discussed, Action Diagrams are more flexible than Decision Trees because they lend themselves to a number of purposes:

- They supplement a Structure Chart to show the sequence of invocations for the program modules and subroutines identified on the structure chart.
- They provide an overview of the structure for a program module or subroutine whose identity is documented on the structure chart.
- They can be used to document the detailed logic of all or part of the processing of an individual program module or subroutine.

The functionality of Decision Trees is more limited. They are important tools, however, because they are easy to understand and can express complex decision logic visually. This makes them viable working documents in a JAD session.

LOGICAL CONTROL STRUCTURES

The notation format of an action diagram is based on the logical control structures of structured programming. A brief review of the constructs of structured programming may clarify this. Structured programming uses four logical control structures: sequence, selection, case structure, and iteration.

Sequence: Executes instructions, subroutines, and so on, in their order of appearance.

Selection: Executes instructions under certain conditions.

Case Structure: Uses the contents of a given field to determine the path to be followed; a special form of a selection construct.

Iteration: Executes a series of steps repeatedly until a specific condition occurs.

ACTION DIAGRAM OVERVIEW

An action diagram is a graphic tool that shows a high-level view of a process solution and the logic details of all or part of specific subroutines or modules. Used to identify the elements of a business process solution, an action diagram is an alternative or a supplement to a structure chart. This offers the advantage of showing the sequence in which the elements are invoked and any conditions governing an invocation. The disadvantage is that it is typically more difficult to understand than a structure chart, and is not as effective as visual presentation for a JAD session because it takes more time for the typical user to understand the presentation format.

Used to show the complete structure of an individual module or subroutine and the details of each routine, an action diagram identifies all basic routines in the module, such as initialization, I/O, field manipulation and editing. In this function, it relies on Structured English to show the actions involved in each of these routines.

An action diagram's ability to identify a module's basic routines is significant with some lower CASE tools. In this instance, the tool automatically prepares an action diagram that shows the structure of the module and the default processing provided for. This action diagram can then be used to enhance the shell to include the additional requirements that the JAD sessions identified as business rules, processing requirements, and so on. The action diagram developed by the CASE tool can also be modified to link program modules and to call 3GL programs to accomplish a complete solution for the business process.

An action diagram can also show the logic for the business rules, special processing requirements, and so on and establish detailed documentation for them. In this function, Action Diagrams are first used in the JAD sessions to verify the logic details of special business requirements. Each action on the diagram is then constructed using either procedure code or an action diagram editor provided by the CASE tool vendor. In the latter instance, the editor is used to enhance the program shell produced by the lower CASE tool.

ACTION DIAGRAM CONSTRUCTS

As Fig. 12.2 shows, the basic building block of an action diagram is a *bracket*. A bracket encloses a set of actions. An action can be a high-level function, such as a program or program module, a subroutine, and the like, or, dropping down into detail, an individual line of procedural code. When Action Diagrams first enter into the life cycle, a primary goal is to document the logic of complex business rules or requirements so the users in the JAD sessions can verify them and the programmers can understand them when construction begins. The appropriate ac-

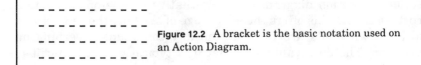

Figure 12.2 A bracket is the basic notation used on an Action Diagram.

—Keywords are used to make the structure clear—for example: IF, THEN, ELSE, ENDIF, REPEAT WHILE, REPEAT UNTIL, ENDREPEAT, EXIT
—Keywords are used for logic—for example: AND, OR, GT (Greater Than), LT (Less Than), GE (Greater than or equal to), LE (Less than or equal to)
—The choice of keywords should be an installation standard.
—The choice of keywords may be selected to conform to a fourth generation language. They do, however, remain language independent descriptions.
—Names of program blocks (modules, internal subroutines, etc.) are capitalized.
—End words such as EXIT, ENDIF, ENDREPEAT, and END are used to make the end of a structure clear.
—Within these constraints, the wording should be chosen so that it is easy for the user the user to understand.

Figure 12.3 Structured English rules used in preparing procedural logic statements on an Action Diagram.

tion level for this is a Structured English or pseudocode statement that easily translates into procedural code. Figure 12.3 contains some of James Martin's (1) rules for writing Structured English.

Figure 12.4 is an example of a basic Action Diagram. The sequence of the action is shown as consecutive steps going down the page.

In some instances, a bracket is executed conditionally. When this occurs, the condition is written at the top of the bracket. If the condition is satisfied, the contents of the bracket are executed. Figure 12.5 is an example of how to express a condition.

Many condition structures have two parts. One says what happens if the condition is true; the other says what happens if it is not true. Figure 12.6 shows the notation used to express this structure.

If there are a number of mutually exclusive conditions (sometimes called a case structure), a bracket can be divided more than once. Figure 12.7 shows this structure.

The final structured programming construct an action diagram needs to show is iteration (or repetition). This structure is diagrammed as shown on Fig. 12.8.

```
┌ Read Screen
│ Validate Customer Date
└ Create New Record
```

Figure 12.4 Example of basic Action Diagram showing several procedural steps to be executed in sequence.

```
┌IF Customer credit is bad
│ Reject Order
│ Create Sales Notification
└EXIT
```

Figure 12.5 Example of a conditional statement on an Action Diagram.

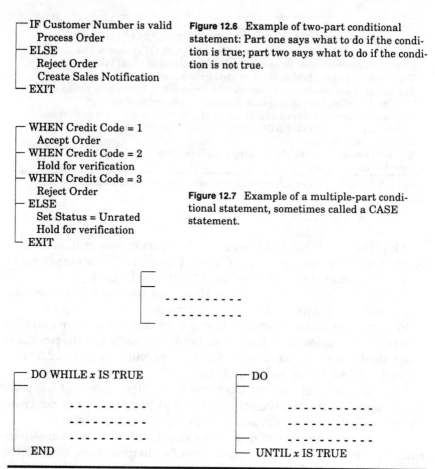

IF Customer Number is valid
  Process Order
ELSE
  Reject Order
  Create Sales Notification
EXIT

Figure 12.6 Example of two-part conditional statement: Part one says what to do if the condition is true; part two says what to do if the condition is not true.

WHEN Credit Code = 1
  Accept Order
WHEN Credit Code = 2
  Hold for verification
WHEN Credit Code = 3
  Reject Order
ELSE
  Set Status = Unrated
  Hold for verification
EXIT

Figure 12.7 Example of a multiple-part conditional statement, sometimes called a CASE statement.

DO WHILE x IS TRUE

END

DO

UNTIL x IS TRUE

Figure 12.8 Notations used on an Action Diagram to represent iterative or repetitive conditions.

In some situations, conditions arise that make continued processing impossible. In this instance, control must go directly to an END rather than continue in sequence. This situation is shown in Fig. 12.9.

SAMPLE ACTION DIAGRAM

In preparing a process solution overview, Action Diagrams supplement a Structure Chart to show more of the control logic of the solution for a business process. To use an Action Diagram for this purpose, a starting point is the Structure Chart which provides a list of the major elements of the solution. The first step in preparing the diagram is shown as Fig. 12.10.

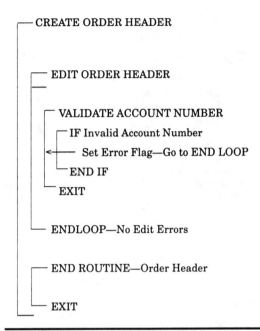

CREATE ORDER HEADER

EDIT ORDER HEADER

VALIDATE ACCOUNT NUMBER
IF Invalid Account Number
Set Error Flag—Go to END LOOP
END IF
EXIT

ENDLOOP—No Edit Errors

END ROUTINE—Order Header

EXIT

Figure 12.9   Notation used on an Action Diagram to show that meeting a condition has caused the normal sequence to be changed.

The next step adds the logic to control the invocation of the elements of the process solution. Figure 12.11 shows the addition of control logic. The final step is to add the control structure for the lower-level elements. The final diagram, with the addition of the lower-level control structures, is shown as Fig. 12.12. (See pages 196–198.)

ABSTRACTION AND INFORMATION HIDING

Abstraction and *information hiding* facilitate the management of complexity during the preparation of an overview of the business process solution. D. Ross and others explain these concepts (2):

... the essence of abstraction is to extract essential properties while omitting inessential details
... and the purpose of hiding is to make inaccessible certain details which should not affect other parts of the system.

Figure 12.13 shows several lines from Fig. 12.12 that demonstrates the use of these concepts in the preparation of an action diagram.

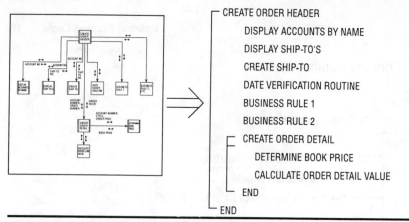

CREATE ORDER HEADER

DISPLAY ACCOUNTS BY NAME

DISPLAY SHIP-TO'S

CREATE SHIP-TO

DATE VERIFICATION ROUTINE

BUSINESS RULE 1

BUSINESS RULE 2

CREATE ORDER DETAIL

DETERMINE BOOK PRICE

CALCULATE ORDER DETAIL VALUE

END

END

Figure 12.10 An Action Diagram can be used to provide a high-level overview of the design solution for a complex business process.

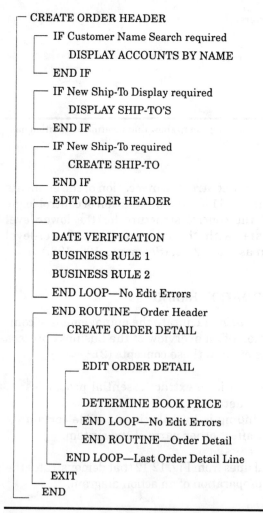

CREATE ORDER HEADER

IF Customer Name Search required

DISPLAY ACCOUNTS BY NAME

END IF

IF New Ship-To Display required

DISPLAY SHIP-TO'S

END IF

IF New Ship-To required

CREATE SHIP-TO

END IF

EDIT ORDER HEADER

DATE VERIFICATION

BUSINESS RULE 1

BUSINESS RULE 2

END LOOP—No Edit Errors

END ROUTINE—Order Header

CREATE ORDER DETAIL

EDIT ORDER DETAIL

DETERMINE BOOK PRICE

END LOOP—No Edit Errors

END ROUTINE—Order Detail

END LOOP—Last Order Detail Line

EXIT

END

Figure 12.11 As a high-level design overview, an Action Diagram shows the components of the solution for a complex business process. It can also show the control logic involved in invoking each element of the design solution.

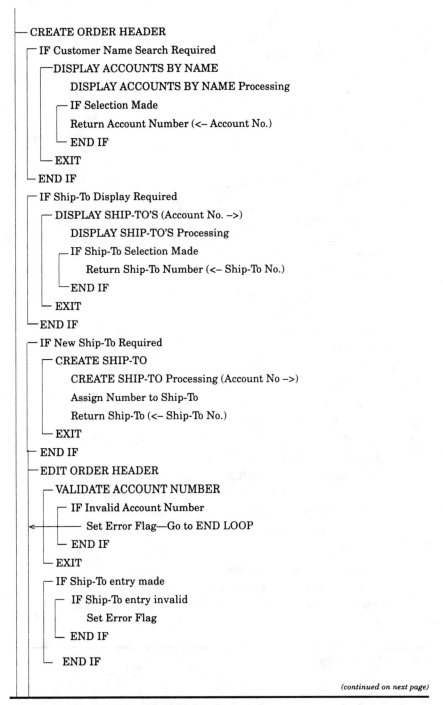

— CREATE ORDER HEADER

  ⌐ IF Customer Name Search Required

    ⌐DISPLAY ACCOUNTS BY NAME

       DISPLAY ACCOUNTS BY NAME Processing

      ⌐ IF Selection Made

       Return Account Number (<– Account No.)

      └ END IF

    └ EXIT

  └ END IF

  ⌐ IF Ship-To Display Required

    ⌐ DISPLAY SHIP-TO'S (Account No. –>)

      DISPLAY SHIP-TO'S Processing

      ⌐ IF Ship-To Selection Made

       Return Ship-To Number (<– Ship-To No.)

      └ END IF

    └ EXIT

  └ END IF

  ⌐ IF New Ship-To Required

    ⌐ CREATE SHIP-TO

      CREATE SHIP-TO Processing (Account No –>)

      Assign Number to Ship-To

      Return Ship-To (<– Ship-To No.)

    └ EXIT

  ⌐ END IF

  ⌐EDIT ORDER HEADER

    ⌐ VALIDATE ACCOUNT NUMBER

      ⌐ IF Invalid Account Number

    ←   Set Error Flag—Go to END LOOP

      └ END IF

    └ EXIT

    ⌐ IF Ship-To entry made

      ⌐ IF Ship-To entry invalid

       Set Error Flag

      └ END IF

    └ END IF

(continued on next page)

Figure 12.12 Sample Action Diagram showing both the components of a design solution and the logic that controls the invocation of each element of the solution.

(contined from prior page)

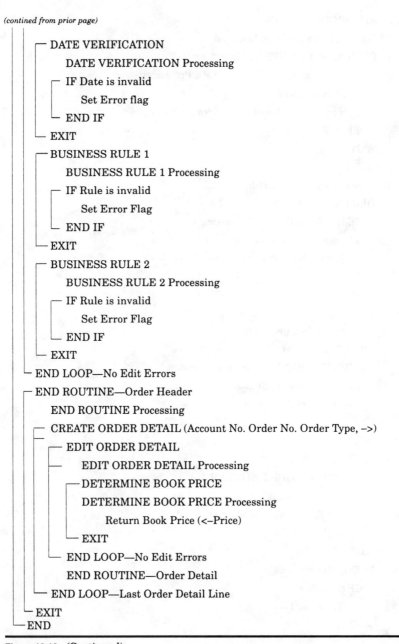

DATE VERIFICATION
    DATE VERIFICATION Processing
    IF Date is invalid
        Set Error flag
    END IF
EXIT
BUSINESS RULE 1
    BUSINESS RULE 1 Processing
    IF Rule is invalid
        Set Error Flag
    END IF
EXIT
BUSINESS RULE 2
    BUSINESS RULE 2 Processing
    IF Rule is invalid
        Set Error Flag
    END IF
EXIT
END LOOP—No Edit Errors
END ROUTINE—Order Header
    END ROUTINE Processing
    CREATE ORDER DETAIL (Account No. Order No. Order Type, –>)
        EDIT ORDER DETAIL
            EDIT ORDER DETAIL Processing
            DETERMINE BOOK PRICE
            DETERMINE BOOK PRICE Processing
                Return Book Price (<–Price)
            EXIT
        END LOOP—No Edit Errors
        END ROUTINE—Order Detail
    END LOOP—Last Order Detail Line
EXIT
END

Figure 12.12 *(Continued)*

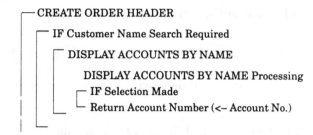

CREATE ORDER HEADER

  IF Customer Name Search Required

    DISPLAY ACCOUNTS BY NAME

      DISPLAY ACCOUNTS BY NAME Processing

        IF Selection Made

          Return Account Number (<– Account No.)

Figure 12.13 The use of the principles of abstraction and information hiding on an Action Diagram. The control logic from the module "Display Accounts by Name" is shown as part of the diagram for the module "Create Order Header."

The two actions, Selection Made and Return Account Number (<– Account Number), are an extraction from a separate structure, Display Accounts By Name. Using an OOD strategy, Display Accounts By Name would typically be a module which is separate from the Create Order Header module, and the commands shown in Fig. 12.13 would be a part of this separate module. Extracting these commands and showing them as part of the higher-level module, Create Order Header, produces a more comprehensive view of the interaction between these two modules. As part of the view of Create Order Header module, the diagram shows that a selection can be made from Display Accounts By Name. And if a selection is made, the account number for the selected account is returned as a parameter for use by the higher-level module, Create Order Header.

Note: The symbol (<– Account No.) indicates that the Display Accounts By Name module is returning the account number of the customer selected as a parameter to the Create Order Header module. This and similar types of remarks can help to clarify the logic of the diagram.

Figure 12.13 also shows an example of information hiding. The command, Display Accounts By Name, hides those details of the processing for this module that do not affect other parts of the system. These details are left for a separate documentation effort.

Abstraction and information hiding facilitate modular programming and code reuse. The details of each element of a solution, such as Display Accounts By Name, become the subject of a separate documentation effort. And, since construction tends to follow the path of least resistance, the boundaries of the documentation effort become the boundaries of the construction effort. This creates a modular programming solution. If the elements of a solution are subsequently reorganized on a structural level or if an element is to be reused as part of the solution for another business process, documentation and code automatically follow the new structure or use.

DEFINING DETAILED LOGIC—DECISION TREES

The following example of a price verification business rule developed for a chemical company shows why most text-oriented business rules produced in a JAD session or in discussions with the user are very ambiguous.

Standard prices are to be established for all products sold by the company. In instances where off-standard materials are to be offered, supplemental prices based on the grade of the material might also have to be developed for a product.

Special prices will be established for some authorized high-volume customers who order in lots of 50 lb or greater. These special wholesale prices might also include supplemental prices for off-standard material.

Long-term contracts will also be negotiated with some customers. These contracts will specify the total volume of a product covered by the contract, the effective end date of the contract, and prices for the product. The base price for a product may be supplemented by special prices for off-specification material. Contract prices apply only to orders of 50 lb or greater.

Prices are to be captured at the time of ordering and remain fixed for the duration of the order.

The decision tree in Fig. 12.14 represents the initial approach to documenting the detailed logic needed to implement this business rule.

The tree represents the various action paths. The existence of conditions identified in the business rule determines which path to follow. The tree specifies several paths, however, that do not lead to the determination of a price and do not specify the action to be taken. Here are some examples:

If there is no price for a contract, is this an error that places the order on hold?

If the date and quantity conditions of a contract are not met, should the customer automatically be given preferential status as an authorized wholesale customer?

If there is no wholesale price for a large order from an authorized wholesale customer, should standard prices be used or should the order be placed on hold until a price can be established? And what is a large order?

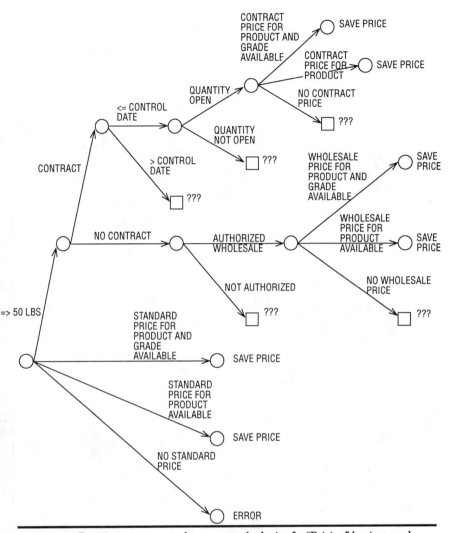

Figure 12.14 Decision tree prepared to express the logic of a "Pricing" business rule. Branches identified with a ??? indicate instances of inadequate definition in the original business rule.

Figure 12.15 resolves these questions. This was done adding new business rules to resolve the ambiguities of which were identified on the original diagram.

If there is no price established for a contract, an error results and the order is placed on hold until the price is resolved.

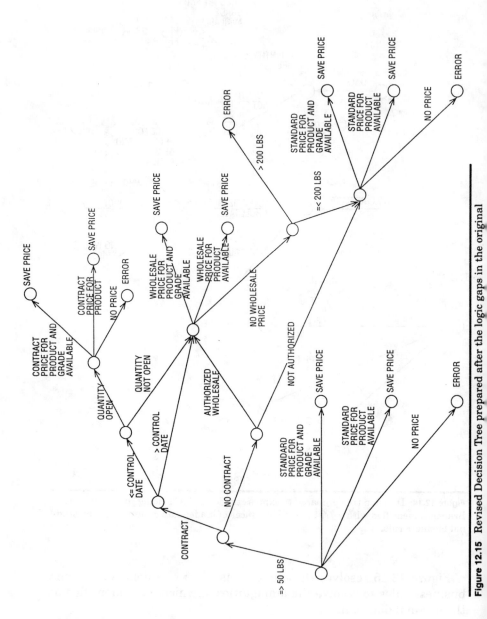

Figure 12.15 Revised Decision Tree prepared after the logic gaps in the original

Contract customers whose contracts have lapsed are treated as authorized wholesale customers.

If an authorized wholesale customer's order exceeds 200 lb, the order is placed on hold if no wholesale price can be found. Otherwise standard prices are used.

If a customer does not have an authorized wholesale account and places an order above 200 lb, prices according to the standard price book apply.

DEFINING DETAILED LOGIC—ACTION DIAGRAMS

Verifying business rules using a decision tree is typically a more effective approach with a user than an Action Diagram because is easier to follow the visual presentation of the logic alternatives. An Action Diagram, on the other hand, is probably more effective for communicating specifications to the programmer because it is closer to the procedural language of programming. Figure 12.16 shows an action diagram to express the price verification logic.

CLOSING THOUGHTS

Every hobby carpenter has heard, "Measure twice, cut once." Experience suggests that it pays to put extra effort into developing a plan. The justification for this extra effort lies in the hope that construction is more efficient if the cut is done right the first time rather than repeated a number of times as part of a trial and error process.

An appropriate corollary for the software developer to the carpenter's axiom is "Verify twice, program once." The validity of this corollary is more than supported by many software studies analyzing the cost of correcting errors. Figure 12.17 summarizes a study by Barry Boehm. (3) This study suggests that it costs four times as much to correct an error in a small project after the system is implemented than it costs to discover and correct this error during analysis. And for large projects, the difference is even greater.

Action Diagrams and Decision Trees help the analyst or programmer formulate a solution to a logic problem. More importantly, however, these notations provide a means for documenting a solution so it can be verified with the user before resources are expended on construction.

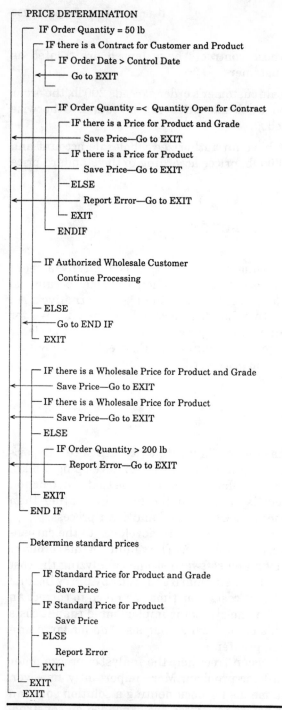

```
┌─ PRICE DETERMINATION
│  ┌─ IF Order Quantity = 50 lb
│  │  ┌─ IF there is a Contract for Customer and Product
│  │  │  ┌─ IF Order Date > Control Date
│ ←┤  │  └──── Go to EXIT
│  │  │
│  │  │  ┌─ IF Order Quantity =< Quantity Open for Contract
│  │  │  │  ┌─ IF there is a Price for Product and Grade
│ ←┤  │  │  └──── Save Price—Go to EXIT
│  │  │  ├─ IF there is a Price for Product
│ ←┤  │  │  └──── Save Price—Go to EXIT
│  │  │  ├─ ELSE
│ ←┤  │  └──── Report Error—Go to EXIT
│  │  │  └─ EXIT
│  │  └─ ENDIF
│  │
│  │  ┌─ IF Authorized Wholesale Customer
│  │  │     Continue Processing
│  │  │
│  │  ├─ ELSE
│ ←┤  │ Go to END IF
│  │  └─ EXIT
│  │
│  │  ┌─ IF there is a Wholesale Price for Product and Grade
│ ←┤  │  └──── Save Price—Go to EXIT
│  │  ├─ IF there is a Wholesale Price for Product
│ ←┤  │  └──── Save Price—Go to EXIT
│  │  ├─ ELSE
│  │  │  ┌─ IF Order Quantity > 200 lb
│ ←┤  │  └──── Report Error—Go to EXIT
│  │  │  └
│  │  └─ EXIT
│  └─ END IF
│
│  ┌─ Determine standard prices
│  │
│  │  ┌─ IF Standard Price for Product and Grade
│  │  │     Save Price
│  │  ├─ IF Standard Price for Product
│  │  │     Save Price
│  │  ├─ ELSE
│  │  │     Report Error
│  │  └─ EXIT
│  └─ EXIT
└─ EXIT
```

Figure 12.16 Sample Action Diagram used as an alternate to the Decision Tree to express the logic of the "Pricing" business rule.

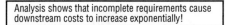

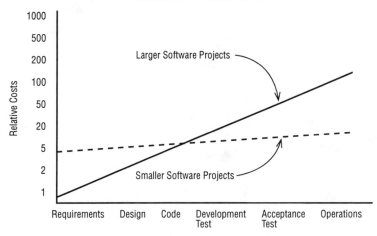

Figure 12.17 The cost of fixing a "requirements" defect increases exponentially through the later phases in the software development life cycle.

Prototyping is an important tool for verifying the look and feel of a system with the user. However, most prototypes do not include the detailed logic that eventually needs to be incorporated into a program. Action Diagrams and Decision Trees, on the other hand, allow the programmer to explain detailed logic to users and review it with them. This verification process prior to programming provides a much more solid basis for proceeding than the typical text or verbal expression of requirements.

REFERENCES

1. Martin, James., and McClure, Carma. *Structured Techniques—The Basis for CASE*, Prentice-Hall: Englewood Cliffs, N.J., 1988, p. 232

2. Ross, D., Goodenough, J. and Irvine, C. "Software Engineering: Process, Principles, and Goals," *Computer*, May 1975, pp. 66, 67

3. Boehm, B.W. *Software Engineering Economics*, Prentice-Hall: Englewood Cliffs, N.J., 1988.

13

CASE Tool Overview

PREREQUISITES FOR CASE

The previous two sections focused on management practices and useful methods for designing commercial software systems. The objective was to suggest an organizational environment and a professional skill set to improve the development of software systems. This last section discusses tools to automate the professional skill set.

The sequence followed in the book is based on the emerging consensus among many professionals experienced with CASE that CASE tools can only be employed successfully if there is a formal software development process which includes a structured approach to software design. Perhaps the best known proponent of this view is Watts Humphrey (1) of the Software Engineering Institute of Carnegie Mellon University. He suggests that the important first step in addressing software productivity problems is to treat the entire software task as a process that can be controlled, measured, and improved. To improve software development capabilities, Humphrey recommends that an organization take six steps:

Step 1: Understand the current status of the development process or processes.

Step 2: Develop a vision of the desired process.

Step 3: Establish a list of required process improvement actions in order of priority.

Step 4: Produce a plan to accomplish the required actions.

Step 5: Commit the resources to execute the plan.

Step 6: Start over at Step 1.

To successfully use CASE tools, the most critical step is the first: Understanding the current status of your development process or processes. Experience shows that advanced tools end up as shelfware if they are introduced into an organization that is not ready for them.

Humphrey proposes a *process maturity structure* (2) to determine the current status of an organization's development process (Fig. 13.1). Since Humphrey presents the definitions associated with these levels in rather academic terms, Fig. 13.1 also includes an interpretation by Read Fleming. (3)

The process maturity structure is a reliable gauge of how much an organization can benefit from CASE tools. CASE experts believe an organization will have significant problems implementing CASE unless it engineers software at Humphrey's level 3 or Fleming's level C or better.

Caper Jones (4) conducted a study that also supports the idea that automation tools *alone* are not the answer to improved software development productivity. He measured the impact of structured methods, upper CASE tools, and lower CASE tools on IS productivity. The unit of measure used in Jones' study was Function Points. The advantage of this measurement of software productivity is that it considers system complexity and is independent of any computer language. Function point analysis considers basic elements: inputs, outputs, files, shared files, and inquiries. The method applies a weight to each occurrence of an element based on its complexity, determines the total of each type of element by complexity level, and then adjusts the total based on the overall system complexity. (A detailed explanation of how to perform a function point analysis is included in Appendix B. For additional information also see references 5 and 6.)

Following is a recapitulation of part of Jones' study which shows the impact of structured methods and tools on software development productivity.

PROCESS MATURITY LEVELS—Watts Humphrey

1. *Initial:* Until the process is under statistical control, orderly progress in process improvement is not possible. While there are many degrees of statistical control, the first step is to achieve a rudimentary predictability of schedules and costs.
2. *Repeatable:* The organization has achieved a stable process with repeatable level of statistical control by initiating project management of commitments, costs sched ules, and changes.
3. *Defined:* The organization has defined the process as a basis for consistent implementation and better understanding. At this point advanced technology can use fully be introduced.
4. *Managed:* The organization has initiate comprehensive process improvement measurements and analysis. This is when the most significant quality improvements be gin.
5. *Optimizing:* The organization now has a foundation for continuing improvement and optimization of the process.

THE FIVE AGES OF METHODOLOGY SOPHISTICATION—
Read Fleming

A. *Age of Anarchy* (60%)—Anything goes.
B. *Age of Folklore* (25%)—Wisdom is passed from one generation of engineer to an other, over beer and pizza.
C. *Age of Methodology* (10%)—The way software is to be engineered is documented, and is actually done that way.
D. *Age of Metrics* (4%)—Both the products and the processes are measured in stand ardized ways.
E. *Age of Engineering* (1%)—Productivity is achieved through continuous quality im provement, much like it is done in manufacturing.

Figure 13.1 Unless an organization is at Humphrey's level "3" or at Fleming's level "C," there will probably be significant problems in using CASE tools.

Productivity Effects of Methods and Tools on Software Development

Function Points per staff month low-high

	No Tools 3GL	Upper CASE plus 3GL	Upper CASE plus 4GL	4GL only
Unstructured Methods	.75-8.0	3.0-12.5	7.0-30.0	5.0-15.0
Structured Methods	4.0-14.0	6.0-20.0	20.0-100.0	10.0-50.0

Experienced Staff

Figure 13.2 The effects of methods and tools on productivity. Typically, tools alone, without new methods for developing software, do not produce the desired productivity gains.

The statistics reveal that the purchase of a 4GL or a code generator raised the productivity of an experienced staff to a level (5.0 to 15.0 function points) that barely exceeds the productivity level achieved by adopting structured methods alone (4.0 to 14.0 function points). And if an upper CASE tool is used to automate the structured methods, the productivity level (6.0 to 20.0 function points) exceeds the results obtained through the purchase of a 4GL or a code generator alone. This point is particularly significant when you consider that the cost of equipping a staff with upper CASE tools is significantly lower than the cost of lower CASE tools. The greatest level of productivity is achieved when structured methods are combined with upper CASE tools to support the design activities and lower CASE tools to support the construction activities.

Humphrey's and Jones' emphasis on structured methods is contrary to much of the CASE focus for the AS/400. Most midrange professional magazines publish advertisements and articles on CASE that emphasize code generators and 4GLs. The message is that the purchase of one of these new technical silver bullets will put an end to productivity problems. Jones' statistics and the empirical experience documented by Humphrey and others, however, indicate that the opposite is true: The place to start is with structured methods and the tools to support these methods. Automating the construction phase of the life cycle with a code generator or 4GL then provides the final increment of productivity increase.

CASE AND THE MANAGEMENT OF CHANGE

By using CASE, an organization can obtain significant benefits if it also uses organizational practices that are appropriate for software development and the people who use the tools have the required design and technical skills. The successful adoption of CASE usually involves making fundamental changes in the way an organization develops software. These fundamental changes involve both cultural and technical elements.

Some of the cultural changes discussed were:

1. An emphasis on planning and system design rather than on construction.

2. An emphasis on team development: The user is a full design participant rather than just a passive customer.

3. The use of a formal software development process rather than ad hoc individual approaches.

4. An emphasis on achieving quality through the design of the development process and the product rather than through postconstruction inspection and testing.

Any organization is limited in its ability to change. And, it is harder to change people than the technical environment. As a result, the successful introduction of CASE tools into an organization depends on the organization's ability to change. Since it is difficult to determine from the beginning how much change an organization can manage, the first question is where to start the change and how this might vary over time.

Figures 13.3 and 13.4 represent two possible scenarios. The first scenario emphasizes people changes, that is, the process for developing software and the base of development knowledge, training, and experience needed to develop software. Technical change is initially minimized and is geared to providing tools to support the evolving skill set of the staff. The second scenario focuses on a technical solution and emphasizes technical change to obtain productivity improvements.

Jones' study can be used to quantitatively present the results of the two alternative routes to achieving increased productivity. Figure 13.5 shows the results of an immediate jump to the code generator or 4GL, Route A. In this strategy the capacity to change is devoted primarily to mastering the technical details of the new tool.

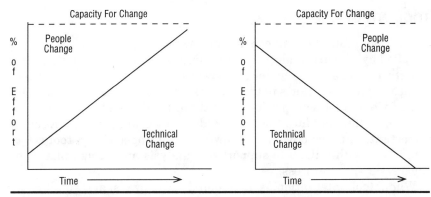

Figure 13.3 The capacity for change focuses on the "people" aspects of software development—improved software design skills, improved management practices, an improved process for software development, etc. New technical skills are not initially emphasized.

Figure 13.4 A technologist's approach to improving software productivity. In many instances, acquiring new technology is an end in itself. Available effort first goes into learning the new technology, then the factors that will make the new technology effective are considered.

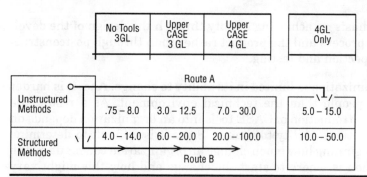

Figure 13.5 Two alternate approaches to improving software development productivity. Using Route A, a new construction tool (a code generator or 4th-generation language) is acquired first. Using Route B, the initial emphasis is on design methods and

Route B focuses first on the software development process and the methods to support this process. Tools are introduced as people develop a need for them to support a new process for software development. The first tools to be adopted on Route B are upper CASE tools that support the analysis and design phases of the software life cycle. Then lower CASE tools are introduced once structured methods and the upper CASE tools have been assimilated into the development process.

TOOL INTEGRATION

When you read the balance of this section which discusses tools supplied by various vendors, an important issue to keep in mind is tool integration. The terms upper and lower CASE essentially reflect two separate mainline efforts in the early development of tools. An obvious issue is how tool sets produced by these separate efforts are to be meshed so they produce the final product, a working system. Equally important, but less obvious, is how well the upper CASE tool set is integrated within itself to support the analysis and design phases of the development process.

When tool integration is considered, two levels are significant: process integration and data integration.

Process integration involves the coordination of separate CASE tools so they support the software development process as a single complex endeavor. This means that the product, or deliverable, from each tool conforms to a common understanding of the development process and that each tool compliments the capabilities of the other tools.

Process integration is the lowest level of integration and frequently is based more on how a tool is used than on any absolute feature of the tool itself. Like the hand tools a carpenter might use, individual tools in a CASE tool set have a fair degree of flexibility. As a consequence, the overall development process selected determines when and how a tool should be used.

Figure 13.6 (repeated from Chap. 12) shows a software development process diagram that can provide a more detailed look at process integration.

In the first phase of this development process, a Data Flow Diagram is used. The diagram shows that the output from this tool, the identification of data and process components, provides input for the next processes in the life cycle. For example, the high-level identification of a data component, such as Customer, is the starting point for the data modeling phase that identifies two customer entities, Customer Master and Ship-To Addresses. These, in turn, are the starting point for the detailed database design activity that identifies attributes for a customer, such as name and address.

The significant process integration problem occurs between the tools and outputs from the process modeling phase and the construction phase. If high-level frame technology is used for construction, the primary process modeling tool is the structure chart. This chart identifies the programming modules to be generated automatically and specifies how they are to be linked to accomplish a business function. The action diagram plays a secondary role and initially documents the logic of exception processing.

On the other hand, if a 3GL is used for construction, the Action Diagram plays a more significant role. Instead of just being used to design and document exception logic, the Action Diagram shows the full structure of a program almost down to a procedural code level. Program sections that some code generators take care of automatically (such as default editing and error processing) are spelled out in the Action Diagram intended for 3GL construction.

Data integration is the more advanced form of tool integration. It allows different tools to share information without manual reentry. This data sharing can take several forms, through interfaces, common access, semantics, and control.

Integration through interfaces is the lowest level of data sharing and is accomplished by passing data from one tool to another, typically by way of a batch transfer. If another tool subsequently changes data that is passed through an interface, the original data is no longer current. Some interfaces are bidirectional, allowing updates to be passed back

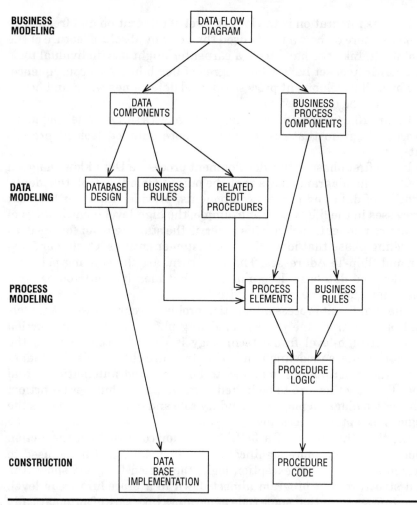

Figure 13.6 To effectively use tools from a variety of vendors, the process for developing software should be formalized. Then tools and methods for using the tools can be evaluated on the basis of their support for a coherent process.

from one tool to the other. Because of the dangers inherent in overwriting data, bidirectional interface cannot be used freely.

Integration through common data access means that different tools access the same data stored in only one place. The common data storage used by different tools has been referred to as a repository, dictionary, knowledge base, and encyclopedia. Data sharing through a common repository greatly reduces the logistics involved in coordinating tools. The problem lies in how to define the data and whether all tools using the repository agree with this definition.

Integration through common data access and common semantics means that tools must be built on consensus on the types and definitions of the shared development data. This description of shared data provides a metamodel. But once tools effectively share data, the issue of control becomes more significant. Data control addresses the issue of ensuring that any changed data is consistent with the metamodel and the individual tools that access the metamodel. Concurrent control deals with multiple users changing data simultaneously. Link management regulates and tracks changes to the repository and preserves the integrity of the repository data.

Efforts to provide data integration for tools have pursued a number of approaches: tool vendor vertical integration, tool vendor cooperative integration, and standards integration.

On the basis of their initial expertise in upper or lower CASE tools, several vendors have established total solutions. They accomplished these total solutions by developing additional products or acquiring (merging) additional products. This approach to tool integration has occurred primarily in the mainframe arena and, for the most part, had no effect on the AS/400 environment.

Some vendors in the AS/400 market practice cooperative integration. Typically, cooperative integration creates links between upper CASE tools designed for mainframe computers and code generators developed specifically for the AS/400.

On September 19, 1989, IBM announced AD/Cycle, an integrated framework for application development. IBM wanted to define a repository that resided on the AS/400 and would link upper and lower CASE tools. For the most part, defining this repository has been very slow. A data definition called the *external source format* (ESF) has been established, but a format for exchanging process definitions is still to come. During the summer of 1992, the original AS/400 repository framework was extended to operate on OS/2 and Unix-based local area networks. Even with this extension, however, it appears that vendor vertical and cooperative data integration will be the more promising approach for the immediate future.

PARADIGM SHIFT

One way to gain a perspective on a CASE tool is to look at the degree to which the mechanics of the tool represent a paradigm shift. Webster defines a *paradigm* as a model or pattern. The switch from RPG II to

RPG III is not a paradigm shift. On the other hand, the adoption of a formal process for software development that separates design activities from construction frequently represents a radical paradigm change.

Since it is difficult to do justice to the many excellent tools available, the selection of reviewed tools is not based on the tools' absolute merits but rather on how great a paradigm shift their use creates.

The upper CASE tools discussed are EasyCASE from Evergreen CASE tools and SILVERRUN form Computer Systems Advisers. The lower CASE tools reviewed are AS/SET and Synon/2E. For additional reviews of AS/400 tools, see references 7 and 8.

EasyCASE is a basic graphics tool that automates the preparation of the diagrams previously described. The basic paradigm shift is from a craft to an engineering methodology. The subsequent transition from manual to automated diagram preparation using Easy-CASE is very straightforward since the technology of this tool does not add to the difficulties of the transition. (For a more thorough discussion see Chap. 14.)

SILVERRUN has methodology and technical features that go beyond that of a hand tool. These additional features significantly add to the tool's efficiency and capabilities. Since these features also add to the tool's cost and learning curve, the tool is more appropriate for the serious designer for the casual user. (For a more thorough discussion see Chap. 15.)

AS/SET and Synon/2E are included in the review because they represent extremes from the perspective of a paradigm shift. AS/SET is a tool that represents an easy transition for most programmers. (For details, see Chap. 16.) On the other hand, Synon is most effective if an organization is able to switch completely to the principles of database design and object oriented design. (For details, see Chap. 17.)

REFERENCES

1. Humphrey, Watts S. *Managing the Software Process.* Addison Wesley: Reading, Mass., 1989, p. 4

2. Ibid., p. 5

3. Fleming, Read T. "Will CASE Come of Age in the 1990's?" *Electronic Design,* January 10, 1991.

4. Jones, Caper. "Using Function Point to Evaluate CASE Tools, Methodologies, and Languages," *Case Trends Magazine,* January-February 1991. pp. 8-16

5. Martin, James. *Rapid Application Development.* MacMillan: New York, 1991, pp. 20-22.

6. Ibid., Appendix II.
7. *NEWS 3X/400,* October 1992. Tools discussed in this issue include SILVERRUN from computer Systems Advisers and PowerDesigner from COGNOS.
8. *NEWS 3X/400,* November 1992. Tools discussed in this issue include PowerHouse 4GL from COGNOS and ADELIA from Hardis Corp.

14

EasyCASE from Evergreen CASE Tools

PRODUCT SYNOPSIS

EasyCASE is a PC-based upper CASE tool that supports the planning (analysis and design) phases of the software development life cycle. It is primarily a graphics tools that can be used to prepare the diagrams discussed in the methods section of this book, as well as other diagrams that have evolved as part of special-purpose methodologies. EasyCASE runs on an IBM PC (AT recommended) or PS/2 and compatibles. A hard disk (3MB space is required), DOS 3.1 or higher, EGA/VGA graphics card connected to an enhanced color monitor, Microsoft or compatible mouse, 640 K RAM, (500 K free) EMS recommended, various printers/plotters supported.

Vendor address
Evergreen CASE Tools, Inc.
8522 154th Ave N.E.
Redmond, WA 98052
USA tel: (206) 881-5149

Price

$750 per copy

PRODUCT DESCRIPTION

EasyCASE is organized as a single module with the following distinct sections: Chart Editor, Analysis Manager, Data Dictionary, and Reports Manager.

The *Chart Editor* is the core section and is used to simplify the production of the following types of diagrams.

Data Flow Diagrams (DFDs)

Entity Relationship Diagrams (ERDs)

Structure Charts (STCs)

Data Structure Diagrams (DSDs)

Data Model Diagrams (DMDs)

Transformation Graphs (TRGs) *

State Transition Diagrams (STDs) *

Note: Transformation graphs are diagrams that contain data and/or control information, as proposed by Ward and Mellor and Hatley to support the modeling of real-time systems. They are used to map the flow of control through a system. This diagram and the STD are outside the scope of this book since they are primarily aids in designing real-time process-control systems rather than commercial systems.

The *Analysis Manager* checks charts for consistency and for conformance to syntactical rules developed for each chart type. An individual chart is checked to ensure that all objects have been correctly labeled, identified, and defined in the data dictionary (repository). For chart objects that have been linked to another chart or text file, the existence of that chart or text file is also checked.

Following is a sampling of the chart verification rules included in the Analysis Manager.

Data Flow Diagram (DFD)

1. Symbols should all be labeled.

2. A data process must have at least one input data flow and one output data flow connected to it.

3. A flow connected to a store must meet one of the following requirements:
   —Be unnamed (assumed to carry the entire contents, if any, of the store).
   —Have the same name as the store.
   —Explode to the same record definition as the store.
   —Be a component of a composite store.

Entity Relationship Diagram (ERD)

1. Entities, relationships, and attributes should all be labeled and identified.

2. Relationships may not be connected.

3. Weak entities may not be connected.

A primary function of the Analysis Manager is to perform level balancing. As was mentioned in the discussion of DFDs, this function is significant when a process on a chart is exploded a lower level chart. The lower level chart provides more details for the object. Level balancing compares the inputs to and outputs from a data process with the inputs to and outputs from the lower level (child).

The *Data Dictionary Manager* lets you add, delete, change, browse, rename, and modify data dictionary (repository) entries. It also lets you pack, sort, import, export, and merge the data dictionary. You can export the entire dictionary in ASCII or SDF file format, or you can export a chart-specific portion in dBASE III file format.

The *Reports Manager* lets you print several basic, predefined chart and data dictionary reports. Following is a sample of the predefined reports.

Chart Objects Summary Report

Chart Objects Alias and Miscellaneous Attributes Report

Chart Objects User Name and Modification Date Attributes Report

GENERAL RELEVANCY AND COMMENTS

EasyCASE evolved from a shareware product developed by an engineer at the Boeing Company. EasyCASE is a very adequate basic drafting tool with excellent screen and print graphic qualities. It automates the preparation of most standard diagrams that are part of an engineering approach to software development. The tool has no embedded methodology biases. Rather, to accommodate various methodologies, EasyCASE provides options for various symbol sets. Diagrams can have the look and feel of the diagrams described in the methodologies texts. For example, when designers are preparing DFDs, they can select either the symbols identified with Gane and Sarson or with Yourdon.

The tool does not contain an action diagrammer to define the detailed logic of complex processes. The data modeling capabilities are very limited and do not provide a reengineering capability or the expanded methods definition capabilities described in Chap. 10. Both of these shortcomings should be resolved by using external tools. As a result, the EasyCASE repository does not contain the full design specifications for a system. An external printed repository, such as a project specification manual, is still required to consolidate all the specifications for a system.

Some features you might find in more expensive tools are also not available. For example, if you want to restructure a diagram by moving an object from one level to another, you must delete the object from one level and add it to the other. The alternative technique of opening up windows that show several levels of a diagram at the same time and then moving an object from one level to another across these windows is not supported.

For an IS department in the early stages of adopting structured methods and a formal approach to software development, EasyCASE is a suitable first acquisition. The capital investment is low, and the training needed to operate the tool is minimal. As a consequence, the emphasis can be on acquiring design skills and on improving the software development process rather than on learning the mechanical or technical skills needed to operate a complex tool.

DESIGNING A SYSTEM

To gain a perspective on the use of EasyCASE, let's briefly go through the process of designing a new system. The basic life cycle tasks and the diagrams used to support these tasks include the following:

Task	Diagram
Define the scope of the proposed system.	DFD
Identify the major components of the proposed system.	DFD

Establish the architectural
structure of the database.

ERD

Identify the database details
(attributes).

EasyCASE can be used for a basic
attribute definition, or use an alternate tool for the detailed analysis.

Establish the architectural
structure of the process
solutions.

Structure Chart.

Establish the detailed logic
of complex processes.

External editor required to prepare
action diagrams; decision trees can
be prepared using graphics
capabilities of one of the other
diagrams, such as a structure chart.

Once you have signed on to EasyCASE and identified the project
being worked on, the first screen is a drawing grid with a menu bar
across the top of the grid and an icons palette that shows the symbols
available for a specific diagram. (See Fig. 14.1.)

The menu bar contains entries for the top-level menu groups. If you
position the mouse pointer on one of the entries on the menu bar and

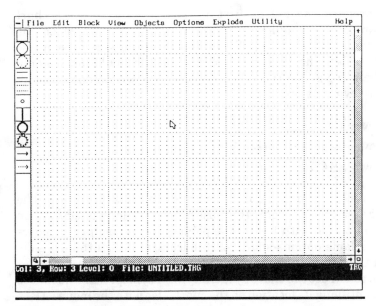

Figure 14.1   The EasyCASE drawing grid.

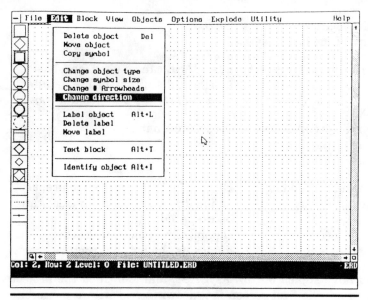

Figure 14.2 Sample of the pull-down menu used by EasyCase.

click, a pull-down menu that identifies details appears. For example, if you select the Edit entry, the pull-down menu shown in Fig. 14.2 appears.

To start preparing a DFD, the first step is to identify the type of chart to be prepared. To accomplish this, use the mouse pointer to select the File entry on the menu bar. A pull-down menu appears, and the mouse pointer can select the Change Type entry on the pull-down menu. Several chart types are then displayed on a new pull-down menu. Three are relevant at this point:

Data Flow—Yourdon/DeMarco (dfd)

Data Flow—Gane and Sarson (dfd)

Data Flow—SSADM v4 (dfd)

The differences among the three options are the symbol sets. The Gane and Sarson symbol set is the most frequently accepted. So, when you select an option with the mouse pointer, a drawing grid appears with the available options shown on the icon palette on the left side. (See Fig. 14.4.)

You then construct the chart by identifying a symbol with the mouse and then identifying its location on the chart, also with the mouse. Data flows are created by selecting the symbol for the data flow and then

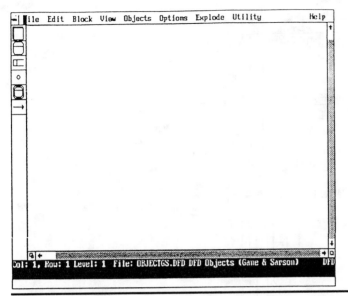

Figure 14.3 Drawing grid with an icon palette for the Gane and Sarson symbols for a Data Flow Diagram.

identifying the origin symbol and the destination symbol for the data flow.

Figure 14.4 shows a typical first-level example of a DFD to establish the boundaries of the proposed system.

Once the high-level boundaries are established, the design process consists of establishing more and more detail for each component you identify for a system. To accomplish the next step in this process, you establish a component breakdown for the process symbol on your first chart. This is a two-step process that consists of the following:

1. Establishing the parent/child linkage for an object by identifying the child's chart name in the data dictionary for the parent

2. Identifying the object for which you want to establish a child chart, and selecting the Explodes item on the menu bar (you then get a new blank diagram for drawing the child diagram, which is already linked to the parent)

To establish the parent/child relationship, the first step is to select the Edit function on the menu bar and then the Identify Object item on the pull-down menu. When this is done, a window appears, identifying the object (Fig. 14.5).

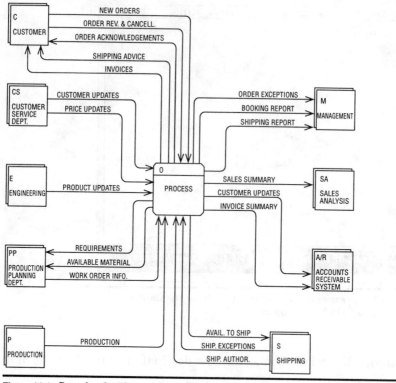

Figure 14.4 Sample of a "Context"-level Data Flow Diagram prepared using Easy-CASE.

Once an entry is made, another window appears (Fig. 14.6), identifying the following:

Object explodes to (Type, Name) : ____

rec (__ name of lower level chart)

On this screen, identify the type, DFD, and the name of the child chart, Essential Functions.

The next step is to create the lower-level diagram. You must first reach the new lower-level. To reach the lower-level chart, select the object to be decomposed to the lower-level by putting the mouse pointer on the symbol and clicking the left button. Then, you select the Explode option on the menu bar and the Down a Level option on the pull-down menu.

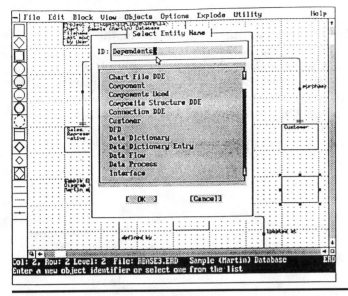

Figure 14.5 Window used to identify a process on a Data Flow Diagram.

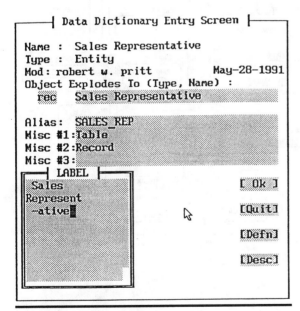

Figure 14.6 Window that identifies the lower-level diagram to be used to decompose a component on a Data Flow Diagram.

When this is down, a new blank chart is established, and the next level of detailing can occur. For this sample system, the results of this next effort are shown as Fig. 14.7.

It is important to note that when this lower-level DFD is being started, EasyCASE provides the option of automatically populating the diagram with the data flows to and from the higher-level process that is being decomposed. On the lower-level diagram, you then manually connect these data flows to the newly created processes which represent the decomposition of the parent process.

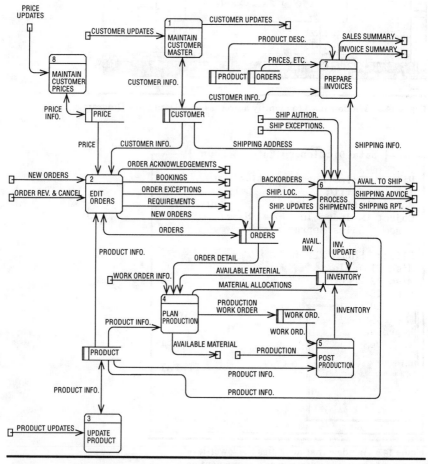

Figure 14.7 Sample "Essential Functions" Diagram representing the explosion of the higher-level process.

A similar approach is used to start developing the Data Model. For each data store, the identification screens establish the linkage to a lower-level ERD. Each data store is exploded, and an ERD is prepared for each data store (see Chap. 8).

Once you have completed the ERDs that establish a structure for each data store, the next step is to create composite charts that show relationships among the entities created for each data store. For example, for a Customer data store, you might have established two entities, Customer and Ship-To. Similarly for an Order data store, you might have established the entities Order Header and Order Detail.

You now need to establish a new ERD that shows the relationship between the Customer entity and the Order Header entity. The easiest way is to select the most complicated ERD created for the individual data stores and create a new chart using the Save As function. This is accomplished by selecting the File function on the menu bar and the Save As function on the pull-down menu.

Once the copy of the original ERD is created, it is necessary to add the entities created for the other data stores. Use the pull-down menu for the File entry on the menu bar and select the Merge Chart function. When this function is selected, a pop-up window appears, listing the other ERDs that were created. Select an ERD from the list, and it is automatically added to the base ERD. This process is repeated until all appropriate ERDs have been added. You complete the chart by establishing the new relationships among all the entities on the chart.

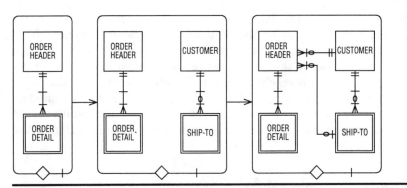

Figure 14.8 Example of the process of creating an enterprise-level Entity Relationship Diagram. Diagrams that show the structure of individual data stores are created first. These individual diagrams are merged, and the additional relationships are then added.

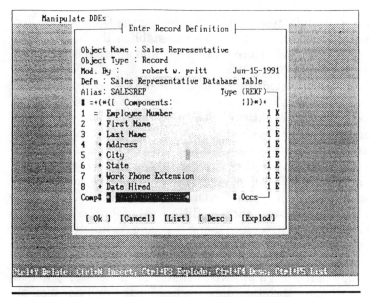

Figure 14.9   The screen provided by EasyCASE for identifying the attributes that are part of an entity.

The next step in the data modeling is to define the attributes for each entity (or, the fields for each file). EasyCASE provides a very basic capability for further definition of the database. This capability is in the data dictionary section. Figure 14.9 shows the format to identify attributes for an entity. The format supports a top-down definition approach and does not include the reengineering capability and the AS/400-specific attribute definition capabilities discussed in Chap. 10.

The final design step in the software development process is to establish the detailed logic of complex business processes. For the lowest-level process on the DFD, use the Data Dictionary Entry Screen to identify the lower-level chart type, a Structure Chart, and the name of the chart. To create a new chart, select the process to be exploded, and use the Explode function on the menu bar. At this point, a new chart will be created, and you can continue the decomposition of the process.

A PRODUCT PERSPECTIVE

While the tasks described for designing a system might appear daunting, learning EasyCASE itself is not a formidable task. If you understand the diagrams and already know what you want to accomplish, you can learn the tool almost intuitively. As I mentioned in the CASE tool overview, its features are almost so basic that it fits in the hand tool category.

In the next chapter, let's take a look at the features of a more advanced tool, SILVERRUN from Computer Systems Advisers.

SILVERRUN from Computer Systems Advisers

PRODUCT SYNOPSIS

SILVERRUN is a PC-based Upper CASE Tool which is used to perform the enterprise modeling phase of the software development life cycle. It is both a graphics tool and a data modeling tool. As a graphics tool it is used to prepared Data Flow Diagrams and Entity Relationship Diagrams. As a data modeling tool it can be used to perform either a top-down design, or use a reengineering approach. Two significant features of the tool are that it fully supports the Object Oriented Design (OOD) concepts which we discussed earlier, and it has an industrial strength repository which makes it an ideal coordination vehicle for larger projects. It runs under either Windows or OS/2, with 6 to 8 MB of memory respectively required for the two versions. It also runs on a Macintosh 68030 processor with at least 2.5 MB of memory.

Vendor address
Computer System Advisers, Inc.
50 Tice Boulevard
Woodcliff Lake, NJ 07675
Tel: (201) 391-2210

PRICE

SILVERRUN is organized as four modules, each of which can be purchased independently. The price for each module is $2500. These individual modules may be used on an individual basis, or used together as an integrated analysis and design tool set. We will discuss these individual modules in the product description section.

PRODUCT DESCRIPTION

The four modules of SILVERRUN are as follows:

DFD: Data Flow Diagram

RDM: Relational Data Modeler

ERX: Entity Relationship Expert

WRM: Workgroup Repository Manager

The Data Flow Diagrammer module is used to automate the preparation of Data Flow Diagrams using Gane and Sarson, Yourdon, or the Merise diagramming techniques. The tool provides many advanced features which facilitate the preparation of these diagrams. One example of such a feature is the ability to move symbols from one diagram level to another. For example, if an Essential Functions Diagram contained so many processes that the diagram is extremely cluttered, a consolidated process would first be created for this high-level view. A lower-level decomposition diagram would then be created, and shown in a separate window on the screen. The original processes that are now represented by the new consolidated process can then be picked up with the mouse pointer and moved to the new diagram. In the process of this move, none of the information originally defined for these detailed processes is lost.

The Relational Data Modeler is used to create and validate a relational database design. This is accomplished by using a palette of graphic tools to establish entities and relationships and a repository window to identify the data elements which are the attributes and key fields for an entity. The data elements in the repository can be entered directly using any of the four modules, or they can be imported into the tool from an ASCII text file.

As a reengineering tool, if an existing database design such as System 36 flat files are down loaded to the PC, they can be used to populate distinct data structures in the repository. These data structures then serve as the basis for generating the equivalent of the

AS/400's Field Reference File called Common Items. When an entity is being defined, the entries in the Common Items table are displayed in a window. The mouse pointer is then used to attach a Common Item field to an entity, and in the process create a new data structure. As an element of a new data structure, a Common Item can then be renamed and redefined. A link is maintained between the new data element and the original Common Item and between the Common Item and the original field in the old format. Thus we have the audit trail which permits an accountability check on the new design and the preparation of planning reports for the data conversion effort.

Other significant features of this module include:

Ability to automatically generate foreign keys once the relationship between modules has been established.

Ability to expand the basic domain definitions of attributes so that methods for editing and operating on data are included. This encapsulation occurs on both a file and a field level.

Export ability so the database design can be uploaded to the AS/400 in an SQL/400 format or in the ESF format for linking to other CASE tools.

The Entity Relationship Expert is a rule based system for building, refining, and validating a Data Model. This module represents an alternate to the RDM module as the starting point for creating a data model. Rather than use an intuitive approach, this module asks the designer a series of questions based on an imbedded expert system. It then generates a first cut database schema.

The first step in this module is to establish a basic database structure using the graphics part of the tool and the table part of the repository. The expert system is then used to refine and validate the model. This validation and refinement is a six step process. The first step, *analyze names*, performs a semantic check of attribute names to ensure that each name contains the name of the entity of which it is a part. The second step, *normalize*, uses a series of expert questions to verify the normalization form of the model. The third step, *verify connectives*, consists of a series of questions which is used to verify the relationships among the entities. The next two steps, *search for identifiers* and *verify identifiers*, are used to establish the primary identifiers (keys) for the entities. The final step, *verify attribute dependencies*, are used to ensure that all nonidentifier attributes are dependent on the primary identifier—the third normal form that we discussed in the chapter on Relational Database concepts.

The Workgroup Repository Manager is the coordination and communication component of the tool set in a multiuser environment. It supports the sharing and consolidation of repository information in a local area network environment. Enterprise level graphical diagrams and design specifications can be down loaded to local project environments for further refinement and to serve as the specifications for the detailed design and construction phases. Changes made on the project level can then be returned to the central repository for review and consolidation.

GENERAL RELEVANCY AND COMMENTS

SILVERRUN represents a significant evolutionary step in the development of tools to support the software development process. Advanced features in the graphics portion of the tool can significantly speed up the process of creating and modifying diagrams. The use of the tool to support database reengineering is an important capability. The support of Object Oriented Design concepts is very unique, and used properly it can be an important factor in planning for software reuse.

The tool does not, however, support the design activities that occur during the process modeling phase of the software development life cycle. Specifically it does not support the development of structure charts and action diagrams. An additional product, POSE, is available from the same vendor to perform these tasks.

For the IS department that is developing a significant new system or reengineering a major old system, SILVERRUN is a suitable tool. Features included in the graphics portion of the tool will significantly add to the productivity of the diagram preparation. More significantly, the Object Oriented Design features provide a more complete specification capability that can be used to guide the subsequent detailing phases of software development. The advanced repository manager allows paper documentation to be eliminated in favor of an electronic store that permits multiple projects to share and update design specifications.

USING THE TOOL

A product such as SILVERRUN is too complex to fully describe all of its features in a book of this nature. However, in order to gain a perspective on the use of SILVERRUN, let's briefly look to see how we would use the tool to support the process which was described in Chaps.7, 10, and 11. As you will recall, those chapters dealt with the

Enterprise Model: The primary phases described in these chapters were the following:

Preparing the Business Model: Establishing the scope of the system and identifying the major components (process and data) using a Data Flow Diagram (DFD).

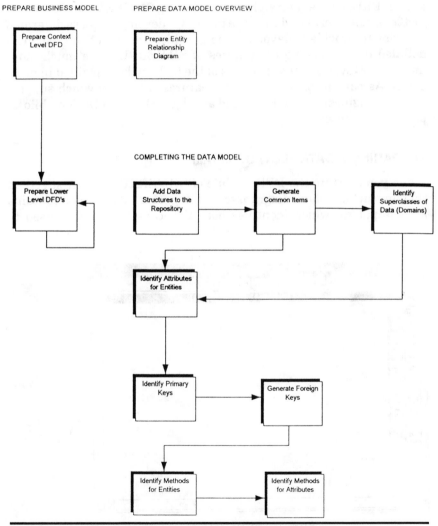

Figure 15.1 An overview of the process for defining an Enterprise Model when SILVERRUN is used as the tool.

Preparing a Data Model overview: Establishing the architectural overview of the database using an Entity Relationship Diagram (ERD).

Completing the Data Model: Identifying attributes for the entities, keys, foreign keys, and so on.

Figure 15.1 shows an overview of the major activities involved in creating an Enterprise Model when SILVERRUN is used as the tool.

Two of the major activities shown in the diagram, preparing a DFD and an ERD, are very straight forward using SILVERRUN. So we will just look at a brief overview of the process of developing these diagrams in order to provide a flavor for the graphics portion of the tool. The detailed data modeling capabilities of SILVERRUN are much more unique, however, so these portions of the tool will be explained in more detail. As part of this explanation, features of the tool which support both a reengineering approach and an Object Oriented Design philosophy will be presented.

PREPARING A DATA FLOW DIAGRAM

When you start up the DFD module of SILVERRUN, the first screen that appears is a blank diagram screen (Fig. 15.2). This screen contains a Tools palette which identifies both the icons that can be used to

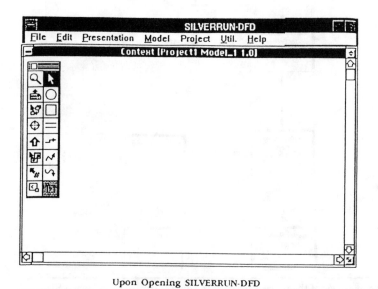

Upon Opening SILVERRUN-DFD

Figure 15.2 SILVERRUN's drawing grid.

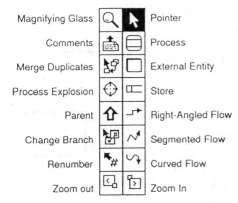

Magnifying Glass	Pointer
Comments	Process
Merge Duplicates	External Entity
Process Explosion	Store
Parent	Right-Angled Flow
Change Branch	Segmented Flow
Renumber	Curved Flow
Zoom out	Zoom In

Figure 15.3 The tools palette provided by SILVERRUN for preparing a Data Flow Diagram (DFD).

The DFD Tools Palette

populate the diagram and auxiliary processes that are used in the preparation of the diagrams (Fig. 15.3).

To start the preparation of our first diagram, select the icon External Entity with the mouse, and then position the icon on the diagram. When the symbol is added to the diagram, a default name is automatically added in order to identify the symbol. This name can be revised by double clicking on the symbols name field. This opens up a window which can be used to rename and describe the symbol. Figure 15.4

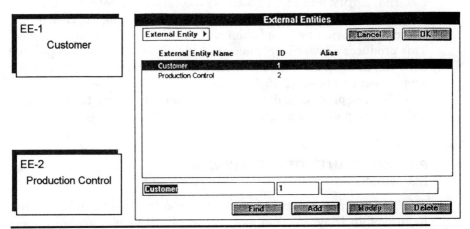

Figure 15.4 The drawing grid for a DFD with a window open to identify the external entity.

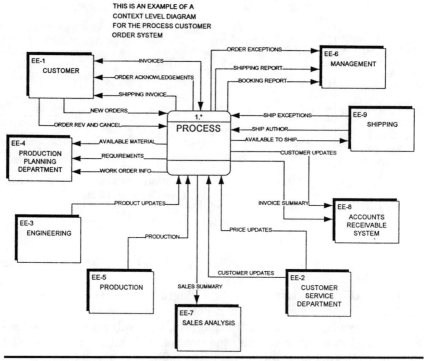

THIS IS AN EXAMPLE OF A
CONTEXT LEVEL DIAGRAM
FOR THE PROCESS CUSTOMER
ORDER SYSTEM

Figure 15.5   Sample of a "Context"-level DFD prepared using SILVERRUN.

shows a diagram with the window open to permit describing an External Entity, and Fig. 15.5 shows a completed Context Diagram.

To decompose a process, you use the tools palette again, click on the Process Explosion tool, and then click on the process to be exploded. This produces a lower-level diagram which is automatically populated with the data flows from the higher-level diagrams as well as their origination points—Fig. 15.6.

Additional processes, data stores, and data flows are then added in order to complete the diagram.

PREPARING AN ENTITY RELATIONSHIP DIAGRAM

SILVERRUN provides two choices when you wish to prepare an Entity Relationship Diagram. You can use the Entity Relationship Expert (ERX) module to help guide you through the normalization process, or you can use the Relational Data Modeler (RDM) module to create the

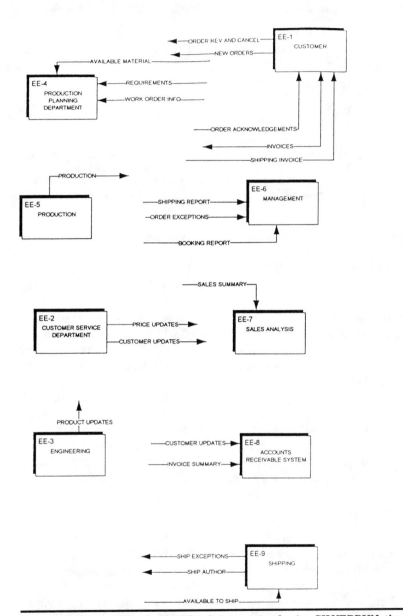

Figure 15.6 When a lower-level DFD is being prepared using SILVERRUN, the tool automatically shows, on the lower-level diagram, the data flows into and out of the higher-level process being decomposed.

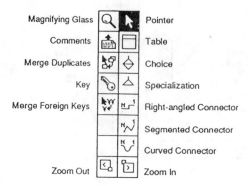

Magnifying Glass — Pointer
Comments — Table
Merge Duplicates — Choice
Key — Specialization
Merge Foreign Keys — Right-angled Connector
— Segmented Connector
— Curved Connector
Zoom Out — Zoom In

RDM Tools Palette

Figure 15.7 The tools palette provided by SILVERRUN for preparing an Entity Relationship Dia-

diagrams directly. For purposes of this explanation, let's look at the RDM module.

When you start up the RDM module, the first screen that appears is a blank diagram screen which includes a tool palette shown in Fig. 15.7.

The first step is to establish the notation to express the cardinality of a relationship. Two choices are offered. The first is called Information Engineering, and uses the crow's foot notation (-) which we discussed earlier. The second formalism is called DATARUN, and uses alpha/numeric's (0,N) to express cardinality. The formalism for a diagram is established by selecting Presentation on the menu bar, and then Preferences on the pull-down menu.

To start the preparation of an ERD, select the Tables icon on the tools palette, and then click the mouse pointer on the location on the graph where you wish to position the entity. This process is repeated until the diagram is populated with the candidate entities which you need to represent the relational database structure for the data stores identified on the DFD.

Note 1: SILVERRUN has no direct way of linking the data stores shown on a DFD to the entities shown on an ERD. As you will recall from our earlier discussion, some tools accomplish this by permitting an ERD to be started by initiating a decomposition of a data store. An alternate approach which can be used with SILVERRUN would be to use the data structures component of the tool's repository in order to establish this linkage. Data structures will be discussed in more detail in the next part of this writeup.

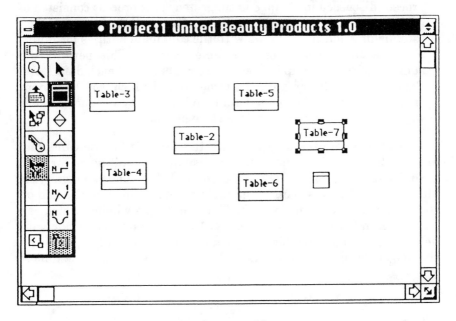

Laid Out Tables

Magnifying Glass Tool

Table Name	client
Coded Name	
Alias	

Table Name Edit Window

Figure 15.8 The default entity names assigned by SILVERRUN are made meaningful by using the mouse pointer to click on "Magnifying Glass" in the tools palette. A Table Name edit window then appears that can be used to assign a meaningful name to an entity.

Note 2: In order to develop manageable diagrams, the assembly process discussed in Chap. 8 is suggested. This process consisted of first establishing the candidate entities for each data store, and then establishing additional views with the candidate entities for multiple data stores shown on the same diagram. This permits the addition of relationship between the components of each data store. For example, between an entity Order Detail which is a component of the data store Customer Order and an entity Product Header which is a component of the data store product.

As you populate the diagram with the symbols for the candidate entities, SILVERRUN automatically assigns a default name for each entity. Meaningful names are assigned by clicking on the magnifying glass tool, and then selecting the table to be renamed by clicking on the table with the mouse pointer. This opens up a window which can then be used to rename the table. Fig. 15.8 illustrates a diagram with default names for the tables, the symbol for the magnifying glass on the tools palette, and the window which is used to rename the table.

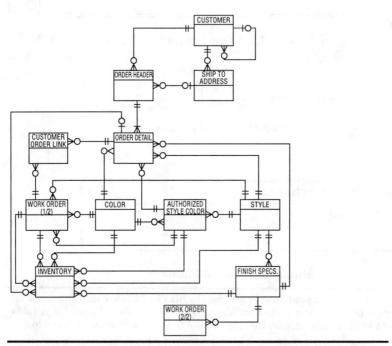

Figure 15.9 Sample Entity Relationship Diagram prepared using SILVERRUN.

Once the candidate entities have been given meaningful names, the next step is to establish the relationships between entities, and identify the cardinality of these relationships. A completed diagram prepared with SILVERRUN is shown in Fig. 15.9.

COMPLETING THE DATA MODEL

When a reengineering approach is being used to complete the data model, there are three tasks to be accomplished initially (Fig. 15.10).

The first of these tasks is to populate the repository with the existing data structures which are to serve as the basis for our reengineering efforts. This can be accomplished in two ways:

Download existing data structures (flat file formats, DDS, physical file layouts, and so on) through PC support, and create an ASCII text file. SILVERRUN can then import this text file directly into its repository.

Enter existing data structures directly into the SILVERRUN repository.

The second task to be accomplished is to use the SILVERRUN facility to create a Common Items file. This file is the equivalent of a Field Reference File on the AS/400. Items in this file are the basis for identifying the attributes for an entity in the same way that a Field Reference File is used to define physical and logical files on the AS/400.

The final task is to identify Super classes of data. These super classes of data are called Domains by SILVERRUN. The purpose of a super class is to support the concept of inheritance which we discussed as part of Object Oriented Design. In effect we want to identify a field such as a Date, and establish common characteristics and editing procedures. A specific instance such as an Order Date in an Order File will then be linked to this super class, with the understanding that any characteristics and editing routines established for Date are to be applied (inherited) by Order Date.

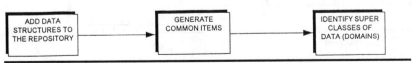

Figure 15.10 Steps involved in using SILVERRUN as a tool to reengineer an existing database.

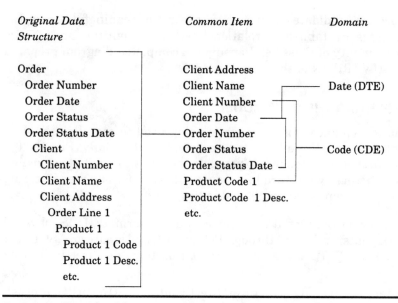

Figure 15.11 Example of the process of data reengineering using SILVERRUN.

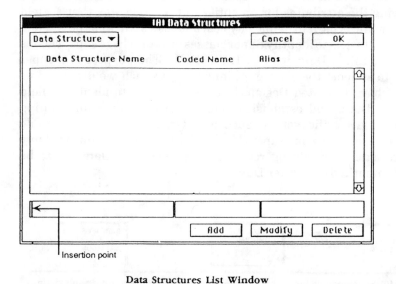

Data Structures List Window

Figure 15.12 Window used by SILVERRUN to enter data structures (typically file names) directly into the repository.

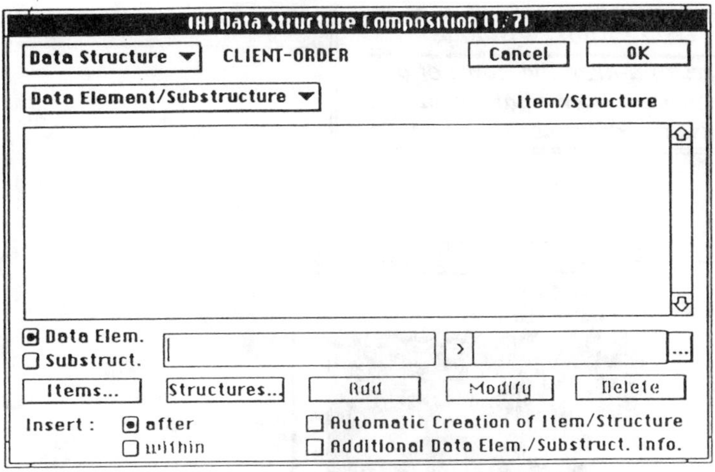

CLIENT-ORDER Composition Window

Figure 15.13 Window used by SILVERRUN to enter directly the fields that are part of a data structure.

Figure 15.11 shows the data transformations that occur in this process.

Figures 15.12 and 15.13 are samples of the windows provided by SILVERRUN to permit direct entry of data structures into the tool's repository.

Once a data structure has been entered into the repository either by direct entry or by importing old data formats, the next step is the creation of the Common Items file. This is accomplished by selecting Project on the menu bar, selecting Generate Common Items on the pull-down menu, and selecting Data Elements on the submenu.

The next step, identifying the attributes for each entity that has been established on the ERD, is accomplished by returning to the ERD diagram. Using the menu bar and the submenus, the Common Items that we have just generated are displayed in a window. The first step in completing an ERD is to identify common items that should be a part of an Entity by selecting them from the window using the mouse pointer. The selected items are then dragged to the appropriate entity (Fig. 15.14).

This process creates a new data structure. Once this has been accomplished, an instance of a common item which is part of this new structure can be renamed and redefined as part of this new data structure while still retaining a link to the common item. Additional attributes can also be added directly to this new data structure.

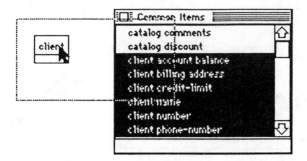

Dragging Common Items to a Table

Figure 15.14 Completing the definition of an Entity by using a window to display fields defined in the repository (data dictionary) and linking them to the entity by dragging with the mouse pointer.

The next step is to designate the primary keys for each new entity or table that we have created. This is accomplished by selecting the Key tool from the palette, and clicking on the attribute(s) in each entity that are to serve as the key. Foreign keys which implement the relationships that we have established between entities can then be generated automatically by SILVERRUN. This is accomplished by selecting this function by using the menu bar and the pull-down menus.

At this point we have accomplished the basic reengineering of an original file or manual form. The Common Item file serves as the link between the fields in the original format, and the fields in the new database design. Reports can be written which provide a cross-reference between the old and the new designs. These serve as the basis for both a data conversion effort and as a way of verifying that we have accounted for all old fields in the new design.

OBJECT ORIENTED DESIGN

An advanced feature of SILVERRUN is the ability to expand at this point the basic design of the database that has just been accomplished.

We do this by adding to the object definitions the methods that operate on these objects. This encapsulation of data and methods is the essence of Object Oriented Design, and represents a significant evolutionary step past the basic approach of Information Engineering.

SILVERRUN accomplishes this method encapsulation on two levels. On an entity or table level, the basic definition can be expanded by defining Actions that operate on the table. On a attribute or column level, the column definition is expanded by identifying Specifications for the column. Let's take a look at the process for identifying these methods which are to be linked to data.

On an entity or table level, the methods specification process starts by selecting the Presentation choice on the menu bar, and then selecting the Display choice on the pull-down menu. A display window now opens as shown in Fig. 15.15.

Click on the Actions check box and the Specifications check box, and then reselect Presentation from the menu bar and Palettes from the pull-down menu. Select Action Categories from the submenu. This results in a display of the Action Categories palette (Fig. 15.16).

One or more of the basic methods that are displayed on the Action Categories palette can now be associated with the entity or table by using the mouse to drag the action from the palette to the table.

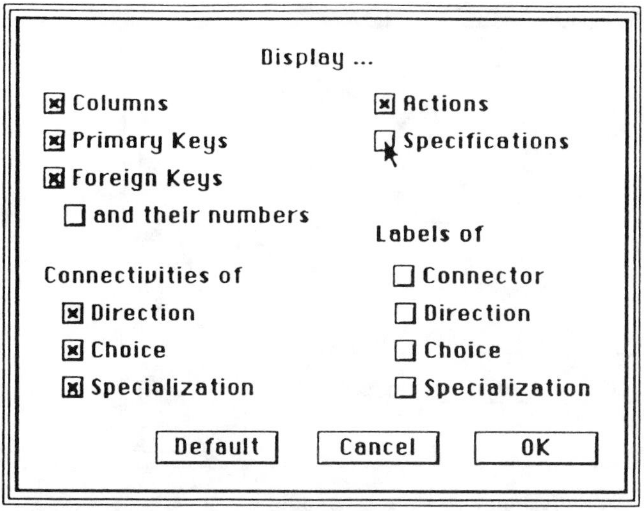

Figure 15.15 The process of defining the methods associated with an object starts by using the mouse pointer to select "Actions."

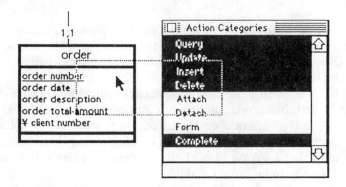

Dragging Actions Categories From Their Palette to a Table

Figure 15.16   This window displays basic methods that can be specified for an entity.

Once a basic method has been linked to a table, it can now be defined in detail. Figure 15.17 illustrates the window which is used to accomplish this definition.

A similar process is also used to establish the methods that are significant for individual attributes or columns. A Specifications Symbols palette is opened, and then relevant symbols are dragged to the individual column. These basic specifications can then in turn be

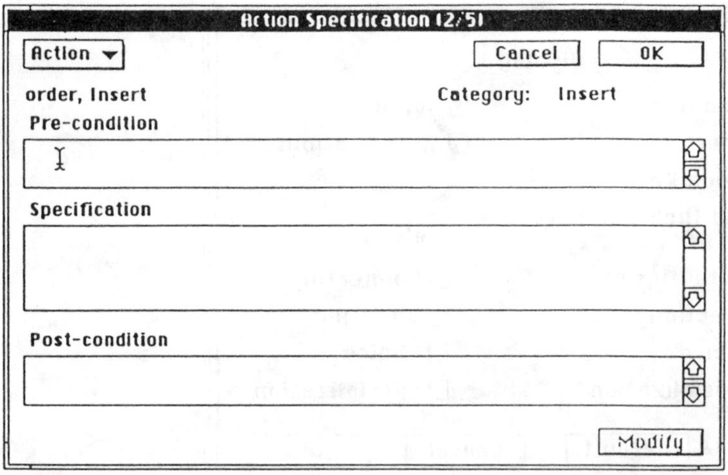

Action Specification Description Window

Figure 15.17   This window is used to define the specifics of a method that has been linked to an entity.

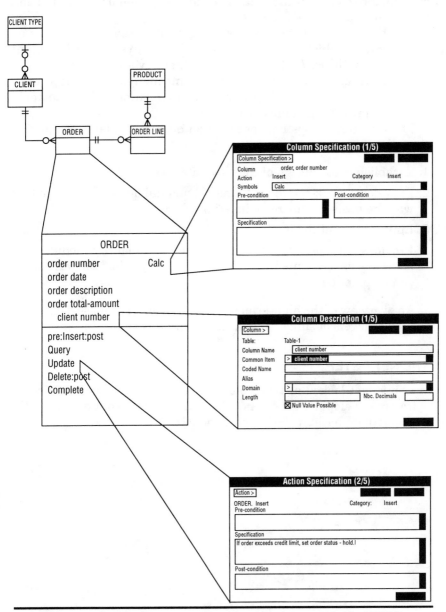

Figure 15.18 The "object" view of an entity or data structure provided by SILVER-RUN. The high-level view of an entity that is first identified on an ERD is defined in greater detail through subsidiary views. These subsidiary views permit the identification of keys, foreign keys, attributes, methods operating on either a file or field level, and the details of the methods.

expanded to establish the details of the calculation or additional edit that is to be performed.

The final result of this process is a graphical representation of an entity or table which can be implemented as a physical file during the construction phase. And as part of this high-level representation, we have identified the existence of significant methods that need to be incorporated into the business process specifications when the application programs are being designed.

Thus we have a system specification document that accomplishes the following:

1. Establishes the design of the new database.

2. Provides a cross-reference to the old manual or flat file design that was the basis for our reengineering effort.

3. Links data and the methods that operate on this data.

4. Provides a repository which can be used to identify modules and subroutines associated with files and fields so that software reuse can be planned.

An overview of the high-level identification of a database design and the lower-levels of supporting documentation is shown in Fig. 15.18.

THE NEXT STEP

We have just looked at two tools that automate the design phases of software development. Let's now look at two tools that automate the construction phase: AS/SET and Synon/2E.

16

AS/SET from System Software Associates

PRODUCT SYNOPSIS

AS/SET (AS/400 Software Engineering Technology) is an AS/400-based lower CASE tool and application code generator. It is used in the construction and maintenance phases of the application development life cycle. It generates RPG/400 source code based on specifications created by designers and programmers. The tool is menu-based and facilitates the adoption of a structured approach to programming. Thus it improves the initial coding effort and the productivity of later maintenance. AS/SET allows programming to start either from scratch with a database that incorporates the concepts of relational database design or with a legacy database that was inherited from earlier development efforts.

Vendor address
System Software Associates, Inc.
500 West Madison
Chicago, IL 60661
tel: (312) 641-2900

PRICE

AS/SET's pricing scheme is tiered according to the size of the AS/400. Prices start at $10,000 for a model B10 and go up to $70,000 for the larger models. Annual maintenance is 15 percent of the software base lease price.

PRODUCT DESCRIPTION

AS/SET is a menu-driven application generator that steps the programmer through all the required functions needed to build an application. It contains a series of panels, or screens, that define the characteristics of an application in terms of a Data Model and screen and report layouts. It also contains a proprietary 4GL that specifies I/O's and establishes the processing logic. These specifications and processing requirements are stored in a repository that is used for code generation and as the documentation center for future maintenance.

Once characteristics and processing requirements are entered into the repository, AS/SET serves several functions:

1. It automatically generates RPG/400 for programs and DDS code for the device files.

2. It automatically creates a data dictionary and generates DDS for additions to the database.

3. It automatically creates new physical, logical, and join logical files.

4. It automatically creates DDS for screen and report layouts.

AS/SET is based on a Structured Design approach to software development. This approach starts with the identification of an individual business function, such as general ledger or inventory control, that is to serve as a partition to segregate the development effort. This partition is called an *application set*. Once this partition is established, the next step is to analyze the data requirements for the individual processes within the Business Area. The purpose of this analysis is to create reusable Data Models that identify the files required for the development area. These Data Models can include either an individual file or multiple files. If multiple files are specified as part of a Data Model, they must be linked by one or more common fields. In this linkage, the common field linking one file to another must be a key field, or foreign key.

Once Data Models are established, a form of transaction analysis (described in Chap. 9) decomposes a business process. Within an interactive program, this transaction analysis identifies the major screens that are part of the programming solution. Once these screens are identified, AS/SET's screen painter is used to format each screen. In the next step, the proprietary language specifies the processing for each screen and establishes screen to screen linkages.

As a menu driven product, AS/SET is organized into five major components:

Product Security: This component allows the definition of application sets that provide the basic partitioning scheme for the development effort. This component also is used to set system wide defaults, identify who can use the system and what functions they can perform, restrict product usage by time, and so on.

Repositories: Each application set has a repository that contains the specifications for the data required for the business function. The repository for an application set can be used to create new files or interface with existing AS/400 files. The repository component also defines the Data Model, provides file and field level security, sets defaults for field characteristics, attributes, and validation. In addition, the repository offers several reports, including audit trails and impact of change reports.

Display Programs: This component creates interactive programs. It contains a full screen painter for laying out an exact screen representation. It uses a higher-level language that identifies actions to be performed to define processing and screen linkage logic. This processing definition is the basis for generating RPG/400 statements.

Report Programs: This component creates programs that produce printed output. This includes customizing the report layout and specifying sorts, level breaks, subtotals, user-defined calculations, and printer characteristics.

Batch Programs: This component creates programs that process files when no screens or reports are required for the function. A batch program can process any number of files to update information in these files or add information to other files. This processing includes user-defined calculations and/or any other required actions.

An important feature of AS/SET is the ability to define a header/detail relationship. When this relationship is established, AS/SET will automatically generate code to maintain a total in a header record when corresponding detail records are added, deleted, or updated. An example of this type of functionality is an inventory summary record for a product supported by zero, one, or many individual lot records. Once the relationship between the summary and the lot records is established, AS/SET will automatically generate code to maintain balances in the summary record when individual lot records are updated.

The higher-level language commands included in AS/SET are called *actions.* These actions specify what processing functions need to be performed for each program. These functions include:

Performing file processing.

Driving the display of file data on the screen.

Progressing from screen to screen within a program.

Manipulating data and performing calculations.

Copying program subroutines and performing program calls.

Executing OS/400 commands.

The structured programming approach used by AS/SET organizes these actions into several groups. A display program, for example, is structured by screen into five different action groups.

Prescreen: Actions that are executed immediately before a panel is displayed.

Post Enter: Actions which are executed each time the user presses the <ENTER> key, assuming that all validation checks are passed.

Post Screen: Actions that are executed each time the screen is exited.

Function Key: Actions that are defined for any function key used on a screen. These actions are executed each time the function key is pressed.

Action Subroutine: Actions that are executed as a subroutine.

Examples of AS/SET action codes include:

@SETLL and @SETGT establish file positioning prior to file read commands.

@GETREC and @GETBLK retrieve records from Data Model files.

@WRITE, @DELETE, and @UPDATE add, delete, and update records in Data Model files.

GENERAL RELEVANCY AND COMMENTS

AS/SET's greatest strength as a construction tool is its use of structured programming for AS/400 development. It also improves the efficiency of the coding process because it uses its own higher-level language that requires fewer statements to define a processing step than conventional 3GL languages such as RPG or COBOL.

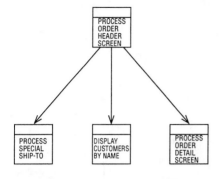

Figure 16.1 Structure chart illustrating the AS/SET approach to structured programming.

AS/SET implements structured programming by providing several discrete coding panels that organize a program into functional sections. These panels are accessed from the screen painter that formats user screens. A look at the structure chart of a Create Customer Order program illustrates AS/SET's approach to structured programming. Figure 16.1 identifies four screens as the basic solution for this process. These screens are:

Order header screen

Special ship-to screen

Customers by name screen

Order detail screen

When the procedural logic for this program is to be coded, the program is developed according to a distinct hierarchy process. First the user screens required as part of the process solution are defined. The procedural logic isthen organized by screen. And for each screen, procedural logic is organized into prescreen, postenter, and other routines. Figure 16.2 shows this hierarchical organization.

Building programs on this structure and maintaining the program on the AS/SET specification level avoids the deterioration of programs and the introduction of spaghetti code. Each part of a program solution has a distinct function which makes it easier for maintenance programmers to identify the part of a program that needs changing.

Adopting the concepts of structured programming as the design foundation for AS/SET provides a great deal of flexibility in how the tool can be used. The tool does not have any rules governing design of

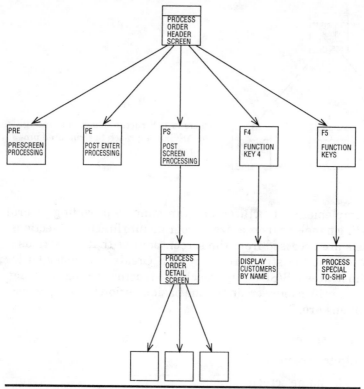

Figure 16.2 Hierarchical structure used by AS/SET in designing a solution for a complex business process.

the database used in conjunction with the tool, so unnormalized or flat files from an old design can be continued. As a result programmers can use either an existing file design which might include redundancies or require the renaming of fields. This is possible because the programming process creates individual Data Models for each program. Each Data Model consists of either a single file or several related files, that is, one file includes a foreign key that is a key in the other file. A Data Model can be based on existing or new file and field definitions. And, using an existing file still allows that individual fields be redefined for that process.

This flexibility is particularly important if a company is committed to a particular package as its basic solution and needs improved productivity for making enhancements to this package.

When a new system is developed, however, the tool's flexibility needs to be controlled to achieve the full potential of productivity improvements. For example, if the database is to serve as a system's architectural structure, data structures should not be reinterpreted or redefined on a process level. If reinterpretation or redefinition is allowed, this increases the probability of uncontrolled design changes during initial development and increases the cost of maintenance later on.

AS/SET does not directly address other significant productivity factors, such as modularization and software reuse. The structure chart in Fig. 16.2 can be constructed as either a monolithic program or as separate modules for each screen. This decision depends on how the tool is used and is not determined by how the tool works. Although flexibility is desirable, it also requires the IS department to have standards and a quality assurance procedure if techniques, such as modularization, are to be the established norm.

Similarly, the tool's flexibility provides no natural programming structure to facilitate software reuse. Programs can incorporate multiple files on a screen and multiple screens. This means that the tool does not include the concept of a software object. Also, it does not maintain a catalog to facilitate the identification of reusable objects that are based on the encapsulation of data structures and the methods associated with these data structures.

Although the tool increases the level of productivity by using structured programming and a higher-level language that is more efficient than a 3GL, it does not address issues like design for manufacturability. To achieve full productivity gains, management controls, quality assurance procedures, and a software catalog of reusable components need to be in place.

BUILDING A SYSTEM

When AS/SET builds a system it goes through several menu-driven processes to accomplish the required tasks. Developing a display program, for example, requires the following processes:

Establish the partition within AS/SET (application set) that segregates this development effort.

Create the required Data Models for the application area by assimilating existing files and fields or by defining new files and fields.

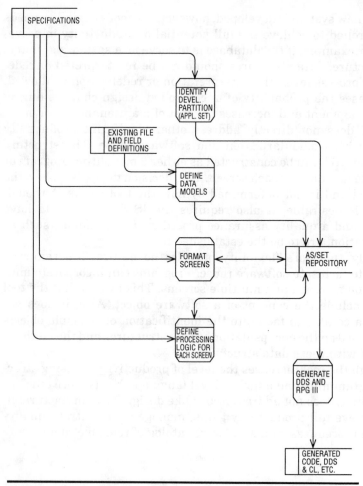

Figure 16.3 The construction (programming) process using AS/SET.

Start the process of developing a program by selecting Data Models and painting a screen.

Use AS/SET's action codes, define prescreen, <ENTER>, postscreen, and the other action group procedures. This definition includes any required call to a next screen.

Figure 16.3 is an overview of this process.

Createa application set. The first step in the construction process is to establish a development partition for the new system or subsystem.

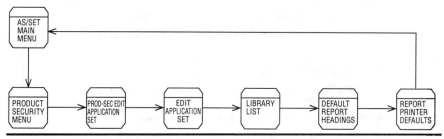

Figure 16.4 Overview of the specification screens used in starting a new project.

This allows the data to be used for the system to be identified and defined and individual programs to be developed. AS/SET's product security component establishes the development partition. Figure 16.4 summarizes the screens that accomplish this function. In addition to the screens shown for the creation of an application set, a number of other screens are available at this time to establish system defaults, and so on.

Following is a sample and a brief description of the function of each AS/SET screen used to establish an application set.

Product security menu: This screen is the top-level menu for the product security component. In the example, option 3 starts the process of establishing an application set (see Fig. 16.5).

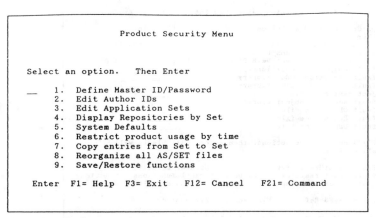

Figure 16.5 Product security menu.

```
        Edit   Delete   Print Definition   Copy   Exit  Help
        ─────────────────────────────────────────────────────────

        Product Security - Edit Application Sets

  Select ("/"); one or more Applications Sets, then select an action. Or
  type one or more action codes.  Then Enter.

      1= Edit    2=Delete  3=Print Definition  4=Copy


     Act   Use   Set Name     Description            Last Used

      1           Ord Ent     Order Entry            10/17/92



  Enter F1=Help F3=Exit F5=Refresh F7=Bkwd F10=Actions F12=Cancel
  F14=Print All Sets F12=Command
```

Figure 16.6 Product security—Edit Application Set: Starts the process
of defining an application.

Product security-edit application set: This screen defines, edits, deletes,
and prints the application sets that AS/SET established. The example
defines a new application set for the order entry function (see Fig. 16.6).

Edit application set: This screen defines essential aspects of the
application set such as default libraries and time restriction on use. It
also is the menu that permits calls to other screens to continue the
definition. These additional functions are included on the bottom of the
screen (see Fig. 16.7).

```
           Edit Application Set  -   Ord Ent

        Application Set Description           Order Entry
        Author                               JP
        Secured by Author                    Y  Y  N  D=Define
        Always save definitions before edit  Y  Y  N
        Time restricted <Effective=E Discontinue=D>  E 00:00 to 24:00
        Default compile  OUTQUE/library      _____  _____
        Default execution JOBQ /library      _____  _____
        Default execution OUTQ /library      _____  _____
        Object naming prefix                 _____
        Default source / object library      _____
        Default CL source file               _____
        Default RPG source file              _____
        Default DDS source file              _____

   Select ('/") one or more options, then Enter.  All blanks will
   select all options.

   __1. Define Set Library List   __4. Report printer defaults
   __2. Default panel features    __5. Default panel functions key Actions
   __3. Default report headings   __6. Compile option defaults

   Enter  F1=Help  F3=Refresh   F12=Cancel   F21=Command
```

Figure 16.7 Edit Application Set: Used to define essential aspects of the
application.

```
          Edit Application Set    Ord Ent

Type a list of library names that will be used within this Application
Set.  Then Enter.  Sequence numbers can be re-sequenced.


Seq        Library          Seq        Library
No                          No

__         _____      __         _____
__         _____      __         _____
__         _____      __         _____
__         _____      __         _____
__         _____      __         _____
__         _____      __         _____


Enter      F1=Help  F3=Exit F5=Refresh    F21=Command
```

Figure 16.8   Edit Application Set—Library List.

Edit application set-library list: This screen identifies the libraries that make up the application set's library list. These lists identify the libraries containing existing files for this set's repository and specify the files used by the generated programs that AS/SET executes (see Fig. 16.8).

Figures 16.9 and 16.10 are used by the programmer to establish characteristics such as date format and page numbering for the reports that are being developed as part of this application set. The default report headings screen specifies where to place default report headings. The report printer defaults screen specifies printer characteristics.

```
          Edit Application Set     Ord Ent

Type the following report headings features that will appear as
defaults when reports are defined within this Application Set.
Then Enter.

                              Line   B/C/E  Position Keyword(Length)
                              No

   Date - numeric format       _     _      *DATE(80)
   Date - business format      1     B      *EDATE(12)
   Time                        _     _      *TIME(8)
   Page numbers                1     E      *PAGE(4)
   Company name                _     _      *COMP(30)
   Author name                 _     _      *AUTHOR(25)
   Application Set name        _     _      *SET(10)
   Report Program name         2     C      *PGMNAME(10)
   Report Program description  _     _      *PGMDESC(30)


Enter   F1=Help  F3=Refresh  F12=Cancel  F21=Command
```

Figure 16.9   Edit Application Set: Used to define default information for a report.

```
        Edit Application Set    Ord Ent


Type the following printer characteristics that will appear as
defaults when reports are defined within this application Set.
Then Enter.

     Left Margin                          1    1-197
     Right Margin                       132    2-198
     Lines per page                      66    1-255
     Last Print line of page             60
     Characters per inch               10.0    5  10  12  15  16.7
     Lines per inch                     6.0    4  6  8  9
     Device Description               *DEVD
     Forms type                        *STD
     Number of copies                    1    1-99
     Hold at printer                 Y         Y  N
     Save after printing             N         Y  N
     Print when spooling begins      N         Y  N
     Spaces between fields               2    1-60
     Default headings on reports     C         C  D (C=Col Hdgs)
                                                  (D=Desc)


Enter   F1=Help   F3=Exit   F12=Cancel   F21=Command
```

Figure 16.10 Edit Application Set: Used to define printer default
characteristics.

Create Data Model.   The next step in system development identifies
and defines the data within AS/SET. This definition can either assimi-
late existing data structures into the tool or define new data structures.
Figure 16.11 provides an overview of the screens that establish the
Data Models that are to be a part of an application set.

Following is a sample and a brief description of the function of each
AS/SET screen used to establish a Data Model.

Repository Menu: This screen is the top-level menu for the repository
component. Option 1 starts the process of defining a Data Model (see
Fig. 16.12).

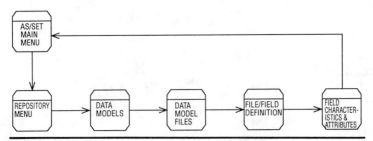

Figure 16.11 Overview of the AS/SET specification screens used to define
a data model.

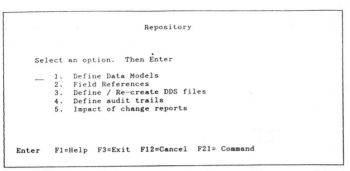

```
                    Repository


Select an option.  Then Enter
    __  1.  Define Data Models
        2.  Field References
        3.  Define / Re-create DDS files
        4.  Define audit trails
        5.  Impact of change reports



Enter    F1=Help  F3=Exit  F12=Cancel  F21= Command
```

Figure 16.12 Repository: Menu screen used to start the process of defining a data model

Data Models: This screen lists and edits existing Data Models and creates new ones. This screen allows copying an existing Data Model into a new one, deleting a Data Model, restricting the use of a Data Model to a specific author, and printing the definition of a Data Model (see Fig. 16.13).

```
Files Copy Delete Secure By Author   Definition Generate Files   Exit Hlp
_____

                      Data Models                    More: _

Select ("/") one or more Data Models, then select an action.  Or type one
or more action codes.  Then Enter

1=Files 2=Copy 3=Delete 4=Secure by Author 5=Def 6=Generate Files

Act    Data Model    Description              Author

_/_    OE11          Order Entry              JP

__     OA11          Stock Allocation         JP

__     OS11          Ship                     JP


Enter F1=Help F3=Exit F7=Bkwd F8=Fwd F10=Actions F12=Cancel
F14=Saved Definitions   F21=Command
```

Figure 16.13 Data Models: Screen used to list, define, copy, etc. Data Models to be used as part of an application set.

```
Fields Delete Auto Load Define Links/Header_Detail_Calcs Def Exit Help
```
```
                    Data Model Files    -  OE11              More: _

Select ("/") one or more Data Model files, then select an action.  Or type
one or more action codes.  Then Enter

1=Fields 2=Delete 3=Auto Load 4=Define Links/Header_Detail_Calcs 5=Def

Act  File Name  Typ   File Description     Member    Rec.Fmt    Library
__   _____   __    _____      *FIRST    *FIRST     ORDER




Enter F1=Help F3=Exit F4=Prompt F7=Bkwd F10=Actions F12=Cancels
F14=Display All Links F21=Command
```

Figure 16.14 Data Model Files: Used to display existing files in a Data Model and to add new ones.

Data Model files: This screen displays existing files within a Data Model and adds new files to it. Figure 16.14 displays the basic screen. Adding an existing file to a Data Model requires the library that contains this file to be identified. In the sample screen, the identified library is called *test.* Pressing function key F4 displays a window that lists all existing DDS files in the test library. This window is shown in Fig. 16.15. A < / > in a file's action field selects this file for inclusion in the Data Model and deletes the window. The selected file is added to the Data Model files screen (Fig. 16.16).

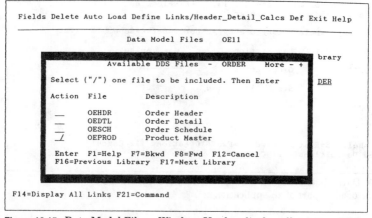

```
Fields Delete Auto Load Define Links/Header_Detail_Calcs Def Exit Help

                 Data Model Files    OE11

      ┌──────────────────────────────────────────────┐ brary
      │        Available DDS Files  -  ORDER   More - +│
      │ Select ("/") one file to be included. Then Enter│ DER
      │                                                │
      │ Action  File        Description                │
      │                                                │
      │        OEHDR        Order Header               │
      │   __   OEDTL        Order Detail               │
      │        OESCH        Order Schedule             │
      │   _/   OEPROD       Product Master             │
      │ Enter  F1=Help  F7=Bkwd  F8=Fwd  F12=Cancel    │
      │ F16=Previous Library  F17=Next Library         │
      └──────────────────────────────────────────────┘

F14=Display All Links F21=Command
```

Figure 16.15 Data Model Files—Window: Used to display all existing DDS files in the specified library.

```
Fields Delete Auto Load Define Links/Header_Detail_Calcs Def Exit Help


                    Data Model Files   -  OE11              More: _

Select ("/") one or more Data Model files, then select an action.  Or type
one or more action codes.  Then Enter

1=Fields 2=Delete 3=Auto Load 4=Define Links/Header_Detail_Calcs 5=Def

Act  File Name  Typ   File Description    Member    Rec.Fmt    Library

 1   OEPROD           Product Master      *FIRST    *FIRST     ORDER




Enter F1=Help F3=Exit F4=Prompt F7=Bkwd F10=Actions F12=Cancels
F14=Display All Links F21=Command
```

Figure 16.16 Data Model Files: Updated screen showing a file (Product Master) added to the files included in a Data Mdel.

File field definition: This screen is reached by keying a 1 on the Data Model screen against a file to be defined. Using this screen, the fields that are to be included in this logical view of the file can be identified by keying in the name of the field to be included or by pressing function key F11 to display a list of previously defined fields. Figures 16.17 and 16.18 show the start of this process and the window that displays the available fields.

```
Include Delete Define_Like Characteristics Attr. Validation Exit Help


            File Field Definition    OEPROD            More:
Select ("/") one or more fields, then select an action.  Or type one or
more action codes.  Then Enter.
 1= Include  2=Delete  3=Define_Like  4=Characteristics  5=Attr  6=Val


Act  Seq  Field Name   Key  Ty  Lngt  Description
__   __   _____      __   __  ___   _____




Enter  F1=Help  F3=Exit  F5=Refresh  F7=Bkwd  F18=Actions
F11=Avail Flds F12=Cancel F14=Delete All Flds F16=Field Reference F211=Cmd
```

Figure 16.17 File Field Definition: Used to define the fields to be included in a logical view of a file.

```
Include Delete Define_Like Characteristics Attr. Validation Exit Help

            File Field Definition     OEPROD            More:

    ┌──────────────────────────────────────────────────────────────┐
    │          Available DDS Fields  OEPROD                         │
    │                                                              │
    │  Select ("/") one or more fields to be included.  Then Enter │
    │                                                              │
    │                                  Strt                        │
    │  Act   Field Name Key   Ty  Lngt Pos      Description        │
    │        PRNUM      1     A   6.0   1      PRODUCT NUMBER       │
    │   __   PRDES            A  30.0   7      DESCRIPTION          │
    │   __   PRDTE            A   6.0  37      STATUS DATE          │
    │   __   PRSTST           A   2.0  43      STATUS              │
    │   __   PRVEN            A   6.0  45      VENDOR CODE          │
    │                                                              │
    │                                                              │
    │  Enter F1=Help F7=Bkwd F8=Fwd F12=Cancel F14=Select All Fields│
    └──────────────────────────────────────────────────────────────┘

F11=Avail Flds F12=Cancel F14=Delete All Flds F16=Field Reference F21=Cmd
```

Figure 16.18 File Field Definition—Window 1: Used to display all fields that previously have been identified as part of a file.

Once the fields that are to be included in this Data Model version of a file are identified, it becomes necessary to verify the characteristics and attributes of each field. Samples of the screens used to accomplish this are shown as Figs. 16.19 and 16.20.

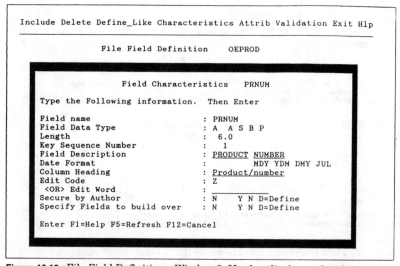

```
Include Delete Define_Like Characteristics Attrib Validation Exit Hlp

            File Field Definition     OEPROD

    ┌──────────────────────────────────────────────────────────────┐
    │               Field Characteristics    PRNUM                 │
    │                                                              │
    │  Type the Following information.  Then Enter                 │
    │                                                              │
    │  Field name                     : PRNUM                      │
    │  Field Data Type                : A  A S B P                 │
    │  Length                         :   6.0                      │
    │  Key Sequence Number            :   1                        │
    │  Field Description              : PRODUCT NUMBER             │
    │  Date Format                    :        MDY YDM DMY JUL     │
    │  Column Heading                 : Product/number            │
    │  Edit Code                      : Z                          │
    │   <OR> Edit Word                :                            │
    │  Secure by Author               : N      Y N D=Define       │
    │  Specify Fields to build over   : N      Y N D=Define       │
    │                                                              │
    │  Enter F1=Help F5=Refresh F12=Cancel                        │
    └──────────────────────────────────────────────────────────────┘
```

Figure 16.19 File Field Definition—Window 2: Used to display and update

```
Include Delete Define_Like Characteristics Attrib Validation Exit Hlp

              File Field Definition     OEPROD

                    Field Attributes   -  PRODNUM
       Position Cursor                      Y    Y N
       Input Allowed                        Y    Y N
       Auto increment                       N    Y N
          Increment value
       Default display attribute
       Default color attribute              N
       Provide field level help             N    Y N
       Define field level help              N    Y N  D= Define
       Mandatory fill                       Y    Y N
       Mandatory entry                      N    Y N
       Allow lower case                     N    Y N
       Auto Advance cursor                  Y    Y N
       Keyboard Checks: Right adjust, blank fill   N   Y N
                        Right adjust, zero fill    Y   Y N
                        Mandatory field exit       N   Y N

       Enter   F1=Help   F5=Refresh   F12=Cancel
```

Figure 16.20   File Field Definition—Window 3: Used to display and update.

Selecting Data Models and painting a screen. Developing a display program starts with the selection of the Data Models that the program will process and the formatting of at least one screen that is to be a part of the program. AS/SET's display programs component accomplishes this step. Figure 16.21 provides an overview of the screen associated with this process.

Following is a sample and brief description of the function of each AS/SET screen that identifies a new program, defines the Data Models this program is to use, and formats the first interactive screen to be used by the program.

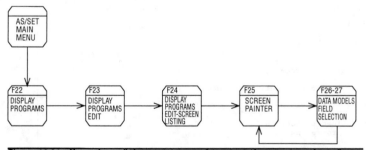

Figure 16.21 Overview of the process used to start the construction of a program by selecting a Data Model and painting a screen.

```
Edit Execute Delete Copy Print Compile_Options Templates Exit Help

                    Display Programs                More

Select ("/") one or more Display Programs, then select an action.  Or
type one or more action codes.  Then Enter

1=Edit   2=Execute 3=Delete 4=Copy 5=Print 6=Compile_Options 7=Templates


Act  Display Pgm.  Description               Password  Last Used  Status

 1   PRMACD        Product Master Maint.                11/15/92   D+ S  O




Enter F1=Help F3=Exit F7=Bkwd F8=Fwd F10=Actions F12=Cancel
F14=Saved Definitions F16=Submitted Generations F21=Command
```

Figure 16.22 Display Programs: Used to define a display program.

Display programs: This screen is accessed from AS/SET's main menu and is the first screen of the process. It defines, edits, deletes, copies, and prints the definition of a display program (see Fig. 16.22).

Display program edit: This screen specifies various characteristics of a display program, such as its description. It also provides the menu for the display program component to access the various tasks involved in specifying a program. For example, task five initiates the process of defining the user screens the program is to include (see Fig. 16.23).

```
                    Display Program Edit


Type the following information, and chose one or more options from
below.  Then Enter

    Display Program name              PRMACD
    Display Program description       Product Master Maint.
    Author                            JP
    Confidential                      N      Y N
    Password (if confidential)
    Execution OUTQ/Library            ASSETOUTQ ASSETO
    Compile OUTQ/Library              ASSETOUTQ ASSETO
    Time Restricted (E=Effective D=Discontinue)  E 00:00 To 24:00
    Display AS/SET file processing messages      Y

Display Set-up Options.  Select ("/") one or more

    _ 1. Display file keywords        / 5. Define screens
    _ 2. Specify Parameters           _ 6. Sel. Crit./Audits/Commit Ctl.
    _ 3. User Defined subroutine      _ 7. Report ruler layouts
    _ 4. Specify program narrative

Enter F1=Help F3=Exit F5=Refresh F12=Cancel  F21=Command
```

Figure 16.23 Display Programs Edit: Used to specify various characteristics of a display

```
        Edit   Delete   Copy   Screen_Keywords   Exit   Help
        ──────────────────────────────────────────────────────────
           Display Program Edit - Screen Listing              More:

     Select ("/") one or more screens.  Then select an action.  Or type one or
     more action codes.  Then Enter.  Sequence numbers can be re-sequenced.
       1=Edit   2=Delete   3=Copy   4=Screen_Keywords


                                          Clr   If Type = "H"
                                          Prv   Start      End
     Act   Seq   Name       Description   typ scr  Lin  Col  Lin  Col

      1          SCREEN1     PRODUCT MASTER  E  _   __    __    __   __




     Enter F1=Help F3=Exit F5=Refresh F7=Bkwd F8=Fwd F10=Actions F12=Cancel
     F17=Include F21=Command F23=Action Diagram (AD)
```

Figure 16.24 Display Programs Edit—Screen Listing: Used to identify the screens that are to be part of a display program.

Display program edit-screen listing: This screen defines the screens a display program is to include (see Fig. 16.24).

Screen painter: This is the work panel that allows the formatting of a screen. Function keys at the bottom of the screen control the process. Function key F10 is used first. This starts the process of identifying the fields to be included on the screen (see Fig. 16.25).

```
     Data_Models Placed_Fields Define_Actions Define_Help Exit Help
     ──────────────────────────────────────────────────────────────
                       Screen Edit - SCREEN 1








     F2=Data Models F3=Ext F5=Refresh F6=Placed Flds F7=Repaint Scrn F8=EditOff
     F11=Avail Flds F12=Cnl F14=Defn Help F16=Dsp Actn Bar F17=Pre Scrn Actions
     F18=Post Scrn Actn F19=Post Enter Actn F20=Func Key Actn F23=AD F24=DS Def
```

Figure 16.25 Screen Painter.

```
     Fields   Delete   Exit   Help
     ─────────────────────────────────────────────────────────────────
                 Data Models / Field Selection   - PRMACD          More:
     ─────────────────────────────────────────────────────────────────
     Select ("/") one or more Data Models, then select an action. Or type one
     or more action codes.  Then Enter. Use F11 to display all available Data
     Models.
         1=Fields    2=Delete
                                                 Start     No Recs  Specify at
     Action   Data Model    Description          Line No   To Disp  File Level

     ──       ──────────    ──────────────────   ──        ──       ──




     Enter F1=Help F3=Exit F7=Bkwd F8=Fwd F10=Actions F11=Avail Data Models
     F12=Cancel  F21=Command
```

Figure 16.26 Data Models/Field Selection: Used to identify the fields in a Data Model to be displayed as part of the screen format.

Data Models/field selection: This screen identifies the Data Models that contain the fields to be included on the user's screen. Figure 16.26 illustrates the basic screen. Figure 16.27 shows the addition of a window that presents all available Data Models that belong to the application set. Selections of Data Models to be included in this screen are made from the window presentation.

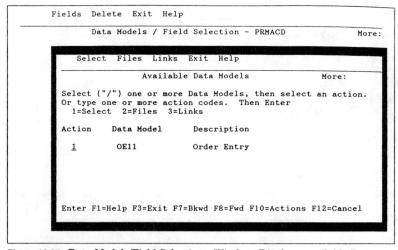

```
     Fields   Delete   Exit   Help
     ─────────────────────────────────────────────────────────────────
                 Data Models / Field Selection - PRMACD          More:
     ─────────────────────────────────────────────────────────────────
     ┌───────────────────────────────────────────────────────────────┐
     │   Select   Files   Links   Exit   Help                        │
     │   ──────────────────────────────────────────────────────────  │
     │               Available Data Models                 More:     │
     │   ──────────────────────────────────────────────────────────  │
     │   Select ("/") one or more Data Models, then select an action.│
     │   Or type one or more action codes.   Then Enter              │
     │      1=Select   2=Files   3=Links                             │
     │                                                               │
     │   Action    Data Model    Description                         │
     │                                                               │
     │   1         OE11          Order Entry                         │
     │                                                               │
     │                                                               │
     │   Enter F1=Help F3=Exit F7=Bkwd F8=Fwd F10=Actions F12=Cancel │
     └───────────────────────────────────────────────────────────────┘
```

Figure 16.27 Data Models/Field Selection—Window: Displays available Data Models that may be used for the screen display.

```
      Fields  Delete  Exit  Help

               Data Models / Field Selection  - PRMACD              More:

Select ("/") one or more Data Models, then select an action. Or type one
or more action codes.  Then Enter. Use F11 to display all available Data
Models.
     1=Fields    2=Delete
                                        Start     No Recs  Specify at
Action  Data Model   Description        Line No   To Disp  File Level

  1     OE11         Order Entry        ___       ___      ___   N




Enter F1=Help F3=Exit F7=Bkwd F8=Fwd F10=Actions F11=Avail Data Models
F12=Cancel  F21=Command
```

Figure 16.28 Updated Data Models/Field Selection screen showing a data model selected for inclusion on the application screen.

Data Model / field selection: Once the Data Models to be used in the screen design are selected, the fields to be included on the screen must be selected from those fields that are a part of the Data Model. This is accomplished by first keying a 1 against a Data Model on the Data Model/field selection screen. This results in the displays of a window that shows the fields already selected. Pressing function key F11 displays another window that shows fields available from the Data

```
      Fields  Delete  Exit  Help

               Data Models / Field Selection - PRMACD           More:
   Include  Delete  Exit  Help

               Data Model Field Selection - OE11      More:
   Select("/") one or more fields. Then select an action. Use F11 to
   display available fields.
        1=Include   2=Delete
   Act Field      Type   Lngt  Field Description       File
    _  ____       ____   ___   _____        _____



   Enter F1=Help F3=Exit F7=Bkwd F8=Fwd F10=Actions
   F11=Avail Fields F12=Cancel F14=Data Model File Links
```

Figure 16.29 Data Models/Field Selection—Window: window used to start the process of identifying the fields to be displayed on an application screen.

```
 ┌─────────────────────────────────────────────────────────────────┐
 │     Fields  Delete  Exit  Help                                    │
 │   ──────────────────────────────────────────────────────────     │
 │              Data Models / Field Selection - PRMACD      More:     │
 │   ┌──────────────────────────────────────────────────────────┐    │
 │   │ Include  Delete  Exit  Help                              │    │
 │   │         Data Model Field Selection - OE11    More:       │    │
 │   │  ┌─────────────────────────────────────────────────────┐ │    │
 │   │  │         Available Fields - OE11         More:        │ │    │
 │   │  │  Select ("/") one or more fields to be included. Then Enter │
 │   │  │  Act  Field      Typ  Lngt     Description      File │ │    │
 │   │  │  /   PRNUM      A    6.0    PRODUCT NUMBER       OEPROD │ │  │
 │   │  │  /   PRDES      A   30.0    PRODUCT DESCRIPTION  OEPROD │ │  │
 │   │  │  /   PRDTE      A    6.0    STATUS DATE          OEPROD │ │  │
 │   │  │  /   PRSTST     A    2.0    STATUS               OEPROD │ │  │
 │   │  │  /   PRVEN      A    6.0    VENDOR CODE          OEPROD │ │  │
 │   │  │  Enter F1=Help F7=Bkwd F8=Fwd F12=Cancel F14=Select All │ │  │
 │   │  └─────────────────────────────────────────────────────┘ │    │
 │   └──────────────────────────────────────────────────────────┘    │
 └─────────────────────────────────────────────────────────────────┘
```

Figure 16.30 Window showing the fields from a Data Model that are available for selection for an application screen.

Model that can be selected for inclusion on the screen. Figures 16.28, 16.29, and 16.30 show examples of this process.

Once the Data Models and fields from the Data Models are identified, AS/SET automatically presents a default screen layout (Fig. 16.31). This initial layout can then be customized to include highlighting, add additional fields, reposition fields, and so on.

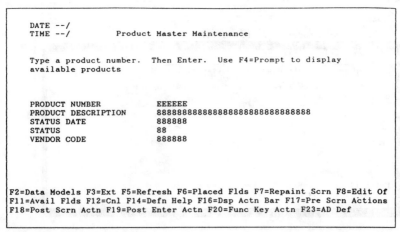

```
 ┌─────────────────────────────────────────────────────────────────┐
 │   DATE --/                                                        │
 │   TIME --/         Product Master Maintenance                     │
 │                                                                   │
 │   Type a product number.  Then Enter.  Use F4=Prompt to display   │
 │   available products                                              │
 │                                                                   │
 │   PRODUCT NUMBER          EEEEEE                                  │
 │   PRODUCT DESCRIPTION     8888888888888888888888888888888888      │
 │   STATUS DATE             888888                                 │
 │   STATUS                  88                                     │
 │   VENDOR CODE             888888                                 │
 │                                                                   │
 │ F2=Data Models F3=Ext F5=Refresh F6=Placed Flds F7=Repaint Scrn F8=Edit Of │
 │ F11=Avail Flds F12=Cnl F14=Defn Help F16=Dsp Actn Bar F17=Pre Scrn Actions │
 │ F18=Post Scrn Actn F19=Post Enter Actn F20=Func Key Actn F23=AD Def │
 └─────────────────────────────────────────────────────────────────┘
```

Figure 16.31 Default screen layout prepared by AS/SET once the fields to be displayed are selected.

```
DATE --/
TIME --/        Product Master Maintenance


Type a product number.  Then Enter.  Use F4=Prompt to display
available products


PRODUCT NUMBER          EEEEEE
PRODUCT DESCRIPTION     8888888888888888888888888888888
STATUS DATE             888888
STATUS                  88
VENDOR CODE             888888




F2=Data Models F3=Ext F5=Refresh F6=Placed Flds F7=Repaint Scrn F8=Edit Of
F11=Avail Flds F12=Cnl F14=Defn Help F16=Dsp Actn F17=Pre Scrn Actions
F18=Post Scrn Actn F19=Post Enter Actn F20=Func Key Actn F23=AD Def
```

Figure 16.32 Once the screen format has been established, use function key F20 to start the process of defining the use of function keys for the application.

Completing the program. Once the program's first screen is formatted, the processing associated with this screen and the help text to be available to the user must be defined. When the first screen is finished, this cycle is repeated until all program screens are constructed. To define the processing associated with a screen, the screen itself serves as the menu driver for the process. Figure 16.32 shows which AS/SET function keys initiate the various process definitions.

Function key F20, for example, starts the definition of the processing that a user can trigger by pressing a function key on the screen.

```
DATE--/
TIME--          Product Master Maintenance

Type a product number.  Then Enter.  Use F4=Prompt to display
available products.

    Edit   Delete   Exit   Help

             Define Actions - Functions Keys
Select ("/") one or more function keys. Then select an action. or type
one or more action codes. Type "Y" for Val to have validation performed

Act Key Val Description Act Key Val Description Act Key Val Description
 _  F1  __ _____  _  F10 __ _____  _  F19 __ _____
 _  F2  __ _____  _  F11 __ _____  _  F20 __ _____
 _  F3  __ _____  _  F12 __ _____  _  F21 __ _____
 _  F4  __ _____  _  F13 __ _____  _  F22 __ _____
 _  F5  __ _____  _  F14 __ _____  _  F23 __ _____
 _  F6  __ _____  _  F15 __ _____  _  F24 __ _____
 _  F7  __ _____  _  F16 __ _____  _  PGUP __ _____
 _  F8  __ _____  _  F17 __ _____  _  PGDN __ _____
 _  F9  __ _____  _  F18 __ _____  _  HELP __ _____

Enter F1=Help F3=Exit F10=Actions F12=Cancel
```

Figure 16.33 The first step in defining procedure logic associated with an application

```
        Define Key Actions - F1     SCREEN 1          More:

   Type the following information. Then enter. Use the line entry field
   to copy, move, delete, and insert new lines

   Line  Type  Char    Field/Keywd   =Action Text (F14=Extended Line)

   ____  __   __    _____   _____
   ____  __   __    _____   _____
   ____  __   __    _____   _____
   ____  __   __    _____   _____
   ____  __   __    _____   _____
   ____  __   __    _____   _____
   ____  __   __    _____   _____


   Scan: _____ Replace:_____  B/F: _

   F2=Mode F3=Exit F4=Prompt F5=RefreshF6=RulersF11=AvlFlds F12=Cnl F16=DspHdg
   F17=Incl F18=Brwse Sbr F19=Syntax Chk Off F20=Scan F22=EdtAll F23=AD D24=DS
```

Figure 16.34 Define Key Actions: Screen used to define procedure logic for a function. key.

Pressing this key makes AS/SET display the specifications screen: Define Actions — Functions Keys Panel (Fig. 16.33). This panel identifies the basic activity associated with the function key. For example, function key F1 might display the help screen and function key F3 might exit the program. Once these basic activities are identified, AS/SET's action codes are used to establish procedural statements that define the processing that is to occur. The next screen in the series, the actions screen, accomplishes this task. Figures 16.34 and 16.35 are examples of action screens that define Help processing and Postenter processing.

```
        Define Key Actions - F1     SCREEN 1          More:

   Type the following information. Then enter. Use the line entry field
   to copy, move, delete, and insert new lines

   Line  Type  Char    Field/Keywd   =Action Text (F14=Extended Line)

   1.00   K    __    @GETREC      DOE11.F.OEPROD.*EQ.PRNUM
   2.00   K    __    @IF          STATUS(D.OE11.F.PRNUM)=*NO
   3.00   K    __    @DSPERR      PRNUM.'Product Not Found'
   4.00   K    __    @END         _____
   ____  __   __    _____   _____
   ____  __   __    _____   _____
   ____  __   __    _____   _____
   ____  __   __    _____   _____


   Scan: _____ Replace:_____  B/F: _

   F2=Mode F3=Exit F4=Prompt F5=RefreshF6=RulersF11=AvlFlds F12=Cnl F16=DspHdg
   F17=Incl F18=Brwse Sbr F19=Syntax Chk Off F20=Scan F22=EdtAll F23=AD D24=DS
```

Figure 16.35 Sample of procedure logic for a function key which has been defined using AS/SET's higher level action statements.

A PRODUCT PERSPECTIVE

AS/SET eliminates spaghetti code by using a structured programming approach to organize procedural code into a consistent format. It also provides its own higher-level language to make coding more efficient.

For the IS organization that wants to improve programming efficiency without a radical cultural change, AS/SET offers significant advantages. AS/SET will also appeal to the organization that wants to improve productivity by enhancing an existing portfolio of programs. AS/SET is very appropriate for this environment since it is effective with existing database designs.

SYNON/2E from Synon Corporation

PRODUCT SYNOPSIS

Synon/2E is an AS/400-based lower CASE tool which supports the construction and maintenance phases of the application development life cycle. It is an application code generator which generates RPG/400 or COBOL programs based on designer and programmer specifications. Conceptually it incorporates many of the Object Oriented Design concepts which were described in Chap. 9. These concepts include framework technology (the use of program shells), the encapsulation of data and methods, and the use of inheritance on a field level. It facilitates program reuse by an object definition approach in which individual program modules are created for each separate file in a system.

Vendor address
Synon Corporation
1100 Larkspur Landing Circle
Larkspur, CA 94939
tel: (415) 461-5000

PRICE

Synon uses a tiered pricing scheme which is based on the size of the AS/400. Prices start at $48,000 for an AS/400 Model B10 and to $75,000 for a Model E90. Annual maintenance is 15 percent of the software cost.

PRODUCT DESCRIPTION

Synon/2E is an application generator which combines specifications created by designers and programmers with Synon's program shells or frameworks. The specifications contain information about stored data, display formats, and processing logic. They are entered into Synon/2E through interactive sessions. In some cases the specifications can be batch-loaded into the front end of Synon/2E. Once the specifications are entered into Synon's repository, Synon will:

1. Automatically create a data dictionary and generate DDS code for the database.

2. Automatically create primary and alternate access paths (logical views) and generate the DDS necessary to support the access paths.

3. Automatically generate DDS code for the device files and HLL code (RPG/400 or COBOL) for programs.

4. Automatically generate code for referential checking (file to file) and for domain checking (field validation).

5. Automatically generate help text and program documentation.

6. Automatically develop a default design for screen and report layouts.

Synon/2E employs a data-oriented approach to development. This requires the creation of a Data Model which is independent of any specific application which might use the data. The Data Model should follow the accepted relational database design rules so that it is fully normalized (third normal form—*see* Chap. 6). There is no need to collect fields appropriate to a program or set of programs into a file, as is done in the typical application development approach. Instead, basic entities (files) and attributes (fields) needed by the business are identified first. Relationships between entities are identified, and the results of the entity, attribute, and relationship identifications are entered into the AS/400 using Synon's Data Modeling language.

Synon's Data Modeling language is similar to the Structured English format described in Chaps. 8 and 10. It consists of the basic format:

SUBJECT	Verb	OBJECT	Modifier Phrase
ex: CUSTOMER	Known By	ACCOUNT NUMBER	

Two of the verbs described earlier, DISPLAYS which is used to identify Virtual and Derived fields, and CONTAINS which is used to identify foreign keys, are not included in Synon's language subset at this time. Instead Synon handles these Data Model specifications through interactive specification screens which enhance the Structured English basic Data Model description.

Once the data has been modeled and described to Synon/2E, an architectural foundation now exists for designing program solutions for the various business functions. This design process starts with an analysis of the low-level business functions (i.e., elementary business processes), which have been identified on a Data Flow Diagram.

The first step of this analysis is to decompose the business function into objects which consist of data and the methods that operate on this data. In this instance the data referred to are the primary files which are created, updated, or displayed as part of the business function. Once the primary files are identified, the next step is to identify the method part of the object.

This is accomplished by identifying which of Synon's prebuilt functions are to be used in conjunction with each of the files that are part of a process solution. Synon's prebuilt functions include all of the commonly used functions operating on a file. They are program shells to which Synon adds processing steps based on the function type and the Data Model definition of the file involved. This basic program can then be enhanced by using lower-level Synon functions similar to an instruction in a 4GL language or by adding user written 3GL code to specific points in the Synon default program.

Based on the Data Model definition and the prebuilt function type which is selected, Synon also creates a default screen design that can then be customized using Synon's interactive editor to move or hide fields, and so on.

Following is a brief description of the Synon's program shells or frameworks which when combined with a file(s) definition in a Structured English format are used to generate program modules. Synon calls these program shells *external functions.*

Edit Record: This shell is used to generate a program module to create, change, or delete a record, one record at a time. Synon provides three versions for different record sizes using one, two or three screen displays.

Edit File: This shell generates a program module that uses subfile to create, change, or delete multiple records at a time through the use of a subfile.

Edit Transaction: This shell generates a program module to create, change, or delete records in two different files at the same module. These records must have an established relationship between each other by the inclusion of the key of the secondary record in the format of the primary record (as a foreign key). A typical use of this shell is a simple order entry process where one entry screen displays the order header fields and the fields for multiple order detail lines.

Display Record: This shell generates a program module to display a record. There are one, two, and three screen versions which can be selected based on the record size.

Display File: This shell generates a program module to display multiple records at a time through the use of a subfile.

Display Transaction: This shell generates a program to display two related record formats on one screen. The screen format permits the display of one primary record (an order header for example) and multiple related records (order detail lines for example).

Print File: This shell generates a program to print a report.

In addition to the program shells which generate complete programs, Synon also includes minor subroutine shells which are used to customize or enhance the basic program modules. These built in functions, as Synon calls them, are similar to 4GL commands. But they are used in conjunction with Synon's Action Diagram Editor rather than in a stand-alone procedural coding environment. These include both conventional programming instructions, mathematical functions, and structured programming constructs. These minor shells include:

Move	Multiply	Case
Convert	Divide	Repeat while
	Add	Iterative Process
	Subtract	

A significant technique used in Synon/2E is a reliance on Action Diagrams. An Action Diagram is a method of presenting a high-level overview of the structure of a program as well as a detailed view of program logic. The basic building block of an Action Diagram is a bracket, which encloses a set of actions. Figure 17.1 shows part of an Action Diagram prepared by Synon.

Each of Synon's program shells have preestablished Action Diagrams. These standard diagrams can be expanded to add to the default editing and processing and to link program modules. Synon provides an Action Diagram editor for this task.

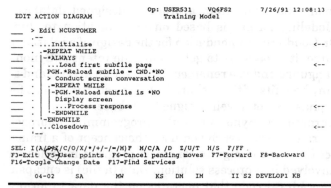

```
                              Op: USER531    VQ6FS2      7/26/91 12:08:13
EDIT ACTION DIAGRAM                    Training Model

___   > Edit NCUSTOMER
___   .--
___   . ...Initialise                                          <--
___   . .-REPEAT WHILE
___   . |-*ALWAYS
___   . |  ...Load first subfile page                          <--
___   . |  PGM.*Reload subfile - CND.*NO
___   . |  > Conduct screen conversation
___   . |  .-REPEAT WHILE
___   . |  |-PGM.*Reload subfile is *NO
___   . |  |  Display screen
___   . |  |  ...Process response                              <--
___   . |  '-ENDWHILE
___   . '-ENDWHILE
___   . ...Closedown                                           <--
___   '--

SEL: I(A/OR/C/O/X/*/+/-/=/M)F  M/C/A /D  Z/U/T  H/S  F/FF
F3=Exit  F5=User points  F6=Cancel pending moves  F7=Forward  F8=Backward
F16=Toggle Change Date  F17=Find Services

    04-02      SA         MW         KS   DM   IM      II S2 DEVELOP1 KB
```

Figure 17.1 Sample Action Diagram prepared by Synon to show the structure of a program module. The Action Diagram is used to enhance the default processing that is automatically generated by Synon.

GENERAL RELEVANCY AND COMMENTS

Synon as a construction tool is predicated upon many of the evolving software development concepts discussed in earlier sections of this book. The first underlying concept is from the principles of Information Engineering which was discussed in Chap. 1. According to this principle:

> Data has an inherent structure. Data analysis, which formally identifies this structure, should be done before process logic is designed. Data Models representing the inherent logical structure of data should be formally designed independently of the processes which operate on the data. (1)

The second set of concepts which has influenced the design of Synon/2E are from Object Oriented Design. These include:

Encapsulation: The organization of data and the methods that operate on this data into discrete objects.

Frameworks: Skeleton Structures of programs which must be fleshed out in order to build complete applications.

Inheritance: The process by which a subclass inherits both the data attributes and the methods of the class of which it is a part.

The concepts underlying Synon's design represents a radical change for the typical programmer. The first change is that any construction effort using Synon must start from a properly designed database. Synon's Data Modeling format is based on normalization to third normal form—Dr. Codd's recommendation for the design of a relational database. Of course, it is possible to get around the intent of Synon's Data Modeling language and use renamed fields, set up arrays, and so on. However, many benefits of the tool are lost if the starting point for the construction phase is not a well-designed database.

For many programmers, Synon's modular programming approach also represents a radical change. Synon uses the concept of a framework from Object Oriented Design to construct program modules for each major file involved in a process solution. Data (a file) is encapsulated with the procedural code that operates on the data to form a module. The means programmers spend a large part of their time creating components (program modules) and then assembling them to arrive at a solution which automates the business process. This approach is more consistent with the way that an engineer arrives at the final design for a new automobile or machine tool rather than the traditional craft approach that a programmer uses to develop a monolithic program.

Another change from traditional approaches is the use of inheritance from OOD. Synon uses this concept by establishing classes for fields and then providing for inheritance on a subclass level for both field attributes and editing methods.

Synon's different approaches to programming represent a paradigm shift in the way that software is developed. It is most appropriate for the environment that has a formal software development process, has adopted structured methods, and is using a well-designed database. In such an environment, Synon reinforces efforts towards modular programming, software reuse, improved program quality, and so on. Synon depends on improved software development methods and reinforces them.

BUILDING A SYSTEM

The construction of a system using Synon consists of following a structured series of steps in which Synon's interactive processes are used to:

Enter data structures into the Synon repository.

Select Synon's prebuilt program shells to construct the program modules.

Customize the default screen prepared by Synon.

Modify the basic program modules in order to add to the default processing.

Modifying the basic program modules to link the modules required for a business process solution.

Figure 17.2 provides an overview of the steps in this process and the system design deliverables used to guide each step.

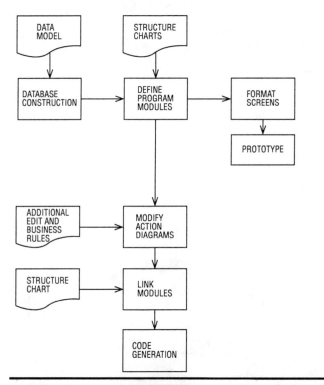

Figure 17.2 Overview of the major construction steps to build a program using Synon and the design documents that contain the specifications required for each major construction step.

Creating a Data Model. The first step in this construction process, entering the Data Model into the Synon repository, involves a series of screens. Let's first look at an overview of the process, and then at a sampling of several screens used for specific steps. Figure 17.3 identifies the processes for entering a Data Model into the repository and creating a basic program module.

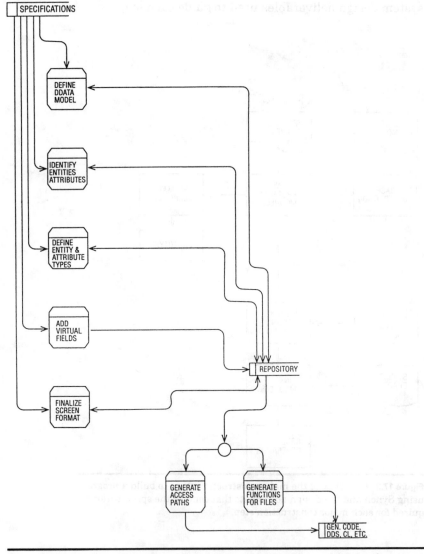

Figure 17.3 Overview of the construction steps to build a data model using Synon.

```
*DSNR  TRAINMDL              Op: USER531   VQ6FS2     7/18/91 15:49:08
EDIT DATABASE RELATIONS          Training Model
->        M                  Rel lvl:
?  Typ Object               Relation    Seq Typ Referenced object
   FIL MCUSTOMER_____ Known by___     FLD M_CUSTOMER_CODE_____
_  FIL MCUSTOMER_____ Refers to__     FIL MSTATE_____
_  FIL MCUSTOMER_____ Refers to__     FIL MSALESMAN_____
_  FIL MCUSTOMER_____ Has_____      FLD M_SEARCH_CODE_____
_  FIL MCUSTOMER_____ Has_____      FLD M_CUS_NAME_____
_  FIL MCUSTOMER_____ Has_____      FLD M_ADDRESS_LINE_1_____
_  FIL MCUSTOMER_____ Has_____      FLD M_ADDRESS_LINE_2_____
_  FIL MCUSTOMER_____ Has_____      FLD M_ADDRESS_LINE_3_____
_  FIL MCUSTOMER_____ Has_____      FLD M_CREATION_DATE_____
_  FIL MCUSTOMER_____ Has_____      FLD M_STATUS_____
_  FIL MCUSTOMER_____ Has_____      FLD M_STATUS_DATE_____
_  FIL MSALESMAN_____ Known by___     FLD M_SALESMAN_CODE_____
_  FIL MSALESMAN_____ Has_____      FLD M_SALESMAN_NAME_____
_  FIL MSALESMAN_____ Has_____      FLD M_COMMISSION_RATE_____
_  FIL MSTATE_____ Known by___     FLD M_STATE_CODE_____



SEL: Z1_3-Details, NO_3-Narr., S1_2-Select, E-Entries, V-Virt.fields, F-Funcs.
F3-Exit  F5-Reload  F7-Fields  F9-Insert  F10-Define obj.  F17-Services

   05-02    SA      MW       KS   DM   IM      II S2 DEVELOP1 KB
```

Figure 17.4 Edit Database Relations: The first step in entering specification for a data model into Synon's repository. The Data Model is defined using a Structured English format.

The first step is to use the EDIT DATABASE RELATIONS screen (Fig. 17.4) to enter the Data Model into the repository. The format is the same as the Structured English format that we discussed earlier.

The next step is to define the file and attribute types using a primary screen -DEFINE OBJECTS- (see Fig. 17.5) and a secondary screen -DISPLAY OBJECT TYPES (see Fig. 17.6). The secondary screen displays Synon's preestablished file and field types. An example of a preestablished field type would be DTE (Date). If a field is identified as a date, it inherits both the attributes and the edit processing (editing method) established for this object class.

```
                            Op: USER531   VQ6FS2     7/18/91 15:25:06
DEFINE OBJECTS                   Training Model
Object  Object             Object    Referenced       Field  Edit
type    name               attr      field            usage  field
FIL     MSTATE_____ ( ? )                            -
FLD     MSTATE_CODE_____     ___       _____    CDE    _
FLD     MSTATE_NAME_____     ___       _____    ATR    -
FIL     MSALESMAN_____ ---
FLD     MSALESMAN_CODE____     ___       _____    CDE    -
FLD     MSALESMAN_NAME____     ___       _____    ATR    -
FLD     MCOMMISSION_RATE__     ___       _____    ATR    _
FIL     MCUSTOMER_____ ---
FLD     MCUSTOMER_CODE____     ___       _____    CDE    -
___     _____      ___       _____    ___    -
___     _____      ___       _____    ___    -
___     _____      ___       _____    ___    -
___     _____      ___       _____    ___  - +

F3-Exit

   06-38    SA      MW       KS   DM   IM      II S2 DEVELOP1 KB
```

Figure 17.5 Define Objects: used to define files and fields according to Synon's predefined categories. The ? opposite the 'State' entry will bring in a secondary screen which displays predefined file types.

```
                              Op: USER531    VQ6FS2      7/26/91 11:46:00
  DISPLAY FUNCTION TYPES                Training Model
  Function type: _____       <-- Position display


  ? Type                    Abbrev       Classification
  _ Change object           CHGOBJ       *INT *DBF
  _ Create object           CRTOBJ       *INT *DBF
  _ Define report format    DFNRPTFMT         *DFN *RPT
  _ Define screen format    DFNSCRFMT         *DFN *SCR
  _ Delete object           DLTOBJ       *INT *DBF
  X Display file            DSPFIL       *EXT *DEV *SCR *DSP
  _ Display record (Old)    DSPRCDOLD    *EXT *DEV *SCR *DSP
  _ Display record(1 screen) DSPRCD      *EXT *DEV *SCR *DSP
  _ Display record(2 screen) DSPRCD2     *EXT *DEV *SCR *DSP
  _ Display record(3 screen) DSPRCD3     *EXT *DEV *SCR *DSP
  _ Display transactions    DSPTRN       *EXT *DEV *SCR *DSP
  _ Edit file               EDTFIL       *EXT *DEV *SCR *UPD

  _ Edit record(1 screen)   EDTRCD       *EXT *DEV *SCR *UPD
  _ Edit record(2 screens)  EDTRCD2      *EXT *DEV *SCR *UPD
  _ Edit record(3 screens)  EDTRCD3      *EXT *DEV *SCR *UPD         +
  SEL: X-Select value, Z-Display description.
  F3-Exit, no selection


      13-02    SA        MW        KS    DM    IM      II S2 DEVELOP1 KB
```

Figure 17.6 Display Object Attributes: used to display predefined file and field types.

As the Data Model is being defined in the Synon repository, a key definition decision is whether the file is to be defined as a Reference or a Capture file. Typically basic Master Files and External Tables are defined as Reference Files. Synon uses this definition to make assumptions about the program structure so it can generate complete programs to create, maintain, or display the file. The programmer's responsibility if the file is defined as a Reference file is to customize the default screen format and to add special editing procedures.

Creating a Program Module. Often it is necessary to specify a new program module rather than relay on the automatic creation of a module that occurs if a file is defined as a Capture file. These instances include:

If a file is defined as a Capture file.

If a reference file is to be retrieved by an alternate access path.

If special screen formats or processing is needed for a reference file.

When this occurs, an additional series of Synon interactive processes are used to define new program modules. Figure 17.7 provides an overview of this process.

The first step in this process is to use the EDIT FUNCTIONS screen to display all existing program modules that have previously been created for this file. If there is no program module that can be reused for the new business function, this same screen is used to start the process of defining a new module. This consists of first giving the new module a name, selecting the Synon program shell that is to be used as the basis for creating the new module, and identifying the access

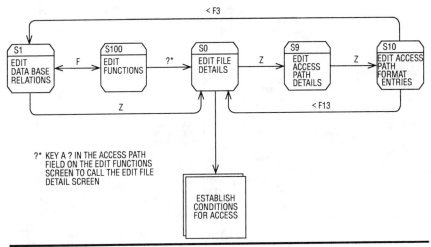

Figure 17.7 Overview of the construction steps involved in creating a program module using a Synon program shell.

path that is to be used for the file. Figures 17.8 and 17.9 show the Synon screens used to start this process.

In Fig. 17.8, the new module is given a name, and a question mark (?) is used to call in the next screen that lists the program shells that can be selected as the basis for creating the program module.

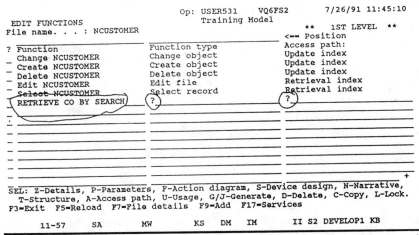

Figure 17.8 Edit Functions: Used to create a new program module. This screen is used to identify the module name, the program shell used, and the access path used.

```
                             Op: USER531    VQ6FS2    7/26/91 11:46:00
  DISPLAY FUNCTION TYPES              Training Model
  Function type: _____   <== Position display


  ? Type                    Abbrev       Classification
  _ Change object           CHGOBJ       *INT *DBF
  _ Create object           CRTOBJ       *INT *DBF
  _ Define report format    DFNRPTFMT         *DFN *RPT
  _ Define screen format    DFNSCRFMT         *DFN *SCR
  _ Delete object           DLTOBJ       *INT *DBF
  X Display file            DSPFIL       *EXT *DEV *SCR *DSP
  _ Display record (Old)    DSPRCDOLD    *EXT *DEV *SCR *DSP
  _ Display record(1 screen) DSPRCD      *EXT *DEV *SCR *DSP
  _ Display record(2 screen) DSPRCD2     *EXT *DEV *SCR *DSP
  _ Display record(3 screen) DSPRCD3     *EXT *DEV *SCR *DSP
  _ Display transactions    DSPTRN       *EXT *DEV *SCR *DSP
  _ Edit file               EDTFIL       *EXT *DEV *SCR *UPD

  _ Edit record(1 screen)   EDTRCD       *EXT *DEV *SCR *UPD
  _ Edit record(2 screens)  EDTRCD2      *EXT *DEV *SCR *UPD
  _ Edit record(3 screens)  EDTRCD3      *EXT *DEV *SCR *UPD           +
  SEL: X-Select value, Z-Display description.
  F3-Exit, no selection

        13-02     SA      MW      KS   DM   IM      II S2 DEVELOP1 KB
```

Figure 17.9 Display Function Types: Used to display the program shells available from Synon. A selection made on this screen is part of the process of defining a new program module.

In Fig. 17.9, we have a display of Synon' program shells, and the X marks the selection.

The next step is to identify the access path that is to be used over the file. In conventional AS/400 terminology, this process is the equivalent of creating a new logical view if a new access path is needed. The first step is to use the EDIT FILE DETAILS screen to display existing access paths. If none are satisfactory, this screen is also used to enter the new access path name and to start the process of identifying the details. Figure 17.10 shows the start of this process.

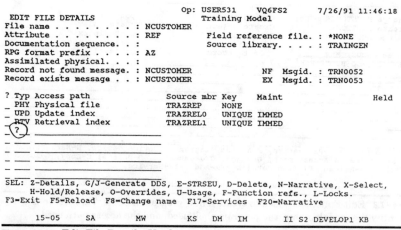

```
                             Op: USER531    VQ6FS2    7/26/91 11:46:18
  EDIT FILE DETAILS                   Training Model
  File name . . . . . . . . : NCUSTOMER
  Attribute . . . . . . . . : REF        Field reference file. : *NONE
  Documentation sequence. . :            Source library. . . . : TRAINGEN
  RPG format prefix . . . . : AZ
  Assimilated physical. . . :
  Record not found message. : NCUSTOMER           NF  Msgid. : TRN0052
  Record exists message . . : NCUSTOMER           EX  Msgid. : TRN0053

  ? Typ Access path              Source mbr Key    Maint           Held
  _ PHY Physical file            TRAZREP    NONE
  _ UPD Update index             TRAZRELO   UNIQUE IMMED
  _ RTV Retrieval index          TRAZREL1   UNIQUE IMMED
  _ ?_____ _____
  _ ___   _____
  _ ___   _____
  _ ___   _____

  SEL: Z-Details, G/J-Generate DDS, E-STRSEU, D-Delete, N-Narrative, X-Select,
       H-Hold/Release, O-Overrides, U-Usage, F-Function refs., L-Locks.
  F3-Exit  F5-Reload  F8-Change name  F17-Services  F20-Narrative

        15-05     SA      MW      KS   DM   IM      II S2 DEVELOP1 KB
```

Figure 17.10 Edit File Details: Used to start the process of defining an alternate access path.

```
                    Op: USER531    VQ6FS2      7/26/91 11:47:13

 DISPLAY ALLOWED VALUES            Training Model
 Field name. . . . . . . . : Access path type
 List name . . . . . . . . : *ALL values

 ?  Value                    Description
 _  PHY                      Physical
    QRY                      Query
 X  RSQ                      Resequence
 _  RTV                      Retrieval
 _  SPN                      Spans
 _  UPD                      Update




 SEL: X-Select value.
 F3-Exit, no selection

    10-02     SA       MW       KS   DM   IM      II S2 DEVELOP1 KB
```

Figure 17.11 Display Allowed Values: Used to display the standard types of access paths provided for by Synon.

A ? in the access path type field triggers a display of the various types of access paths Synon provides. These types are show in Fig. 17.11.

In the example shown, the data is to be retrieved by an alternate key rather than by the primary key, so a resequence access path is selected. With this type selected with an X, the system returns to the previous screen where the name of the new access path is also entered. This is shown as Fig. 17.12.

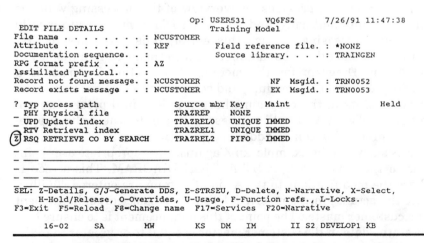

```
                         Op: USER531    VQ6FS2      7/26/91 11:47:38
 EDIT FILE DETAILS                 Training Model
 File name . . . . . . . . : NCUSTOMER
 Attribute . . . . . . . . : REF        Field reference file. : *NONE
 Documentation sequence. . :            Source library. . . . : TRAINGEN
 RPG format prefix . . . . : AZ
 Assimilated physical. . . :
 Record not found message. : NCUSTOMER              NF  Msgid. : TRN0052
 Record exists message . . : NCUSTOMER              EX  Msgid. : TRN0053

 ? Typ Access path              Source mbr Key    Maint           Held
 _ PHY Physical file            TRAZREP    NONE
 _ UPD Update index             TRAZREL0   UNIQUE IMMED
   RTV Retrieval index          TRAZREL1   UNIQUE IMMED
 Z RSQ RETRIEVE CO BY SEARCH    TRAZREL2   FIFO   IMMED
 _ ___  _____
 _ ___  _____
 _ ___  _____

 SEL: Z-Details, G/J-Generate DDS, E-STRSEU, D-Delete, N-Narrative, X-Select,
      H-Hold/Release, O-Overrides, U-Usage, F-Function refs., L-Locks.
 F3-Exit F5-Reload F8-Change name F17-Services F20-Narrative

    16-02     SA       MW       KS   DM   IM      II S2 DEVELOP1 KB
```

Figure 17.12 Once the file access type is determined, the system returns to the previous screen in the process—Edit File Details. A 'Z' against the name of the new access path starts the process of defining the details of this new access path.

```
                             Op: USER531    VQ6FS2         7/26/91 11:48:45
EDIT ACCESS PATH FORMAT ENTRIES        Training Model
File name . . . . . . . . : NCUSTOMER                 Attribute . : REF
Access path name. . . . . : RETRIEVE CO BY SEARCH     Type. . . . : RSQ
Format text . . . . . . . : NCUSTOMER
Based on. . . . . . . . . : NCUSTOMER                 Format No . :   1

                                     DDS           Key    Altcol Ref
? Field                              Name    Type  no. Dsc seq  cnt
_ NCUSTOMER CODE          CDE        ARCD    A          _        1
_ NSTATE CODE             CDE        AUCD    A          _        1
_ NSTATE NAME             TXT        APTX    V                   1
_ NSALESMAN CODE          CDE        ATCD    A          _        1
_ NSALESMAN NAME          TXT        AOTX    V                   1
_ NSEARCH CODE            CDE        ASCD    K      ( 1 ) _       1
_ NCUST NAME              TXT        AKTX    A          _        1
_ NADDRESS LINE 1         TXT        ALTX    A          _        1
_ NADDRESS LINE 2         TXT        AMTX    A          _        1
_ NADDRESS LINE 3         TXT        ANTX    A          _        1
_ NCREATION DATE          DTE        AMDT    A          _        1    +

SEL: Z-Field details.
F3=Exit  F7=Relations

      10-02    SA      MW      KS    DM    IM       II S2 DEVELOP1 KB
```

Figure 17.l3 Edit Access Path Format Entries: Used to identify the fields that are to be used as the keys for the new access path.

The next step is to identify the field(s) that is (are) to be a part of this new access path. Figure 17.13 shows the display of the fields in the file and the selection of a field for the new access path by putting a 1 in the new key field.

Adding to the Default Editing. In a program module generated by Synon, domain and referential integrity editing are provided for automatically. When additional editing routines, mathematical calculations, and the like, are needed, the basic program generated by Synon must be supplemented. To accomplish this, Synon provides an Action Diagram that provides an overview of the processing which is generated automatically, and an Action Diagram editor to modify the basic processing. To use this editor, it is necessary to first identify the module to be modified, and to then call in a display of the Action Diagram for the module. This Action Diagram is a structured view of the module, and contains an identification of the specific points in the program where supplemental processing can be added. Figure 17.14 shows these user points where the supplemental processing can be added.

As is shown in the example, an X against the appropriate user point calls in the next screen, EDIT ACTION DIAGRAM. This screen is where the modifications to the Action Diagram are entered. To illustrate the actual process involved, let's take a basic edit enhancement for a customer master. The point of this enhancement is to ensure that the status date in the customer master is equal to or greater than the creation date.

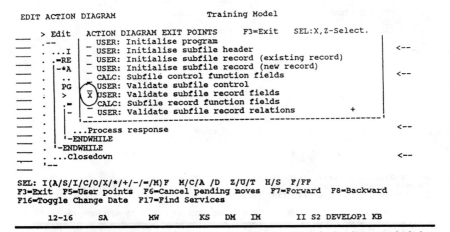

Figure 17.14 Action Diagram: The first step in adding to the default editing included in a Synon program shell.

(Text continued on next page.)

```
                              Op: USER531    VQ6FS2        7/26/91 13:11:08
    EDIT ACTION DIAGRAM            Training Model
```
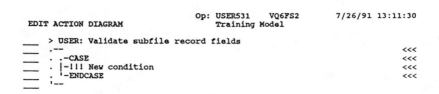
```
  (IC) > USER: Validate subfile record fields
        .--                                                              <<<
        '--
```

```
    SEL: I(A/S/I/C/O/X/*/+/-/=/M)F  M/C/A /D  Z/U/T  H/S  F/FF
    F3-Exit  F5-User points  F6-Cancel pending moves   F7-Forward  F8-Backward
    F16-Toggle Change Date  F17-Find Services

        04-04     SA      MW       KS   DM   IM       II S2 DEVELOP1 KB
```

Figure 17.15 Edit Action Diagram: The basic screen which is used to define additional processing. In this example a CASE statement will be added.

When the EDIT ACTION DIAGRAM screen is displayed, the first step is to use one of Synon's constructs to begin modifying the diagram. These constructs include: (1) IA=Insert action, (2) IC=Insert case, (3) IS=Insert a sequence of actions, (4) II=Insert iteration, (5) IX=Insert a new condition within a case bracket.

In the example, we are adding a condition to the processing, so the construct to use is Insert Case. Adding this construct and the results of the addition are shown as Figs. 17.15 and 17.16.

```
                              Op: USER531    VQ6FS2        7/26/91 13:11:30
    EDIT ACTION DIAGRAM            Training Model

    ____ > USER: Validate subfile record fields
    ____   .--                                                          <<<
    ____   . .-CASE                                                     <<<
    ____   . |-III New condition                                       <<<
    ____   . '-ENDCASE                                                  <<<
    ____   '--
```

```
    SEL: I(A/S/I/C/O/X/*/+/-/=/M)F  M/C/A /D  Z/U/T  H/S  F/FF
    F3-Exit  F5-User points  F6-Cancel pending moves   F7-Forward  F8-Backward
    F16-Toggle Change Date  F17-Find Services

        05-02     SA      MW       KS   DM   IM       II S2 DEVELOP1 KB
```

Figure 17.16 Edit Action Diagram: A new condition has been added to the Action Diagram. This condition must now be defined.

```
                              Op: USER531     VQ6FS2        7/26/91 13:11:30
___   EDIT ACTION DIAGRAM                 Training Model
___     > USER: Validate subfile record fields
___     .--                                                         <<<
___     . .-CASE                                                    <<<
(IA)    . |-III New condition                                       <<<
___     . '-ENDCASE                                                 <<<
___     '--
```

```
SEL: I(A/S/I/C/O/X/*/+/-/-/M)F  M/C/A /D  Z/U/T  H/S  F/FF
F3-Exit  F5-User points  F6-Cancel pending moves  F7-Forward  F8-Backward
F16-Toggle Change Date  F17-Find Services

    07-04     SA       MW       KS   DM   IM       II S2 DEVELOP1 KB
```

Figure 17.17 Edit Action Diagram: This screen starts the process of defining the action to be taken if the condition is met.

The next step is to provide for an action to be performed if the condition is met. Figure 17.17 shows this step, and Fig. 17.18 shows the result.

```
                              Op: USER531     VQ6FS2        7/26/91 13:11:45
___   EDIT ACTION DIAGRAM                 Training Model
___     > USER: Validate subfile record fields
___     .--                                                         <<<
___     . .-CASE                                                    <<<
___     . |-III New condition                                       <<<
___     . | III Undetermined action                                <<<
___     . '-ENDCASE                                                 <<<
___     '--
```

```
SEL: I(A/S/I/C/O/X/*/+/-/-/M)F  M/C/A /D  Z/U/T  H/S  F/FF
F3-Exit  F5-User points  F6-Cancel pending moves  F7-Forward  F8-Backward
F16-Toggle Change Date  F17-Find Services

    07-02     SA       MW       KS   DM   IM       II S2 DEVELOP1 KB
```

Figure 17.18 Edit Action Diagram: A new undefined condition and action have been added to the Action Diagram.

```
                              Op: USER531    VQ6FS2      7/26/91 13:13:07
EDIT ACTION - CONDITION               Training Model

Displayed title . . :  !!! New condition

Context . . . . . . :(RCD) Field. :(?)

Condition . . . . . : ?_____
  OR
Comparison. . . . . : ??  Context : ___  Field : _____




F3-Exit

'?' type FLD not found.
    06-38      SA        MW        KS    DM    IM       II S2 DEVELOP1 KB
```

Figure 17.19   Edit Action-Condition: The first step in defining the condition is to identify the field to be tested.

To specify the details of the conditional test, two additional screens are used. The first, EDIT ACTION - CONDITION, identifies if the test is a comparison of two fields or a test of the existence of a condition. The second screen identifies the field(s) to be tested. Figures 17.19 and 17.20 are examples of these two screens.

The results of this process are shown as Fig. 17.21. The undetermined action has now been replaced by a conditional statement that identifies the two fields to be tested—the status date and the creation date. The type of test, LT (Less Than) has also been identified. The next step is to now define the action to be performed if the condition is met. This action, the sending of an error message, is defined in a similar manner using a separate set of interactive screens.

```
                              Op: USER531    VQ6FS2      7/26/91 13:13:14
DISPLAY FIELDS WITHIN CONTEXT         Training Model
Context . : RCD  SCREEN  Subfile record.
For . . . :  Condition
                                         DDS
?  Field                       Attr name
_  *SFLSEL                      STS  *SFLSEL
_  NCUSTOMER CODE               CDE  ARCD
_  NCUST NAME                   TXT  AKTX
_  NSEARCH CODE                 CDE  ASCD
_  NSALESMAN CODE               CDE  ATCD
_  NSALESMAN NAME               TXT  AOTX
_  NADDRESS LINE 1              TXT  ALTX
_  NADDRESS LINE 2              TXT  AMTX
_  NADDRESS LINE 3              TXT  ANTX
_  NSTATE CODE                  CDE  AUCD
_  NSTATE NAME                  TXT  APTX
_  NCREATION DATE               DTE  AMDT
(X) NSTATUS                     STS  ACST
_  NSTATUS DATE                 DTE  ANDT
SEL: X-Select field.
F3-Exit, no selection


    20-02      SA        MW        KS    DM    IM       II S2 DEVELOP1 KB
```

Figure 17.20   Display Fields Within Context: Used to display the fields that can be used as the basis for the conditional test. In the example the status date fields is to be selected.

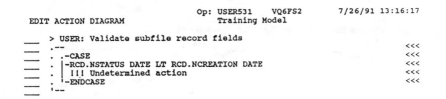

```
                              Op: USER531    VQ6FS2      7/26/91 13:16:17
EDIT ACTION DIAGRAM                         Training Model

___   > USER: Validate subfile record fields
___   .--                                                         <<<
___   . .-CASE                                                    <<<
___   . |-RCD.NSTATUS DATE LT RCD.NCREATION DATE                  <<<
___   . | !!! Undetermined action                                <<<
___   . '-ENDCASE                                                 <<<
___   '--


SEL: I(A/S/I/C/O/X/*/+/-/=/M)F  M/C/A /D  Z/U/T  H/S  F/FF
F3-Exit  F5-User points  F6-Cancel pending moves  F7-Forward  F8-Backward
F16-Toggle Change Date  F17-Find Services

     07-02      SA       MW       KS   DM   IM       II S2 DEVELOP1 KB
```

Figure 17.21   Edit Action Diagram: The completed conditional statement once the field (Status Date) to be tested, the type of test (less than) and the field (Creation Date) being tested are identified.

Linking Program Modules.   A characteristic of Synon is that relatively small program modules are generated. Usually a program module consists of the processing required to create, modify, retrieve or delete the record(s) of a single file. As a consequence the solution for a complex business process typically involves a number of modules. Figure 17.22 is a structure chart which shows a modular solution for an order entry process.

The process solution includes separate modules for processing the order header, the order detail, creating a ship-to over ride, a customer name search, and so on. To link these modules together, Synon uses its own set of screens in order to generate a program call. These screens are part of

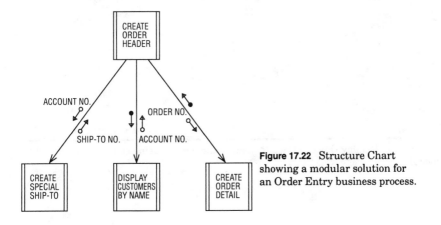

Figure 17.22   Structure Chart showing a modular solution for an Order Entry business process.

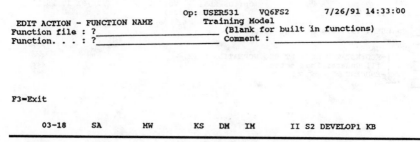

```
                              Op: USER531    VQ6FS2        7/26/91 14:33:00
   EDIT ACTION - FUNCTION NAME     Training Model
   Function file : ?_____ (Blank for built in functions)
   Function. . . : ?_____ Comment : _____



   F3-Exit

        03-18    SA      MW      KS   DM   IM      II S2 DEVELOP1 KB
```

Figure 17.23 Edit Action—Function Name: Used to initiate the process of identifying the program module being called by the Order header module.

the Action Diagram editor, and follow a processing sequence similar to the Action Diagram modification previously described. An example is a call from an order header Create module to a module which displays customer by name. In Fig. 17.23 and 17.24, the first steps are accomplished, starting the process and identifying the file that is being called.

Once the customer file is identified, Synon displays all previously created modules that deal with the customer file. Keying a P against the appropriate program module, as shown in Fig. 17.25 identifies the module to be called and starts the process of identifying the parameters to be passed to this module.

```
                              Op: USER531    VQ6FS2        7/26/91 14:33:27
   DISPLAY OBJECTS                Training Model

   ?  Type Description            Attr
          NC_____         <-- Position display
   (X) FIL  NCUSTOMER             REF
   _   FIL  NORDER HEADER         CPT
   _   FIL  NSALESMAN             REF
   _   FIL  NSTATE                REF
   _   FIL  NUMBER FILE           REF
   _   FIL  ORDER DETAIL          CPT
   _   FIL  ORDER HEADER          CPT
   _   FIL  ORDER SCHEDULE        CPT
   _   FIL  PRODUCT MASTER        CPT
   _   FIL  xcompany              REF
   _   FIL  xsalesperson          REF
   _   FIL  xsalesperson code     REF
   _   FIL  xstate                REF
   _   FIL  ZCOMPANY              REF
   _   FIL  znumber file          CPT                              +

   SEL: X-Select value, N-Narrative.
   F3-Exit, no selection

        07-02    SA      MW      KS   DM   IM      II S2 DEVELOP1 KB
```

Figure 17.24 Display Objects: Used to identify the module being called by the initial module.

```
                         Op: USER531    VQ6FS2         7/26/91 14:33:34
  EDIT FUNCTIONS                        Training Model
  File name. . . : NCUSTOMER                              **   2ND LEVEL  **
                                                        <-- Position
  ? Function                    Function type           Access path:
  _ Change NCUSTOMER            Change object           Update index
  _ Create NCUSTOMER            Create object           Update index
  _ Delete NCUSTOMER            Delete object           Update index
    Edit NCUSTOMER       ·      Edit file               Retrieval index
  P RETRIEVE CO BY SEARCH       Display file            RETRIEVE CO BY SEARCH
    Select NCUSTOMER            Select record           Retrieval index
  _ _____            _____        _____
  _ _____            _____        _____
  _ _____            _____        _____
  _ _____            _____        _____
  _ _____            _____        _____
  _ _____            _____        _____ +

  SEL: P-Parameters, N-Narrative, X-Select, U-Where used, C-Copy, L-Locks.
  F3=Exit  F5=Reload  F9=Add function

     11-02       SA        MW       KS   DM   IM       II S2 DEVELOP1 KB
```

Figure 17.25 Edit Functions: The 'P' against the object -Retrieve Co. by Search- starts the process of identifying the parameters to be passed to the module being called.

Once parameters are identified using the standard Synon screens, the EDIT ACTION DIAGRAM screen is redisplayed with the action to be performed fully specified (Fig. 17.26).

```
  F3=Exit  F9=Edit parameters, ENTER to accept   F12=Previous

  Some parameters have been defaulted.  Press ENTER to accept
     07-37       SA        MW       KS   DM   IM       II S2 DEVELOP1 KB

                         Op: USER531    VQ6FS2         7/26/91 14:41:43
  EDIT ACTION DIAGRAM                   Training Model
  ___     > USER: Validate subfile record relations
  ___       .--                                                        <<<
  ___       . .-CASE                                                   <<<
  ___       . |-RCD.*SFLSEL is *Zoom                                   <<<
  ___       . |   RETRIEVE CO BY SEARCH - NCUSTOMER  *                 <<<
  ___       . '-ENDCASE                                                <<<
  ___       '--
```

Figure 17.26 A modified Action Diagram showing the statements used to establish the call to another program module.

A PRODUCT PERSPECTIVE

Synon/2E represents a significant paradigm shift for many AS/400 programmers. The learning period can be significant, not because of the product complexity per se, but because it takes a new approach to the process of constructing programs. A significant element in this new approach is a well-designed database that follows the rules of normalization associated with relational database design. The incorporation of the rules of normalization as a building block for use of the product also means that typically Synon is not appropriate as a productivity enhancer in the environment where there is a large portfolio of old programs with a poorly-designed database.

In the environment where systems are being redesigned and where the emphasis is on a well-designed database, Synon can be a very valuable tool. It will certainly speed up the coding process. But more significantly, it will typically result in a higher quality product than is usually produced with conventional coding, and it can have a significant impact on development costs by fostering software reuse. Synon does not represent the technical silver bullet. But it can be a significant element for a radically improved way of developing software.

In our next and closing chapter, let's try to put all the elements of a new way to produce software in perspective.

REFERENCE

1. Martin, James. *Information Engineering,* Book 1. Prentice-Hall: Englewood Cliffs, N.J., 1991.

18

A Perspective on Change

As I was completing this book in the fall and winter of 1992-93, several events occurred which might give us pause for thought when we consider the management of our careers. The events were the management changes in a number of major companies. In these instances corporate leaders identified with the status quo were rejected. They were replaced by new leaders who emphasize change and seem more in tune with the competitive challenges facing their companies. And what do these national events have to do with us on either a Information Services department level or on a personal career level?

These events reflect a change in the ground rules by which our society will operate. Productivity is the key economic issue, and the social bias will be towards those who are open to change rather than to the defenders of the status quo. It means that the professionals should periodically go through a period of introspection that addresses two questions:

1. What should I be doing?
2. How should I do it?

Two recent books can help put these questions in perspective. The first, Yourden's, *The Decline and Fall of the American Programmer* (1), discusses the competitive challenges that programmers face from discusses the competitive challenges that programmers face from international competition. The message is that many companies are already finding out that they can farm out laborious programming to cheap subcontractors in India, Ireland, Taiwan, and elsewhere.

The competitive solution Yourden suggests for the U.S. programmer is to develop new skills which focus on the planning and design aspects of systems development. And these new planning skills must be accompanied by the new CASE tools which automate the grunt work associated with programming.

A second book, *Strategic Choices* (2), uses several graphic illustrations to provide insight into the answers to the questions.

The first illustration is a curve called Waves of Innovation, and is used to portray the way in which the use of a technology matures over time. When this curve is applied to Information Technology, two distinct waves illustrate the historical focus of computerization efforts (Fig. 18.1).

As shown in the first curve, the initial focus of Information Technology was on the automation of routine business functions. These functions included many of the accounting activities such as payroll, accounts payable, and general ledger. The emphasis during this initial period was on clerical and administrative savings, and in most instances existing functions were automated as is, rather than fundamentally restructured before they were computerized.

The second Wave of Innovation started in the 1970s and focused on asset management. Many of the inventory managements systems and production and asset scheduling systems installed during this period

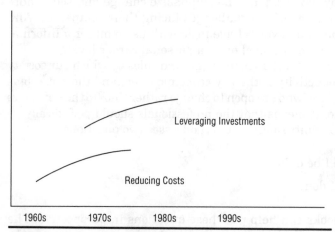

Figure 18.1 Waves of Innovation. The way that a technology matures over time.

were examples of this focus. The objective and the justification for these systems were not clerical savings. Rather, inventory turns, reducing holding costs, more effective use of warehouse space, better scheduling of production equipment, and so forth were the objectives. To put these two Waves of Innovation in perspective, let's add to the basic illustration the Parieto chart that we discussed in Chap. 3 (see Fig. 18.2).

Whether we talk about the Law of Diminishing Returns or the 80:20 Rule, the bottom line is that after a point in time the opportunities for obtaining further benefits from an automation focus diminish significantly. Most of us who have been involved in an Information Services Department for a period of time are well aware of this phenomenon. When a new application is first considered, it is typically possible to identify major benefits for the project. But after the initial system is installed and maintenance support starts, requests for additional displays and reports, enhancements, and so on become increasingly difficult to justify on a tangible basis.

So a basic issue in planning the focus of Information Technology projects is whether we continue to pursue innovation curves that have a diminishing value to the organization, or do we look for new direc-

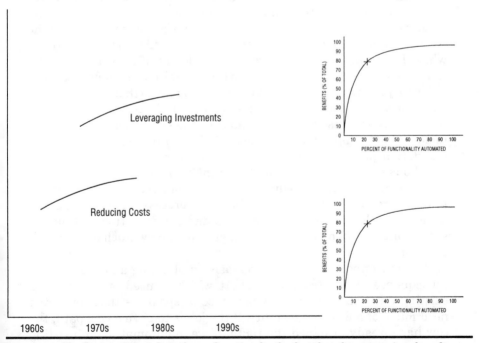

Figure 18.2 The Parieto Principle is the explanation for the fact that the economic value of a technology focus declines over time.

tions? And in terms of new directions to look at, what are the opportunities that we might pursue?

There are perhaps two major areas of focus that offer significant opportunities for us in the decade ahead. These are:

Business Process Reengineering

Enhancing Products and Services

Business process reengineering seeks to obtain quantum improvements in productivity by fundamentally reengineering business processes. This is done not by automating accounts payable, for example, but by a fundamental improvement in the way vendors are paid, which eliminates many traditional activities such as the matching of receiving reports and invoices. Advances in information technology, such as enhanced communications and industry data interchange standards, are part of the basis for this reengineering. Perhaps even more significant are changing management attitudes concerning the organization of work, the use of teams, flatter organizational structures, and the empowerment of employees.

Another major opportunity for the Information Technology professional is in the use of the computer to enhance business products and services. In this area, technology can have a significant impact on the competitiveness of the organization. One distribution company for which I did some consulting work decided that, if they added a new front end to their order entry system that permitted customers to place orders using a touch tone telephone, it would reduce their clerical costs. Once the service was in place, to the surprise of the company, the major benefit was increased orders because of the convenience to the customer and the higher-level of service. This initial effort became the foundation for an new service in which the company took over the warehousing functions of a number of their customers.

However, if we start to redirect the focus of our professional activities towards the new opportunities of business process reengineering and using technology to enhance products and services, this will have a significant impact on how we do things and on how much our services can cost.

The first impact will be an emphasis on planning and design. One consequence of our traditional effort which focused on automating existing functions (paving cow paths, so to speak) is that you didn't need much of a design capability. If the job is to pave a cow path, the cow has already designed the route. If we're automating an existing function without any fundamental process or organizational changes, some organization or procedure specialist has already designed the basic system, typically in the distant past and based on outmoded technology. But if the competitive advantages of business process reengineering are to be obtained, and if the information technology is to be used in new ways to support the business in the market place, we cannot rely on an existing business process structure as the basis for our automation effort.

The use of Information Technology to enhance a company's products and services will also significantly impact the cost pressures we face as professionals. We have always been subject to deadlines and to cost pressures. But to the degree that we were a back room operation which was outside the mainstream of the organization, our performance did not significantly affect the competitive position of the company.

But if Information Technology becomes a competitive weapon that operates in the forefront of the business, our overall productivity will be more of an issue. To understand the cost implications of this changing role, let's look at the value-added breakdown of the distribution company that I mentioned earlier. Historically, the function that they performed was the physical handling of goods, and the information component of the service provided was minimal (Fig. 18.3).

As the business is currently evolving, however, the major strategic opportunity for this distributor is to take over the complete warehousing function of their customers and provide a Just-in-Time inventory service. And as this service is being provided, there is a radical change in the value-added content of the distributor's service (Fig. 18.4).

This increase in the information content of the service being provided is due to the fact that the distributor is now performing many of the functions that were formerly part of the customer's warehousing operation. These include internal requisitioning, internal departmental billing, forecasting, and usage analysis.

A major concern for this company as the information content of the service being offered increases is:

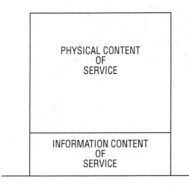

Figure 18.3 Information content of a business service in the early days of computers.

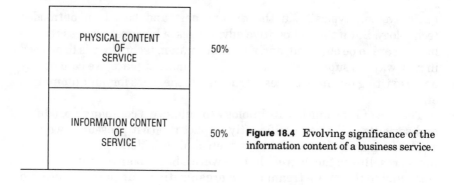

Figure 18.4 Evolving significance of the information content of a business service.

What will be the cost of the information component?

And if the company is not in a dominant market position or if there are no detailed industry standards which control intercompany electronic data interchange transactions, the concern becomes:

> How do you obtain the capability of responding quickly and efficiently to new customer requirements as they arise?

Again the book *Strategic Choices* provides us with a general concept that we can apply to Information Services. This concept is the notion of an experience curve. Figure 18.5 is an illustration of the historical experience curves for several of the companies in the auto industry. (3)

In the Information Services area, we also have an experience curve which shows the relationship between cost per unit (or program) and time. As with a corporate experience curve, the IS curve is based on management practices, the skill and training of the staff, tools available, and so on. A typical experience curve for an AS/400 is shown as Fig. 18.6.

In the experience curve that applies to most AS/400 installations, initially the costs of developing programs declines significantly as new skills are acquired and the technology of the machine is mastered. After a point in time, however, unit or per program costs level off and then start to rise. This occurs because the portfolio of programs is increasing, and typically in a craft-oriented environment the larger the portfolio, the more difficult the program maintenance.

To meet the challenges of business process reengineering and to provide our companies with a competitive edge as Information Technology becomes a more significant component of products and services being offered, it is the thesis of this book that a new experience curve is possible (Fig. 18.7).

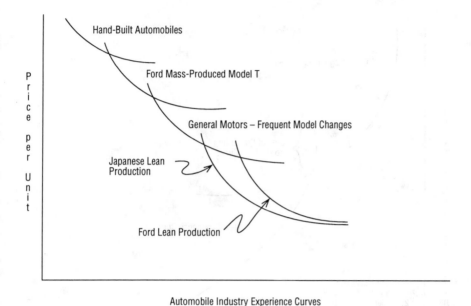

Automobile Industry Experience Curves

Cumulative Output

Figure 18.5 Experience or Learning Curve. Typically the cost per unit to produce a product or service declines over time.

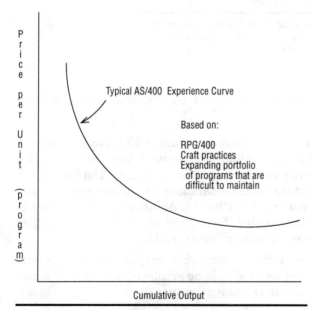

Cumulative Output

Figure 18.6 Typical Experience Curve for As/400 program construction using conventional 3rd generation technology.

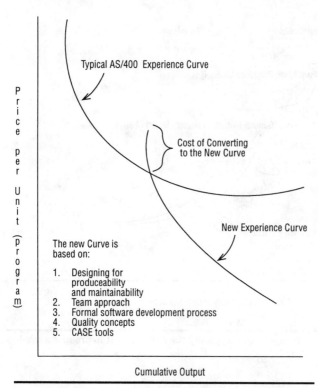

P
r
i
c
e

p
e
r

U
n
i
t

$\widehat{p}$
r
o
g
r
a
$\underline{m}$

Typical AS/400 Experience Curve

Cost of Converting
to the New Curve

New Experience Curve

The new Curve is
based on:

1. Designing for
    produceability
    and maintainability
2. Team approach
3. Formal software development process
4. Quality concepts
5. CASE tools

Cumulative Output

Figure 18.7 A new Experience for AS/400 program construction is based on better design, improved management practices, and the use of CASE tools.

This new experience curve is based on the areas that we have discussed including:

1. *Designing for produceability and maintainability.* This is the software equivalent of designing for manufacturability, which the automobile companies are now realizing is so significant. The foundation of this design concept is relational database technology and the rules for normalization discussed in Chap. 6. Another significant part of this concept is Object Oriented Design and an emphasis on modular programming so that software reuse is facilitated.

2. *A team approach to software development.* The knowledge and insight of the software users should be employed during the formulation stage of software development, rather than during the correction stage.

3. *The use of a formal software development process.* A formal process for software development can be evaluated and subject to a program of continuous improvement.

4. *The adoption of quality concepts to the software product being developed and the development process.* A reliance on testing at the end of the programming activity is too little too late. A quality program should include quality assurance at the beginning of the design process and a process improvement program that addresses quality issues by improving the process rather than by inspecting the product.

5. *Effective use of tools.*

CASE tools provide a significant opportunity for improving quality, facilitating software reuse, easing maintenance problems, and reducing the labor-intensive activities of the construction phase.

As is shown on Fig. 18.7, adjusting to a new experience curve has a cost. And this cost typically involves both a financial cost to the company and an emotional cost to the professional. But the alternative to these costs are a deteriorating competitive position for the company and the risk of skills obsolescence for the individual.

REFERENCES

1. Yourdon, Edward. *The Decline and Fall of the American Programmer.* Yourdon Press, Prentice-Hall: Englewood Cliffs, N.J., 1992.

2. Primozic, Kenneth, Primozic, Edward, and Leben, Joe. *Strategic Choice.* McGraw-Hill: New York, 1991.

3. Ibid., p. 47.

Midrange Software Packages (White Paper)

A major feature of IBM's midrange computer offering is a vast library of software application packages that are available from independent vendors. These packages permit a customer to obtain a total solution for their business information processing needs without the expense of custom developing the software.

The purpose of this White Paper is to examine the current relevancy of software application packages, and to discuss the need for fundamental changes in the way that these packages are developed and marketed. The need for this discussion is evidenced by several trends:

Increasing evidence of consumer dissatisfaction with existing software package offerings.

Fundamental shifts in the market which application packages are intended to serve.

An evolution in the State of the Art of software development which is not reflected in the design approach taken by most software packages.

Consumer Dissatisfaction—A recent study (1) of 90 users of mid-range manufacturing packages (with names supplied by the package vendors) provided the following results:

Fifty percent felt that their original objectives were not met.

Thirty three percent would not buy the same package again.

Ten percent failed in their first implementation.

While this is a relatively small sample compared to the number of packages sold, it is significant that the names were provided by the vendor. And typically, a vendor would provide names that are perceived to be satisfied customers.

Looking at these statistics, it is hard to visualize another industry or profession surviving with a comparable level of consumer satisfaction. Undoubtedly the ultimate fault is with the consumer for a poor purchasing decision. But the risk to the industry is that without a higher-level of consumer satisfaction, the market is completely open to new forms and types of competition.

Shifts in the Market—In the early days of midrange computers (IBM System 34 and others) the typical installation might have ten terminals, and serve the needs of a $5- to $10-million a year company. The most frequent packages which were purchased for these installations were financials: accounts receivable, general ledger, and so on. If a package didn't quite fit the needs of a company of this size, the solution was something called a *workaround*. And what a workaround consisted of was additional clerical work to perform additional tasks or programming enhancements to produce additional reports. A cardinal rule of these programming enhancements, however, was that the new programs should supplement the original system rather than change it. If the original package was modified, typically the vendor's warranty no longer applied.

The current world of the IBM AS/400 is vastly different from these early System 34 days. The horsepower of the E series makes it an appropriate solution for the $100-million company and larger. The application focus has also shifted dramatically. The early focus of Information Technology was on reducing costs and on leveraging investments. As industry progresses through the decade of the 1990s, the emphasis is changing to the use of Information Technology to support business process reengineering and to enhance business products and services. (2)

Both the increased size of the companies being served and the new application focus of these companies has significant implications for the package customer. First the financial penalty of a clerical workaround is much greater. Secondly, if Information Technology is to provide a company with a competitive edge, it cannot settle for the lowest common denominator or the approved functionality typically incorporated into a package.

Evolution of the Software "State of the Art"—Many software packages had their intellectual genesis in the Structured Design concepts of the early 1980s. As in Structured Design, the emphasis of the typical package is on the process. More specifically, the way many packages have evolved and are currently sold is based on the functionality of the software. New releases and new versions typically add to the original functionality, and reflect a consensus of a users group that has survived the veto power of the vendor. And the customer is frequently in the position that, to take advantage of a fix to errors in their current version, it is necessary to install a new version that might include unwanted new functionality.

Perhaps the first thing to question is should a software purchase be based on functionality as the major criterion? In their book, DeGrace and Stahl (3) point out a number of problems with this approach.

"Having computers in the environment affects the requirements."

"People are just not used to specifying things."

The newer design strategies of Information Engineering and Object Oriented Design represent a significant evolution past the process or functionality focus of Structured Design. Information Engineering emphasizes the database design as the architectural focus of software. One of its precepts is that data is a strategic resource of an organization. And a corollary is that the data of an organization is very stable, and that processes tend to be significantly more volatile. Thus, a software solution that incorporates the underlying data structure of an organization has long-term value. A software solution that focuses on the process or on functionality, on the other hand, is geared to the transitory needs of the organization at a specific point in time.

The concepts of Object Oriented Design (OOD) also have a significant impact on the long-term viability of a software solution. The essence of OOD is the encapsulation of data and the methods that operate on this data. It provides basic guidelines for software modularization. The significance of this modularization is that the solution to a business process requirement consists of an assembly of parts. And if either the data or the procedural element of a part needs to be changed, the change can be isolated. OOD concepts mean that a software solution can continuously evolve without the economic penalty of a major software rewrite.

A PARADIGM SHIFT

Webster defines a paradigm as a model or pattern. A paradigm shift represents a radical change in a pattern or model. Used in an industrial sense, a paradigm shift typically represents a radical change in the way that a product is developed or marketed. Perhaps the best known industrial paradigm shifts have occurred in the automobile industry. These shifts have been graphically described in the book *Strategic Choices* (4) through the use of experience curves. These curves show the relationship between price per unit and cumulative output (Fig. A.1).

The first automobiles were hand built by craftsmen, with essentially no two automobiles built the same. The first experience curve of the craftsmen was later superseded by Ford when he standardized the product, and revolutionized the industry by introducing mass production. This significantly lowered the cost of the product to the consumer. A characteristic of the Ford mass production methods, however, was strict limits on consumer choices. In effect, the consumer could select any color he or she liked as long as it was black.

General Motors successfully challenged Ford's market supremacy by introducing the idea of choice. The variety of styles and colors appealed to a more affluent market, and permitted General Motors to dominate the market for 50 years. The difference between the underlying production techniques and manufacturing philosophy was minimal however. Both companies relied on a command organizational

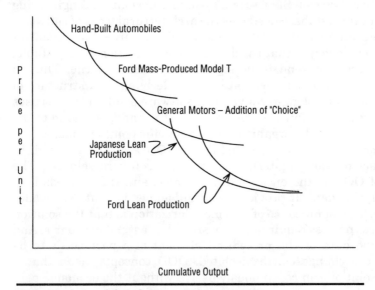

Figure A.1 Automobile industry experience curve.

style, and rigid production techniques. Parts manufacturing was characterized by inflexible tooling and long production runs, and product adaptations to changing markets took five years or longer.

The new experience curve in the automobile industry is called *Lean Production*. This experience curve was pioneered by the Japanese, and successfully adopted by Ford. On a macro management level, this curve is significant because once again in our own time it establishes that existing practices are not sacred. New players with new insights can successfully challenge existing market leaders. From a micro management perspective, two concepts from Lean Production are directly applicable to software production. These two concepts are:

Design for manufacturability.

Flexible manufacturing.

In the book *The Machine That Changed the World* (5), the authors described a study done by General Motors to determine reasons for the difference in productivity levels between GM and Ford. The reason for the study was that GM takes almost twice as long to assemble an automobile as does Ford. One significant difference noted in the study was that Ford has successfully adopted the concept of design for manufacturability. In the example cited, the design for the bumper assembly was evaluated. In the GM assembly, there were 100 parts. In the Ford bumper assembly, there were only 10 parts, and the 10 parts were simpler and easier to assemble. The bottom line—there is no production technology that can successfully compensate for an inefficient initial design.

The concept of Just-in-Time inventory management which is so popular a subject of discussion does not just represent a change in the underlying production technology. The change in the underlying production technology might be called *flexible manufacturing*. To illustrate this change in production technology, let's again use an example that was cited in *The Machine That Changed the World.* (6) This example deals with the stamping presses used to process roles of sheet steel into fenders, doors, and other parts.

In traditional mass production, presses were set up to continuously produce the same part for a significant period of time. To change from the production of one part to another, the services of specialists were required, and the changeover typically took a day or longer. Since the rigidity of traditional mass production was inappropriate for the much smaller Japanese automobile market, Toyota spent considerable effort to develop more flexible manufacturing technology so that more frequent machine setup did not adversely affect manufacturing costs. The result of this effort is as follows:

The production change that took a day or more and required the services of specialists can now be accomplished by Toyota in three minutes, and now requires only the skills of the traditional factory worker.

With the example of the change in automobile production as a guide, let's now look at how the two concepts, design for manufacturability and flexible production, call into question the current approaches taken in software package production.

THE SOFTWARE SOLUTION

When software solutions are classified according to experience curves, three distinct curves are evident (Fig. A.2). The first experience curve, custom developed software, is comparable to the hand-built experience curve of the automobile industry. Each product produced is unique, and there are no economies of scale. While it offers the consumer the

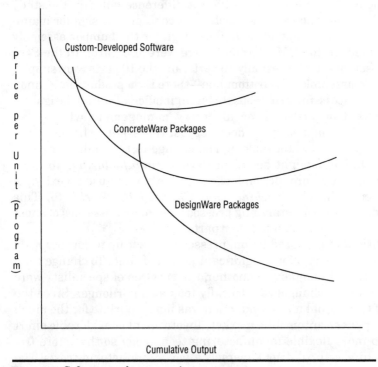

Figure A.2 Software package experience curve.

opportunity to decide exactly what the product is to look like, in most instances the associated costs are prohibitively expensive.

The ConcreteWare Packages experience curve represents the current generation of software packages. The term ConcreteWare is used to describe this generation of packages because of their similarities to the properties of concrete. As all are aware, concrete in its initial state is a fluid substance, and can be molded into almost any shape imaginable. But once the product is completed, it is essentially presented to the market as a rigid product, with the same inflexibility that characterizes a concrete structure.

The ConcreteWare product offering and its associated experience curve are in many ways comparable to the old mass production experience curves. Some measure of choice is available in that there frequently is a set of optional modules beyond the base package. But the underlying production technology typically has not progressed past the custom experience curve. In the instance of the ConcreteWare, this typically means a 3GL such as COBOL or RPG, and the use of Structured Design as the underlying methodology. The consequence of these old production approaches is that the ability to change or modify is more in line with the day- and one-half setups of mass production technology than the three minute setups of lean production technology.

DesignWare as a new experience curve represents the next generation of software packages. The two underlying tenants that distinguish these products from the previous generation are the Information Technology equivalent of several of the factors from Lean Production which were discussed earlier. These factors are:

Design for manufacturability.

Flexible production.

The design emphasis of the new experience curve reflects the insights of Information Engineering. As was discussed earlier, the data structures of an organization are typically the most stable part of the information environment of an organization. So the first part of a DesignWare offering is a fully normalized Relational Database Model which reflects the vendor's knowledge and understanding of an application area. And the first step in reaching a DesignWare solution is to compare the DesignWare Data Model with the customer's existing data structures. The results of this comparison are then used to update the DesignWare Data Model. In this process, the emphasis is on getting the database design "right" so that there is a viable architectural foundation for all future software developments.

The next step in a DesignWare solution is to focus on the processing side. The vendor's offering includes a library of prebuilt business process solutions or templates that consists of program modules and subroutines that have been developed according to the guidelines of Object Oriented Design (OOD). The significance of the OOD guidelines is that modules and subroutines are built around individual files and fields, and are then assembled to arrive at a business process solution. Where a required part or module needs to be modified because of customization performed on the database, it is only this module or subroutine that needs to be modified. And if new files are added to the initial database design, only modules and subroutines associated with the new file need be added to the vendor's initial library.

In a DesignWare solution, Information Engineering and OOD concepts are accompanied by new production technology which permits more effective program construction. Lower CASE (Computer Aided Software Engineering) tools are used as part of the process of arriving at a solution for the customer's needs. These tools consist of either code generators which produce COBOL or RPG programs from high-level specifications, or fourth generation languages which produce object code directly from the high-level specification. The vendor's basic process solutions are initially established as specifications for the tool, and customer modifications which represent changes or additions to these initial specifications are then added. Once a final set of specifications is agreed to, the CASE tool produces the operational programs.

The use of CASE technology as a part of the DesignWare solution is significant for a number of reasons:

CASE represents an order of magnitude increase in programming productivity. (7)

The number of defects is significantly lower and the completeness of functions such as editing is significantly higher compared to programs produced by writing procedural code directly using 3GLs such as COBOL or RPG.

Changes required by a customer do not result in a deterioration of the structure or quality of existing programs since complete new programs are produced once the specifications have been finalized.

IMPLICATIONS FOR THE VENDOR

Changing to a new way of doing business will have significant implications for the vendor. These implications fall into the following categories:

Competitive advantage.

Organizational and management.

Revenue stream.

Competitive advantage—As in the automobile industry, the early adaptors to a new experience curve have a significant competitive advantage. As was discussed earlier, Ford displaced the craft automobile producers, and when GM's new capabilities were developed, it took Ford 50 years to catch up.

As DesignWare vendors develop their marketing skills, stressing the true cost of a ConcreteWare solution will give them a competitive advantage. These true costs for ConcreteWare include not only the initial package cost, but also workaround costs, modifications costs, and high maintenance because of the inflexibility of the older packages.

Organization and management—The primary customer interface for the ConcreteWare vendor consists of sales personnel whose role is to convince the customer that the functionality offered by the package is the appropriate solution. In addition there typically is a technical support staff whose role is to explain the package, and assist the customer to adapt to the package.

In the DesignWare environment, there is no fixed solution, so the primary customer interface requirement is for sales engineers. The new role for the sales engineer is to work with the customer in order to understand the problem, and then to assemble a solution from the vendor's library of reusable parts. In this process the need for architectural revisions to the database will be determined, as well as changes and additions to the vendor's process solution. In this new role, the technical support staff will need skills beyond the ability to understand and explain the vendor's product. True software design skills are needed, as well as the ability to work as a team member with customer personnel to reach the most beneficial solution. The management problems of controlling a library of thousands of reusable components rather than a few versions of a basic product are significant. It took years for Ford to adjust to the multiple style offerings of General Motors because of the need for internal procedural changes and a reshaping of the management mind set. In the same vein, the procedures needed to document and control the reusable components of a DesignWare solution are significantly more complex than the version control procedures currently in existence. In addition, designing elements of the software solution so that they are reusable is a significant cultural and technical adjustment.

Revenue stream—The nature of the DesignWare market will have a significant impact on traditional sources of revenue of the package vendor. An important source of the revenue for the ConcreteWare vendor is an annual fee for maintenance of the package. This service is typically sold on the basis that the customer will receive periodic improvements to the basic functionality of the package, as well as corrections of defects.

In the DesignWare environment, there is no standard product which the vendor evolves in lockstep with their customers. Rather, each solution will tend to be unique, and the customer will tend to evolve the initial solution according to the company's unique requirements. And typically a solution developed with a lower CASE tool will be of higher quality, providing less concern about the problem of embedded defects. Both of these changes will make the selling of the basic maintenance services more difficult.

The potential loss of maintenance revenue is more than offset by two services that can be offered by the DesignWare vendor, however. One of the major selling obstacles to a DesignWare solution is the capital cost to the customer if the lower CASE tool is also purchased. But without the CASE tool, the customer is faced with the older experience curve when it comes to maintenance and enhancements to their solution. The DesignWare vendor can turn this problem to their advantage by developing a service bureau offering in which they retain a copy of the customer's unique solution, and provide TIMESHARING access to the CASE tool which is resident on the vendor's equipment. This service would not only provide a source of revenue—it would eliminate a major selling obstacle for the vendor.

Along the same lines, a DesignWare vendor can develop a new source of revenue by providing a maintenance out-scoring service. The vendor would retain a copy of the customer's solution, and make changes and enhancements using their own personnel. This would make economic sense for many potential customers since it avoids the capital expense of the tool. More significantly, the vendor because of a larger staff can typically maintain a greater depth of technical expertise, and as a consequence, be more cost-effective than the in-house personnel.

IMPLICATIONS FOR THE CUSTOMER

DesignWare solutions offer the promise of significantly greater flexibility and an order of magnitude improvement in cost-effectiveness. The improved cost-effectiveness is particularly true when the costs of modifications and of long-term maintenance is added to the basic cost of a ConcreteWare solution.

But to take advantage of the opportunities offered, there are a number of implications for the potential customer. Instead of being a reactive evaluator of an established design, the customer now becomes a proactive participant in developing the solution. This typically means that the customer's staff will need to develop new design skills, and become familiar with the graphic expressions (Data Flow Diagrams, Entity Relationship Diagrams, and so on) used by the vendors to develop a design solution.

In addition, the vendor's use of advanced production technology will impact the skills needed by the customer's Information Services Department. Typically the DesignWare vendor will offer to the customer either high-level design specifications in the format required by the lower CASE tool, or the source code programs generated by the CASE tool. If the customer is to take advantage of the efficiencies of the CASE tool for future maintenance, their staff will need to learn the tool. This will permit them to work with the design specifications rather than the source code, and eliminate the labor-intensive procedural coding that currently consumes most of the Information Services resources. As the customer faces the development of new skills and the adjustment to a new experience curve, taking advantage of a TIMESHARING offering from a DesignWare vendor will minimize the problems of this transition, however. By taking advantage of the vendor's established installation, the customer will start with proven software designs, established standards, and the mentoring of experienced technicians on the vendor's staff. This will significantly ease the problems of technology transfer.

THE NEAR TERM OUTLOOK

A number of independent vendors are already pursuing this new path. DataWright in Chicago, Cantoc in Toronto, Marcam in Newton, Mass., Gemma International in Westmont, Ill., and CommercialWare in Boston already have or will shortly have the new solutions available. The CASE tool vendors are now actively pursuing package developers, and will undoubtedly realize that in the long term these developers will be the greatest single source of market stimulation among end users. This will no doubt result in the offering of incentives to package developers that hastens the conversion to the new technology. The benefit to the companies purchasing the new products would be a significant improvement in cost-effectiveness and an enhanced ability to use Information Technology as a competitive weapon.

REFERENCES

1. Capron, William. "Follow the Rules to Avoid Failure," *32X/400 Information Systems,* December 1991.

2. Hammer, Dr. Michael. "Making the Quantum Leap," *Beyond Computing,* March-April 1992.

3. DeGrace, Peter and Hulet Stahl, Leslie. *Wicked Problems, Righteous Solutions.* Yourdon Press Computing Series, Prentice-Hall: Englewood Cliffs, N.J., 1990, p. 69.

4. Primozic, Kenneth, Primozic, Edward, and Leben, Joe. *Strategic Choices.* McGraw-Hill: New York, 1991.

5. Womack, James, Jones, Daniel, and Ross, Daniel. *The Machine That Changed the World.* Harper Collins Publishers: New York, N.Y., 1990.

6. Ibid., p. 63.

7. Jones, Caper. "Using Function Points to Evaluate CASE Tools, Methodologies, and Languages," *CASE Trends Magazine,* January-February 199, pp. 8-16.

A Metrics Program for Information Services (White Paper)

INTRODUCTION

An organized effort to improve the performance and productivity of an Information Services Department should include as a component a metrics program to measure key factors for the department. The purpose of this metrics program is to quantitatively define where and how resources are currently used, and to track the results of any productivity improvement program. The need for this type of information is almost an issue of basic navigation. As every sailor knows, you can't figure out how to get to where you want to be if you don't know where you are now. And if you don't take periodic sightings along the way, you can drift off course without realizing it until it's too late.

So to with an Information Services Department. If you don't have a quantitative evaluation of both the starting point and of efforts to improve, an improvement program will be based strictly on subjective opinions. And unfortunately the opinion that is most frequently expressed is:

> I'm already working as hard as I can now, how do you expect me to produce more?

The answer—Work more effectively, not harder. And the purpose of a metrics program is to help define what "more effectively" represents.

So let's look at how to establish a metrics program that might help us asses the effectiveness of the Information Services Department. And we'll look at how to perform this assessment from three perspectives:

A strategic assessment

A process assessment

A productivity assessment

A Strategic Assessment

THE RANGE OF OPTIONS

As we start to consider the ways to improve performance, a number of options are available. As technical specialists, frequently the first options considered tend to be technical. These options include new tools such as code generators and report writers, and tend to focus on the programming or construction phase of the software development life cycle.

In many instances, however, the greatest potential for improvement tends to come from the people elements of software development.

These elements include improved training, a more effective process for software development, more effective participation from the users, and the selection of projects with a greater cost/benefit ratio.

In order to put a technology bias in perspective, it might be appropriate to briefly examine the experience of two companies that embarked on productivity improvement programs in the 1980s. The two companies that took radically different approaches to productivity improvement were General Motors and Ford.

In the GM program, the emphasis was on the use of technology to increase the automation level of the factories. Approximately $80 billion was spent on robots, material handling equipment, automatic welders, and so on.

The Ford attempt had a completely different focus. Perhaps because of a lack of money as much as anything else, Ford concentrated on adopting the concepts of Lean Production from the Japanese. These concepts essentially involved people changes. Included in the changes was a focus on quality and the prevention of defects, adoption of the concepts of Just-in-Time inventory and design for manufacturability, the use of teams, and so on.

The results of the two efforts: Ford currently assembles an automobile in roughly half the time required by GM. And equally significant, the major increases in productivity which were achieved by Ford through improvements in the people part of the process are now a source of funds for investment in new technology to further improve productivity levels.

THE NATURE OF THE WORK

Perhaps the most frequently quoted statistic in an Information Services Department is:

80% of our effort is devoted to maintenance!

This oft-cited statistic has some very significant implications. Perhaps the first is that it carries a message to both management and to the users that if only things were done right the first time, we would not have to spend so much time fixing things after the fact. Equally important, this statistic seems to identify a sink hole for resources that cannot be controlled. So perhaps a first step in a metrics program is to establish a classification scheme for the activities that both improves our public image and provides us with the insights needed to start a program of continuous improvement.

When we start to think about the use of an expanded vocabulary in order to classify our activities, a comparison with terms used by a more mature industry—home building—might be of value.

Home-building terms	Data processing terms
New construction	New system
Gut rehabilitation	Maintenance
Build an addition	Maintenance
Remodel/redecorate (as in remodel the bath or paint or carpet)	Maintenance
Refurbish (as in put on a new roof)	Maintenance
Maintenance (as in fix the faucet or furnace)	Maintenance

In the home-building industry, the label attached to proposed work is important because it lets the consumer (user) exercise judgement as to whether to pursue the matter further. The consumer can make this judgement because, through experience, he or she has developed a mental table that associates tasks with costs. Here's a typical consumer's idea of the costs associated with the various activities of the home-building industry:

New construction $200,000 +
Gut rehabilitation $100,000 +
Addition $ 35,000 +
Remodel $ 10,000 +
Refurbish, etc. $ 2,000
Maintenance $ 500

When a request comes into our shop and it gets labeled as maintenance, guess what cost the consumer associates with the request. And
if we are not able to accomplish the task for $500, the reaction is often
that Information Services is indulging in another example of overpric-
ing and under performing. But perhaps more important from our own
perspective, this catch-all label reveals little about the nature of the
work, its criticality, the skills required, and the significance to the
organization.

The National Bureau of Standards has moved in the direction of a
more descriptive classification by providing the following classifications for software maintenance:

Corrective: Bug fixes.

Perfective: Enhancements to an application that are outside the
scope of the original system.

Adaptive: Modifications to an existing systems required to keep it
viable.

The classification of the NBS, while more definitive in terms of the
criticality of the work, tells us little about the scope of the activity or
skill required for the task. So let's return to the home building example,
and develop a comparable classification scheme: (1)

Home building	Data processing
New construction	*New system:* Develop a new system for which there is no existing model. Typically there is higher risk and a greater problem in developing both the requirements and a working design.
Gut rehabilitation	*Redesign:* Reprogram an existing system, typically to take advantage of newer technology (flat files versus relational databases) and to add functions that are practical with the improved price/performance of newer equipment.
Build an addition	*New Function:* Typically this would involve new files as well as new processing. This activity also typically involves new interfaces to the old files and perhaps minor changes to the old files.

Home building	Data processing
Remodel/redecorate	*Enhancement:* Add a new report or display to an existing system or make a minor improvement in the processing functionality. Typically this does not involve any significant change to the existing file structure.
Refurbish	*Adaptation:* This category covers adoptive maintenance needed to keep a system viable. It might involve changes in processing logic in a payroll system, for example, to adopt to a new tax requirement. Or it might involve installing a new release of the operating system or of a software package.
Maintenance	*Correction:* Bug fixing.

When we establish a more rigorous classification of our activities, we enrich the vocabulary that we use to discuss projects with our users and management. More importantly, for our purposes, we have a classification scheme that can be useful in gauging the strategic value of the Information Services Department. But before we explore this use of the classification scheme, let's first take a look an another way of classifying our activities based on their business focus.

THE FOCUS FOR OUR EFFORTS

The focus for the application of Information Technology may be classified as follows:

Reducing costs through routine automation.   The initial objective for most Information Technology applications was to reduce organizational costs through the automation of routine functions. This was the era of the payroll automation expert. During this period, the emphasis was on identifying stand-alone applications with significant clerical costs associated with them. These functions would then be automated without significantly impacting either the basic organizational structure or the overall work flows of the organization. Typical applications included accounts receivable, accounts payable, general ledger, payroll, billing, and so on.

Leveraging investments.   With many of the significant clerical operations automated, the second focus for Information Technology emphasized the effective management of assets. In the industrial sector, major emphasis was placed on systems to manage inventory, schedule equipment, and so on. In the service sector, the emphasis changed to areas such as cash management, sales analysis, service scheduling, and so forth.

Enhancing products and services.   The next focus for Information Technology innovation, a significant current focus for many organizations, is the enhancement of products and services. In many instances this current focus represents a response to market pressures. Perhaps the most significant example of a market pressure is the current emphasis on Just-in-Time inventory. This has resulted in the creation of EDI links between many customers and suppliers, and significant revamping of inventory management systems. A number of companies are now carrying this information integration between customer and supplier to the point where the supplier is offering, as part of their services, the management of the customer's inventory. Numerous other examples have been written up in trade literature where modern technology has permitted a company to efficiently assume systems responsibilities that formerly were the province of their customer.

Business process reengineering.   Competitive pressures are encouraging organizations to fundamentally reexamine traditional organizational structures and ways of doing things. Instead of automating an existing activity, the search is for completely new ways to accomplish the desired objective. An example of this fundamental restructuring or redesign of a business process was Ford's approach to accounts payable. An initial study was made to determine the impact of additional automation on this function. When the potential improvements were benchmarked against a Japanese automobile company, it was found that expected costs still exceeded the benchmark company's costs by an order of magnitude. A more basic assessment was then made, and fundamental process changes made. The result of this second review was a new process for A/P in which vendors are automatically paid by matching receiving reports to purchase orders. The traditional process of receiving invoices, matching the invoices to receiving reports, and verifying prices against purchase orders was eliminated. A similar improvement was achieved by Motorola by examining the processes involved in fulfilling a customer order. The result of this examination was the reduction of the steps involved from 209 to 39.

ASSESSING THE STRATEGIC FOCUS

When we combine our new activity classifications with the development focus which we just discussed, we are able to produce a grid which can be used for a strategic assessment of an Information Services Department (Fig. B.1).

	Reduce costs Leverage investments	Enhance products and services	Reengineer business processes
New system design	B	A	A
New function enhancement	C	A	A
Adaptation/correction	—— D ——		

Figure B.1

Using this grid, the activities for perhaps the past six months plus anticipated activities for the next year should be assessed, and the percentage devoted to each combination in the matrix should be filled in. The results of this assessment can then serve as the basis for determining the strategic relevancy of the Information Services Department to the company, and the contribution of Information Technology to the organization's ability to meet competitive challenges.

As a guide to how this evaluation can be used for a strategic assessment, let's take a look at each of these categories. To set the stage for review, however, let's first review one of the more famous economic principles, the Parieto Principle. This principle, also known as the 80:20 rule, states that a small proportion of a cause is responsible for a disproportionate portion of the results. This principle has had its greatest impact on manufacturing, since it encourages a focus on the small number of processes that are responsible for the greatest number of defects.

The Parieto Principle can also be used as a guide for evaluating our automation efforts. As is shown in Fig. B.2, when we start to automate the various functions of a business process, typically automating the first 20 percent of the functionality will produce 80 percent of the benefits.

In many instances automation efforts past the first 20 percent of the functionality are to eliminate nuisance activities for the user rather than to produce any real economic benefits. So with this thought in mind, let's take a look again at the matrix in Fig. B.2, and develop some ideas on how to assess the strategic value of the department.

Category D—correction and adaptation

This category is somewhat like fixing potholes on an old highway. When the need arises, it should absolutely take first priority. But this category also reflects the continuation of a past level of achievement, not an emphasis on present and future competitive problems. In effect it is a support for the status quo. Unfortunately, however, an organization that is not progressing is not just standing still. Compared to its competition, it is probably going backwards. So if this category requires a significant use of resources, it is at the expense of the positive contribution that Informational Technology should be making.

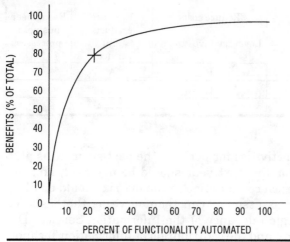

Figure B.2 The Parieto Principle.

Category C—enhancements and new functions within traditional application boundaries

In many Information Services Departments, this category represent the major activity. Existing organizational boundaries and business processes are accepted as the architectural framework for automating efforts involving Information Technology. But as we discussed earlier, the Parieto Principle tells us that the major economic benefits from the applications currently being enhanced were probably already realized once the first 20 percent of the functionality was automated.

Typically there is a valid organizational need for new reports and for the mechanization of additional isolated functions. But the involvement of Information Services in these activities is based on a traditional ownership of the only computer.

Now, however, there is the option to use powerful PCs and work stations which are equipped with inexpensive software packages such as spread sheets. As a result the involvement of Information Services in these activities should be questioned.

Category B—redesign or develop new systems within traditional application boundaries

This activity typically occurs based on the need to make a switch to a new technology. The occasion might be a platform vendor's inability or unwillingness to continue to provide maintenance support, or a significant improvement in the price/performance ration of newer technology. When this activity occurs, it typically can be justified on the basis of either hard-dollar savings or because there is no choice (the hardware is obsolete).

Where a choice is possible, however, is how this activity is approached. One option is to approach this type of project on the basis of converting existing functionality to a new system with perhaps minor design concessions to a new technology such as converting flat files to a relational database design. A second option is to use the need to redesign a system as the occasion to fundamentally reassess the business processes, and look for quantum improvements in the business efficiency.

Category A—enhancement of products and services, business process reengineering

The Information Services Department that is devoting 60 to 70 percent of its software development resources to these two areas is in a position to make a major contribution to the organizations bottom line. In the first instance, the enhancement of products and services, the goal is for the organization to make money through Information Technology. Perhaps the best known example of this use of technology is the SABRE reservation system from American Airlines. It has resulted not only in better control of passenger seats, but it is also a source of revenue, and provides a competitive advantage against other airlines.

Business process reengineering represents another major opportunity for the Information Services Department. Many organizational structures and business functions go back 50 or 100 years, and are based on outdated constraints of time and distance. An example of the effect of a time and distance constraint on an organization would be many of the old record-keeping sections in warehouses. This type of function was needed because central records of orders, shipments, and so on, were too far away, or they couldn't be updated fast enough. But with the advent of on-line systems, however, this type of function is no longer necessary.

Another justification for a fundamental assessment of the business processes is that many of them are based on the turn of the century ideas of Frederick Taylor. Taylor's ideas of work organization and task decomposition became the basis for not only organizing the factory, but they also were used to help organize the office. Using Taylor's ideas, efforts to improve productivity in the office resulted in the breaking up of complex jobs into small pieces that could be handled by rote. Successive layers of management were then added to handle all but completely routine matters.

This decomposition approach undoubtedly introduced efficiencies at the time, but it also added significantly to the cycle time for most business processes. The new trend is to now consolidate functionality in order to eliminate delays between steps, to provide better service, and to flatten the organizational structure. An example of this change was an insurance company which replaced the multistep data entry and actuarial processing with a new customer service representative function equipped with a computerized expert system. Where it typically took two weeks to process a policy, it is now done in one day for 80 percent of the new policies.

A STRATEGIC DIRECTION

Doing the wrong things efficiently is not the best way to maximize the contribution of Information Technology to the organization's bottom line. The purpose of a strategic assessment is to understand how resources are currently utilized, and to establish a future direction. Figure B.3 is a suggested direction the Information Services Department.

There are two main thrusts to the strategic direction that is suggested in Fig. B.3. The first is to move towards end user computing for many of the traditional reporting and department functions that currently are a significant drain on IS resources. With the advent of powerful PCs, the availability of inexpensive software packages, and a significantly higher computer literacy on the part of users, the traditional role is no longer necessary.

A strategic move towards the use of Information Technology to enhance products and services and to enable the reengineering of business processes represents an effort to use technology to gain competitive advantage. In the process, the Information Services Department can change from a back-office overhead operation to a front-office competitive player. This change is the goal of the strategic assessment.

In many ways, automating historic procedures within the constraints of established organizational structures is comparable to the paving of cow paths. But typically we can't use an established cow patch a the route for our new superhighway. Nor can we use present tasks as the basis for a new business process design. As a result, an emphasis on system design is required, and typically an Information Services Department will need a new process for software development which includes a partnering with our users. The process for software development is the subject of our next section.

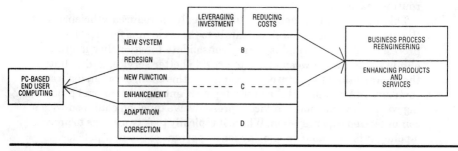

Figure B.3

A Process Assessment

THE QUALITY PROBLEM

The Process for developing software in many organizations has been described as:

Ready! Fire! Aim!

In effect there frequently is an emphasis on immediate visible coding results. But the price of this immediate focus on production without adequate prior planning is frequently poor quality, with consequent delays in installation and additional expenses for rework.

So a first step in a process assessment should be a quality evaluation, particularly a determination of the cost of poor quality.

In order to provide a framework for a quality assessment, let's first take a look at two definitions of quality that were developed by two pioneers of the quality movement, J.M. Juran and Phil Crosby.

Juran's definition of quality, fitness for use, provides the more strategic view of quality. In the software arena, this definition should be evaluated in terms of two types of customers who are significant when the software is delivered. The first is the ultimate customer or user of the software, and the quality definition asks the question: Is the software fit for use as initially delivered, or is additional rework required? The second user of software is an intermediate user, the maintenance programmer. And for this user, the definition is used to determine if the design, structure, and documentation of the software facilitates future maintenance.

Crosby's definition of quality, conformance to requirements, is a more tactical view, and appears to stem from his manufacturing background at ITT Corporation. This view of quality is process oriented, and emphasizes the early establishment of specifications and designs. These specifications then serve as a control for the balance of the construction and installation phases of the process.

When we start to consider the issue of software quality, some of the published studies on software development might provide an indication of the significance of quality to a process assessment.

In one study of a company's software efforts, 64 percent of the errors were in analysis and design, even though the users had formally signed off on the documentation. (2)

A more comprehensive study (3) of 2500 + commercial systems projects developed during 1980-1990 provided the following breakdown of the source of defects:

Requirements	Design	Coding	Documents	Bad Fixes
30%	25%	30%	5%	10%

Using these studies as a guide, it appears that more than 55 percent of the errors in software development can be traced to inadequate planning during the early phases of a project before programming begins. And according to one study, this results in an error removal effort that constitutes up to 40% of the cost of a system. (4)

To reduce this cost, errors need to be detected earlier through better planning. The emphasis on early detection is due to the fact that the point in the development of a system when an error is detected has a significant impact on the cost of correction. As is shown in Fig. B.4, the cost of correcting errors increases exponentially (6) the later in the process that the correction is made.

So a process assessment that determines the phase in a project when errors are detected and the cost of correction at the time of detection

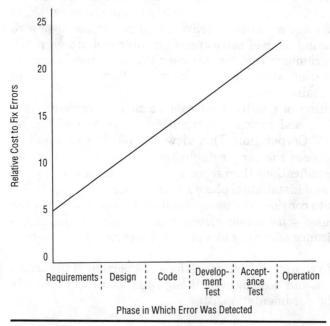

Figure B.4

can be an important guide for use in improving the effectiveness of the development process.

PRIMARY MEASURES OF QUALITY

In order to determine if a general industry quality problem is also an issue that needs to be addressed in your own organization, measurements need to be collected which permit a process assessment. Two potential types of measurement can be used. The first is resource based, either in terms of time or dollars. The second is in terms of defects per thousand source lines of executable code. The first measurement is the more valuable in that it is more apt to raise people's consciousness concerning quality—the first step in addressing a problem. The second is of more limited value, although it does permit a comparison of your quality level with that of other organizations. In this discussion, the emphasis will be on a resource-based measurement. For further information on defects per thousand lines of source code, see reference 6.

As a first step in establishing a resource oriented process measurement effort, let's define some of the terms involved:

Project: In a software development sense, a project should be defined as a planned undertaking which is initiated in order to accomplish specific objectives. This means that a project per se cannot be opened until there is at least a reasonable idea of what the objectives are, and for our purposes it should include the intention of installing a new or revised piece of software at the end. General investigations to establish an initial feasibility or scope should be classified as a study, and are outside the scope of the process measurement which we are discussing. And the project ends when the software has been installed and accepted by the user.

Project phases: These are the major activities of a development project. The high-level activities which are to be used as a basis of organizing resource statistics are:

Planning: This phase includes the requirements definition and system design phases of the project.

Construction: This phase includes programming, testing, and preparing the system and user documentation. This phase ends when the system is ready to install.

Installation: This phase includes all activities from ready to install to acceptance by the user.

Note: This classification is a minimum type of breakdown. If an organization uses a formal methodology with a more detailed set of phases, they should be used instead.

Resource: The unit of measure that is suggested for a Process Assessment is net work hours. All the work effort involved in a project should be recorded. This includes both developers time and all user time devoted to the project. Users time to be captured includes all time devoted to preparing specifications and designs, testing time, training time, data conversion, and installation.

Note 1: Time spent on general training, vacations, and so on, should not be recorded against the project.

Note 2: The net work hours collected for the process assessment will also be used for the productivity assessment to be discussed in the next section.

Chart of accounts: The net work hours collected against each phase of the project should be broken down into the following classifications:

Planning phase: No breakdown required. It might be of value to break this category down, however, into more detail for further analysis. Following are two suggested breakdowns:

Requirements		JAD preparation
Design	or	JAD sessions
Prototyping		JAD follow up

JAD = Joint Application Design

Construction phase: Total construction time should be captured and classified as follows:

Specification rework: This breakout should identify any changes or clarifications required by the programmers based on the criteria—fitness for use.

Productive: This category should include the balance of the time not identified as specification rework. It might also be of value, however, to break this time down into Coding and Testing so that the breakout can be used for additional analysis.

Installation phase: Total installation time should be captured and classified as follows:

Specification changes: This category should include all time spent because of specification changes requested by the user as a condition for installation. In effect, this time category covers all efforts required because the user is saying that the system in not fit for use. This category represents deficiencies in the design process.

Program changes: This category should include all changes that are required either because the programs do not work properly or because they do not conform to the design specifications. This classification also includes all time spent revising programs because they do not conform to IS Department standards.

Specification enhancements: This category includes all effort which is expended to improve the functionality of the system based on initial experience with the working version. It represents improvements that are evident based on operational experience, not changes required before the system can be installed.

Productive: This category covers the balance of the time for the phase. It might be of value to also break this time down further as follows:

Training

Pilot installation

System roll out (multiple sites)

In order to evaluate the process used to develop a system, the following ratios are suggested:

1. Cost of (poor) quality =
$$\frac{\text{Spec rework} + \text{spec chge} + \text{program chge} + \text{spec enhance.}}{\text{Total time on project}}$$

This ratio represents the percentage of total project time which is required because a prior phase was not done right the first time. In effect, it represents defects which are passed on to the next phase of a project. Currently there is no accepted benchmark standard in Information Services for an acceptable ratio. When this ratio is determined, however, it is appropriate to refer back to Fig. B.5 which shows that the cost of correcting a defect increases exponentially in later phases of a project. As a result perhaps the appropriate standard is the one which is now the accepted goal in manufacturing—zero defects.

2. Design quality =
$$\frac{\text{Spec rework} + \text{spec chge} + \text{spec enhance}}{\text{Total Planning Time}}$$

This ratio represents failures in the planning phase of the process. Remedies that are evolving for these types of problems typically include the following:

- Adoption of a more effective partnering relationship with the user, frequently referred to as Joint Application Design (JAD)
- Adoption of improved structured methods for design, particularly graphics (Data Flow Diagrams, Entity Relationship Diagrams, Structure Charts)
- Use of prototyping to verify the user interfaces of the system (screen and report formats, and so on.)
- Use of Action Diagrams and Decision Trees to verify complex processing logic before programming begins
- Establishment of a quality assurance program so that requirements and designs benefit from an independent review before construction begins

3. Programming quality =

$$\frac{\text{Programming changes}}{\text{Total construction time}}$$

This ratio represents failures in the programming phase of the development. It represents either failure to conform to established specifications when developing the program, failure to test adequately, or failure to conform to established programming and documentation standards. It should be noted that it does not represent any problem with the adequacy or completeness of the design specifications. Any problems with the specifications should have been resolved first, with the time involved captured as specification rework time. Typical solutions to problems of this type include the use of formal test plans, additional training, and the adoption of a formal quality assurance review before programs are released for installation.

4. Project ratios

$$\text{Planning ratio} = \frac{\text{Planning phase time}}{\text{Total time on project}}$$

$$\text{Construction ratio} = \frac{\text{Construction phase time}}{\text{Total time on Project}}$$

$$\text{Installation ratio} = \frac{\text{Installation phase time}}{\text{Total time on project}}$$

As a general goal, the objective of a process assessment is to reduce construction and installation time through better planning. One visible way to determine progress is to see planning become a more significant percentage of a total project. The other way is to see an absolute increase in the productivity level of the software projects. The measurement of productivity levels will be discussed in detail in the next section.

AN ADDITIONAL QUALITY MEASURE

When we are determining the cost of quality, we need to look not only at the initial development costs for a system, but also at the costs associated with support during its life. Typically, support costs equal or significantly exceed the original costs associated with a system. When a software package solution is used, costs to initially customize and install plus later support costs can be a major use of Information Services resources.

In the section on strategic assessment, we discussed the first approach that can be used to control these costs. As you will recall, applying the Parieto test provides an indication of whether or not enhancements and additional functionality contribute to the organization's bottom line.

For those support projects surviving this initial test, further evaluation can contribute to our understanding of the software development process, and provide a basis for improving the process. This can be accomplished by evaluating all post installation projects for a system, and developing a classification scheme for them. The purpose of this classification is to identify what portion should be considered acceptable because of changing business requirements, and what portion should be considered to be a "quality" cost. The portion identified as quality costs represents, in effect, defects introduced into the system during the original project. If the support represents software package customizing that was unplanned at the time of the purchase, these costs also represent a quality problem. In this latter instance, however, these costs identify problems in the purchasing process.

Before we start to consider an analysis of software support costs, it might first be appropriate to examine a statistical phenomenon (Fig. B.5) concerning software support which was documented by DeMarco. (7)

As shown in this study, revisions to a system tend to be concentrated in the first six to twelve months after a system is installed. During this period of time, typically 5 percent or less of the original code is revised. So changes or additions equalling 5 percent of the original code tend to cost the same as the original 95 percent of the basic system.

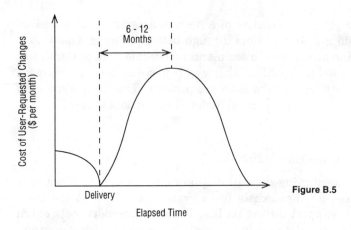

Figure B.5

When we analyze these support costs, certainly any corrections should be considered a programming quality problem. DeMarco also suggests that enhancements and new functions that are added during this period typically are requirements that always existed, and were not properly determined during the initial specification process. As a result, these expenses should also be considered a cost of quality.

The qualifier to the automatic identification of enhancements and new functions as quality problems is the current use by many Information Services Departments of an iterative process for software development. Using this approach, the core functionality is programmed and installed first, and this core is then expanded through successive iterations of development until full functionality is achieved. The advantage of this approach is that a working system is obtained more quickly, and as a consequence the benefits of the system start accruing sooner. In addition, both the users and the developers have the benefit of operational experience before the next part of the system is developed.

So when we attempt to get a handle on the true cost of quality, care must be taken to avoid penalizing the valid use of an iterative development approach. As a result, the planned expansions of the functionality of the first working version should be considered a subproject of the original development. These subprojects are then controlled as part of the basic management of the original project. Cost overruns of this nature should typically be tied back to the initial study which established the project and are not specification quality concerns.

In the same vein, many software package purchases are accompanied by significant programming expenses which are needed to meet the unique requirements of the organization. The question concerning these efforts: Do they represent a planned effort which is established

	Programming Defect	Specification Defect	Original Project	New Business Requirement
Correction	Hours			
Enhancement		Hours	Hours	Hours
New Function		Hours	Hours	Hours
Package Support		Hours	Hours	Hours

Figure B.6

when the package is considered, or do they represent problems in the purchasing process?

So once again we can use a grid to get a handle on the maintenance expenses, and determine the need for process improvements. The suggested grid is shown as Fig. B.6.

The hours shown in the shaded area should be considered to be part of a quality problem. These costs should be used and included in the appropriate ratios for the process assessment.

A Productivity Assessment

VARIATIONS IN PRODUCTIVITY

In the first two sections of this paper, we discussed two types of assessment, a strategic assessment and a process assessment. The first is significant because if Information Services is not focusing on the areas that make the most significant contribution to the organization's competitive capability, not much else matters. The second is significant because if the basic software development process is unstable and a significant effort must be devoted to rework, experience shows that the first step should be to eliminate the cause of the rework, not improve rework efficiency.

The third area for assessment which we will discuss in this section is used to determine the basic productivity of an Information Services Department. This permits both a comparison of a departments productivity level to established benchmarks from other organizations and the establishment of goals for a continuous improvement program. The benchmark that can be used to compare productivity levels with other organization is Function Points per Worker/Month.

Before we discuss the method for calculating this benchmark, let's first take a look at the significance of a productivity assessment. Following are statistics gathered for various categories of Information Services Departments (3):

Type of IS Department	Productivity range (Function points per worker/month)
Low skill level Ad hoc development process No CASE tools	.25 to 5.0
High skills level Ad hoc development process No CASE tools	.75 to 8.0
High skills level Structured development process Upper and lower CASE tools	20.0 to 100.0

These statistics show a range of 4000 percent in the productivity levels of Information Services Departments. Or putting it another way, one company might be paying $4000 for something that its competitor is getting for $1. And to put the reliability of these numbers in perspective, they represent an evaluation conducted on over 2500 projects.

Perhaps even more startling is the comparison between category 3, the highest producers, and category 2, the high skilled department using an ad hoc development process without the benefit of advanced CASE (Computer-Aided Software Engineering) tools. This category perhaps best describes the craft environment of most AS/400 installations. The difference in the productivity level is a factor of 12.50. This means that benchmarking indicates that there is a potential improvement of 1250 percent in the productivity level for the typical AS/400 installation.

HISTORY OF PRODUCTIVITY METRICS

The first efforts at developing a language independent measure of the productivity of software development occurred at IBM in the late 1970s. Until this point, if any measurements were made at all, they tended to be based on the lines of code produced by a project. But as a base for measurement, lines of code have a number of problems:

Software can be produced by a variety of languages and tools. A "lines of code" metric does not permit comparisons of productivity between different projects and different organizations.

As an economic measure of productivity, lines of code are inherently deceptive. With a higher-level language, fewer lines of code are needed to solve a problem. But from an economic standpoint, when the higher-level language is used, the same user benefit is obtained. A measurement yardstick based on lines of code, however, would actually show a decline in productivity since fewer lines of code were written.

The solution to these problems was presented by A.J. Albrecht in a formal paper in October, 1979. (8) The metrics solution, called function points, had been used informally within IBM for several years. Subsequently it has gone through a number of iterations, most notably in 1984 in an IBM revision. Currently functions points are a guide project, and an International Function Points Users Group has been formed to establish standards and to share productivity studies. (9)

Note: For a more detailed history of the development of software metrics as well as a significant amount of information for use in benchmarking, see reference 3.

FUNCTION POINTS OVERVIEW

Function points are determined for an application by listing the inputs and outputs to the system, and then adjusting each input or output based on a classification scheme that measures the complexity of the I/O. This results in a total count of unadjusted function points. This unadjusted total is then adjusted by an additional factor for the complete system which considers the use of on-line data entry, the significance of end-user efficiency, and so on. Once the final adjusted function points have been calculated, they are then divided by the time in worker-months (planned or actual) used to develop the system. This final calculation results in the measure of productivity—

Function points per Worker Month

This calculation may be expressed as:

$$\frac{FP}{\text{Worker month}} = \frac{(\text{I/O} \times \text{level factor}) \times \text{general char. factor}}{\text{Total worker months}}$$

Determining function points/worker month for a system consists of a six step process:

1. Identify each I/O for a system, categorize the I/O according to preestablished function types and complexity. List the I/O on a work sheet.
2. Tabulate the work sheet by function type and level of complexity.
3. Use the associated weighing factor for each combination of function type and complexity level to calculate the unadjusted function points for the system.
4. Determine a weighing factor for the complete project based on characteristics such as transaction rates, on-line data entry, and so on.
5. Multiply the project weighing factor (called the general information processing function) by the total from step 2 to get the total function points for the system.
6. Divide the function points total by the worker months for the project.

Let's take a look at each of these steps in detail.

Step 1: Classify and list I/Os according to function type and classify each function type that is listed according to complexity.

Step 2: Tabulate the work sheet by function type and level of complexity.
Following is a list of function types which are used to classify the I/Os for a system, and guidelines for determining the complexity. Also shown are some of the significant guidelines developed by the International Function Point Users Group (IFPUG) for counting function types. The full guidelines can be obtained by contacting the IFPUG (9) or one of the consultants specializing in this area. (10)

a. *Internal Logical Files (ILF):* User identifiable group of logically related data or control information maintained and utilized within the boundary of the application. User identifiable group of logically related data refers to data related at such a level that an experienced user would identify the data as fulfilling a specific user requirement of the application. The data analyses equivalent to such high-level logical groupings are singularly named data stores on a Data Flow Diagram.
Complexity level:

	1-10 DET	20-50 DET	>50 DET
1 RET	L	L	L
2-5 RET	L	A	H
>5 RET	A	H	H

DET= attributes or fields; RET= entities or physical files

Counting rules:	Count as:
Logical entity of data from the user's viewpoint	1 ILF
Internal Logical Files generated or maintained by the appreciation	1 ILF
Files accessible to the user through keywords or parameters	1 ILF
Files used for data or control by sequential (batch) application	1 ILF
Each hierarchical path (alternate access path) through a database derived from user requirements (include paths formed by secondary indices and logical relationships)	1 ILF
Backup files (if requested by user to meet business requirements)	1 ILF
Hierarchical paths not derived from user requirements	0 ILF
Intermediate or sort work file	0 ILF
Alternate index (path)	0 ILF
Backup files for restart/recovery	0 ILF

b. *External Interface Files (EIF):* Unique identifiable group of logically related data or control information utilized by the application, but maintained by another application. User identifiable group of logically related data is defined as data related at such a level that an experienced used would identify the data as fulfilling a specific user requirement of the application.

Complexity level:

	1-10 DET	20-50 DET	>50 DET
1 RET	L	L	L
2-5 RET	L	A	H
>5 RET	A	H	H

DET= attributes or fields; RET= entities or physical files

Counting rules:	Count as:
File of records from another application	1 EIF
Database shared from another application	1 EIF
Super File (Each File Read)	1 EIF

For a Super File, if the DET (fields) > 100, then the file is a Super File. Each RET (Record) = 1 FTR (File Types Referenced) Check top row of matrix—If DETs IN RET>50, then 'A'. Else 'L' User requested backup of file = 1 'H'.

c. *External Inputs (EI):* Process data or process control information which enters the application's external boundary. The processed data through a unique logical process, maintains an internal logical file. Control information data is used by a process within an application boundary to assure compliance with business function requirements specified by the user. Control information may or may not directly maintain an internal logical file. An external input should be considered unique if it has a different format or if the logical design requires processing different from other external inputs of the same format.

An External Input is considered unique if the data maintained on an Internal Logical File and the input format is unique or the processing logic is unique.

Complexity level:

	1-4 DET	5-16 DET	16 or more
0 or 1 FTR	L	L	A
2 FTR	L	A	H
3 or more FTRs	A	H	H

FTR = File Types Referenced

Counting rules	Count as:
Data screen input	1 EI
Multiple data screens entered, accumulated, and processed as one transaction with no processing of individual screens.	1 EI
Function screen input	1 EI
Function screen with multiple different functions	1 EI
Automatic data or function transactions from other applications	1 EI
Inquiry followed by an update function	1 EQ, 1 EI
Alternate input with the same processing logic as the primary input, if this is a special request by the user	1 EI
PF key duplicate of a screen already counted as a input	0 EI
Two input screens with the same format and processing logic	1 EI
Two input screens with the same format and different processing logic	2 EI
Screen that is both input and output	1 EI, 1 EO

d. *External Outputs (EO):* Process or control information that exits the application's external boundary. An external output should be considered unique if it has a different format or if the logical design requires processing that is different from other external outputs of the same format. An external output is considered unique if:
   1. The output format is unique.
   2. The processing logic is unique.

Complexity level:

	1-5 DET	6-19 DET	20 or more
0 or 1 FTR	L	L	A
2 or 3 FTR	L	A	H
4 or more FTRs	A	H	H

Counting rules	Count as:
Data screen output	1 EO
Automatic data or function transaction to other applications.	1 EO
Operator message frame (format) from the application for multiple similar operator messages *Note:* The complexity level of the information processing function is determined by creating different messages as different element types.	1 EO
Message frame (format) for multiple error messages,or confirmation messages associated with one EI *Note:*The complexity level of the information processing function is determined by treating different messages as different data element types.	1 EO
Individual error message within a message frame	0 EO
Individual confirmation message output within a message frame	0 EO
Batch printed report	1 EO
Batch run report	1 EO
Batch error report	1 EO
Terminal printed report	1 EO
Control total output	1 EO
Audit list or check list report	1 EO
Repeat screen output	0 EO
Start (log on) screen output	0 EO
End screen output	1 EO

e. *External Inquiries (EIF):* Unique input/output combinations that result in the retrieval of data required output, do not contain derived data, and do not update an internal logical file. An External Inquiry is considered unique if it has a format different from other External Inquiries in either its input or its output parts or if the logical design requires edits and sorts different from other external inquiries.

An input/output combination is considered unique if:

1. The input format is unique.
2. The output format is unique.

Complexity level (Use matrix for external inputs)

Counting rules:	Count as:
Online input and output with no updating of data in files	1 EQ
Inquiry followed by an update input	1 EQ, 1 EI
Selection menu screen input and output	1 EQ
User maintained table or file—Potentially	1 ILF, 1 EI, 1EO, 1 EQ

Note: A major query facility or language should be decomposed into its hierarchical structure of EIs, EOs, EQs, using the existing definitions and current practices.

As each I/O is evaluated, it is listed on a work sheet. Figure B.7 represents a sample work sheet for this purpose.

FUNCTION TYPE WORK SHEET

System_____   System I.D._____

Prepared By: _____   _/_/_

Reviewed By: _____   _/_/_

Function List				Classification				
Type	ID	Ref	Description	Low	Ave	High	Est	Act

Figure B.7

As you will note on the form, there are columns to indicate if the functions that are listed represent an initial estimate, or the actual functions that have been measured after the system is built.

Step 3: Use the associated weighing factor to determine unadjusted function points

Once the Function type counts by complexity level have been determined, the weighing factors shown in Fig. B.8 are used to calculate the total unadjusted function points for the system.

Step 4: Determine a weighing factor for the complete project

Once the total unadjusted function points for the system has been determined, the next step is to apply a weighing factor to this total. This weighing factor is based on the characteristics of the project, and adjusts the function point count up or down by a factor of 35 percent. Figure B.9 shows the characteristics that are considered in determining a system weighing factor, and a points system used to identify quantify these characteristics.

The degree of influence points are totaled for the system, and the weighing factor is calculated as follows:

$$\text{GCA} = \text{general characteristic adjustment} = 0.65 \times (0.01 \times \text{GC})$$

$$\text{GC} = \text{the total of the points assigned to each characteristic}$$

FUNCTION TYPE RECAP AND CALCULATION					
System_____			System I.D._____		
Prepared By: _____ _/_/_					
Reviewed By: _____ _/_/_					
Function Type Recap					
ID	Description	Low	Ave	High	Total
EI	External Input	___×3=___	___× 4=___	× 6=___	
EO	External Output	___×4=___	___× 5=___	× 7=___	
ILF	Int. Log. Fle.	___×7=___	___×10=___	×15=___	
EIF	Ext. Inter. Fle	___×5=___	___× 7=___	×10=___	
EIF	External Inq.	___×3=___	___× 4=___	× 6=___	
FC	Total Unadjusted Function Points				—

Figure B.8

GENERAL INFORMATION PROCESSING FUNCTION

System_____   System I.D._____

Prepared By: _____   _/_/_

Reviewed By: _____   _/_/_

General Information Processing Function

ID	Characteristic	DI	ID	Characteristic	DI
C1	Data Communications	_____	C8	Online Update	
C2	Distributed Functions	_____	C9	Complex Processing	
C3	Performance	_____	C10	Reuseability	
C4	Heavily Used Config.	_____	C11	Installation Ease	
C5	Transaction Rate	_____	C12	Operational Ease	
C6	Online Data Entry	_____	C13	Multiple Sites	
C7	End User Efficiency	_____	C14	Facilitate Change	_____
GC	General Characteristic			Degree of influence	_____

DI Values

Not present, or no influence	= 0	Average influence		= 3
Insignificant influence	= 1	Significant influence		= 4
Moderate influence	= 2	Strong influence		= 5

CGA   General Characteristic Adjustment $= 0.65 \times (0.01 \times GC)$

$$= \text{_____}$$

Figure B.9

Step 5: Determine total function points for system

The function points for the system are determined by using the formula:

$$FP = FC \text{ (from step 2)} \times GCA \text{ (from step 4)}$$

where   FP = function points
FC = unadjusted function points
GCA = general characteristic adjustment

Step 6: Determine productivity

Two basic measures are needed to determine productivity. The first is work product output, which in our case equals function points. The second is work input, which is measured in work months. The figure to use for work months is the net work months, which excludes vacations, general training, and so on.

Net work months on a project is determined as follows:

$$\text{NWM} = \frac{\text{Total net hours on project}}{\text{Average work hours per month}}$$

1. Total net hours includes all user time, test time, installation time, and the like, as well as IS time. This time is the same as the time used in performing the process assessment.
2. The average work hours per month excludes vacation, and so on. Typically this equals 75 percent of the possible gross work hours.

The calculation of productivity is as follows:

$$\text{Productivity} = \frac{\text{FP}}{\text{NWM}} = \frac{\text{Total function points for system}}{\text{Net work /worker/months for system}}$$

A PROGRAM OF CONTINUOUS IMPROVEMENT

When we first start to measure quality as part of a process assessment, the stage is set for a self-reinforcing program of continuous improvement. To gain a perspective on an improvement program, let's take a look at the history of the quality movement in manufacturing.

Three plateaus are generally recognized to describe the focus of the quality movement in industry:

Circa 1920: Product inspection—examine the intermediate and final product in order to detect defects.

Circa 1960: Process control—monitor defect rates for specific processes in order to identify defective process elements and to control the process.

Circa 1980: Design improvement—engineer the design of the product and the process in order to prevent defects.

Adopting the insights of manufacturing to Information Services, the solution focus for quality problems should be on the engineering of the product and the process in order to prevent defects. To improve the design of the product, the design must be easily visible, not buried in thousands

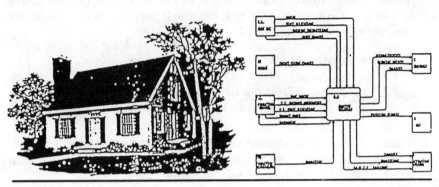

Figure B.10

of lines of third generation procedural code. To make a design visible, graphic techniques comparable to those used in manufacturing and in the construction industry need to be adopted (see Figs. B.10 and B.11).

And once graphic techniques are adopted, a more effective partnering with the user can be established compared to what occurs when the user is asked to sign off on a voluminous text specification of a system.

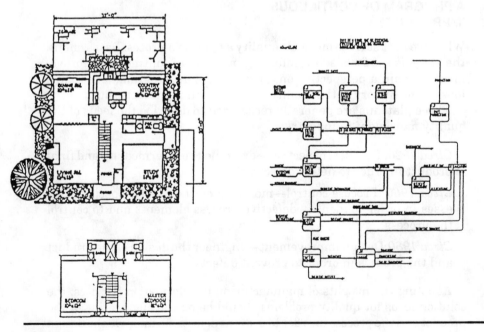

Figure B.11

Thus the first attempt to improve the quality of the design leads naturally to the first improvements in the process for developing the system, the adoption of structured methods for designing the system. The use of graphic techniques then makes the participation of the users in the definition and design of the system more effective.

These first process improvements also provide an opportunity for a significant increase in the reliability of the estimates that are used to plan resources and schedules for a project. Estimating by its nature is a process of successive approximations. Initially the best that can be done is to use general rules of thumb such as:

Two days to write and install a simple report

These initial guidelines are comparable to the rules of thumb used initially by the construction industry such as:

The average new house in the area costs $200,000

The average house is 2000 square feet, and typical construction costs are $95 per square foot

But a contractor will not use these general guidelines in order to set a price for building a specific house. More must be known about the house to be built in order to establish the estimate to be used to establish personnel and material requirements. This "more is known" equates to a detailed set of plans and specifications for the house.

In Information Services, on the other hand, we are frequently asked to provide firm estimates for a project when little is known about the scope of the effort. This initial problem is then compounded when an informal craft process is used which intermingles design and construction. In this instance what's to be built is not known until after it's built. This makes any efforts at reliable estimating an impractical task.

When structured techniques are established in order to improve the quality of the design, we also have the basis for improving the quality of our estimating. Initial design diagrams such as a Data Flow Diagrams and Entity Relationship Diagrams contain all the information needed to identify the function points in the proposed system. Once function points are determined by deriving them from the design, historical productivity measures of function points per worker month can be used to calculated resource requirements and schedules.

A FINAL THOUGHT ON METRICS

Many attempts at establishing a metrics program in organizations have been unsuccessful. There are perhaps a number of reasons for these failures. Perhaps the first is the lack of clear goals, and an inability to follow through to correct the problems that have been identified through metrics.

Perhaps even more significant is how metrics are used. In a command management structure, metrics are used to pressure employees to produce more. What frequently happens in this instance is that it is in the employees self interest to sabotage the metrics program.

The more successful approach to a metrics program is to create a participatory or team approach that involves not only the Information Services personnel, but the users as well. Metrics are made highly visible, and are first used to develop a sense of awareness of the problems of effectiveness and productivity. This visibility is accompanied by an effort to ensure that everyone feels that they have a stake and a voice in the program of continuous improvement.

REFERENCES

1. Primozic, Kenneth, Primozic, Edward, and Leben, Joe. *Strategic Choices.* McGraw-Hill: New York, 1991.

2. Martin, James. *Systems Design from Provable Correct Constraints.* Prentice Hall: Englewood Cliffs, N.J., 1985.

3. Jones, Caper. *Applied Software Measurement.* McGraw-Hill, New York, 1991, p. 136.

4. Rush, Gary. "A Fast Way to Define Computer Requirements," *Computerworld,* October 7, 1985, pp. 11-16.

5. Boehm, B.W. *Software Engineering Economic.* Prentice Hall: Englewood Cliffs, N.J., 1981, p. 40.

6. DeMarco, Tom. *Controlling Software Projects.* Yourdon Press, Prentice-Hall: Englewood Cliffs, N.J., 1982, p. 200.

7. Ibid., p. 199.

8. Albrecht, A. J. "Measuring Application Development Productivity," *Proceedings of the Joint SHARE/Guide and IBM Application Development Symposium,* October 1979, pp. 83-92.

9. International Function Point Users Group (IFPUG) 5008-28. Pine Creek Drive Waterville, OH 43081-4899, tel: (614) 895-71301.

Glossary

Action Diagram   A diagramming technique which uses a form of Structured English or pseudocode to describe the detailed logic of a complete business process or a complex business rule or processing task. (Chap. 11)

Application   A terms used to describe a partition of an overall business system according to the historic organizational structure and division of tasks. (Chap. 3)

Application or project planning   A life cycle phase in which an overall system is broken down into small subsystems which can be organized as separate projects for independent analysis, design, construction, and installation. This phase is preceded by a business modeling and a data modeling phase. These prior phases establish the scope of the system, dependencies among the subsystems which are organized as separate projects, and the design of the database. The database design then provides the structure which permits the independently developed subsystem to work together. (Chap. 2)

Business Modeling   A life cycle phase (typically the first) in which the boundaries of a proposed system are established and the components (processes and data) needed to accomplish a business objective are identified. (Chap. 2)

Business process reengineering   The radical redesign of business processes to achieve dramatic performance and efficiency improvements. The antithesis of cow path automation (*see* Cow path automation). (Chap. 1)

Cardinality   The nature of the relationship between two entities that are part of a database design. The nature of the relationship between entiyies is typically expressed on an Entity Relationship Diagram (*see* Entity Relationship Diagram). An example of a typical relationship is that between the entities order and Customer. An order can be related to only one customer, but a customer can be related to many orders. (Chap. 8)

CASE—Computer-Aided Software Engineering   Computer tools to aid in the analysis, design, and programming of commercial software systems.

Cow path automation   The routine automation of an existing business process within the framework of established organization boundaries and procedures without examining whether or not the established processes are appropriate for meeting the business objective.

Composite object   A term used in Object Oriented Design (*see* Object oriented design) to identify an object which is made up not only of its own data and the methods which operate on this data, but also of other objects consisting of data and methods. This term would be analogous to the term "assembly" used in hard goods manufacturing to identify an item which consists of multiple parts, each with its own design specifications and methods for manufacturing. (Chap. 9)

Context Level Diagram   The first level of a Data Flow Diagram (*see* Data Flow Diagram). This diagram is used to identify the scope of a system by identifying the environment which is external to the system and the data interfaces between the environment and the system. (Chap. 7)

Data Flow Diagram (DFD)   A graphics notation used to define the scope of a proposed system and the major components (data structures and processes) that are included in the system. This diagram was initially developed prior to World War I by industrial engineers as a paper flow analysis tool. It was popularized in computer automation by the Structured Design movement in the late 1970s. It is included in the generic category of diagrams called dependency diagrams. A notable feature of the diagram is that it established the structural dependencies among the components of a system, that is, the process Prepare Invoice is dependent on data created by the process Enter Orders, and so forth. Dependency relationships are a significant consideration in partitioning a system into small projects and establishing the sequence for undertaking these small projects. (Chap. 7)

Data modeling   A life cycle phase in which the data structures identified as components of a system are analyzed and organized into a database design. (Chap. 2)

Data store   A symbol used on a Data Flow Diagram to indicate that a data structure which is a part of a system is physically stored or at rest between processes in a system. There are no implications made as to the storage media, it might take the form of a paper order which is stored in a file cabinet. (Chap. 7)

Decision tree   A special form of graphical notation used to express the logic involved in a multiple-decision situation. (Chap. 11)

Derived field   A field that is not entered as part of a data structure but that is calculated based on other fields in the data structure. An example might be the extended value for an order line that is calculated based on the price and the quantity ordered. Typically a derived field is not physically stored in a database but is calculated by the application program each time it is needed. (Chap. 6)

Domain Integrity   The allowed values that data can have in a system. The allowed values identify the editing parameters for a field including field length, type, attributes, and so on. (Chap. 6)

Enterprise modeling   A term associated with an Information Engineering approach to software development. During this modeling phase, data is analyzed and organized into its simplest form. This simplest form then becomes the basis for a database design. Historically this term has been associated with an analysis scope that covers either a complete enterprise or at least a major segment of the enterprise such as a business area. (Chap. 3)

Entity   A symbol used on an Entity Relationship Diagram (see Entity Relationship Diagram) to identify a class of people, things, and so forth, with characteristics in common, about which data is stored. (Chap. 8)

Entity relationship diagram   A systems design graphics notation which is used to show how the information retained by a system is organized and how the organizational elements relate to each other. This diagram is based on the table and relational concepts of a Relational Database Management System (RDBMS). (Chap. 8)

Essential Functions Diagram   The second level of a Data Flow Diagram. This diagram is used to identify the major compontnts of a system (data structures and high-level processes or functions). It also links the data interfaces to the environment with the major functions that use or provide the data interfaces. This diagram is also called a Level 0 diagram. (Chap. 7)

Information Engineering   The application of an interlocking set of formal techniques for the planning, analysis, design, and construction of information systems on an enterprise basis or across a major section of the enterprise. Information Engineering emphasizes the analysis of the data in an organization and the design of the database in its simplest form in order to establish a structural foundation for all subsequent software systems. (Chap. 1)

Inheritance   A term used in Object Oriented Design (*see* Object oriented Design) to indicate the ability of a class of objects (data and the methods that operate on the data) to use the methods and variables of a higher class of which it is a part. (Chap. 9)

Integrated CASE   Software development tools that support both the analysis and design phases of software development as well as the construction phase. A significant feature of these tools is a common repository where the analysis and design portion of the tool stores the system specifications so that the construction tool can then retrieve them in order to generate or compile working programs. (Chap. 1)

Joint Application Design   A team approach to software development. Key users, designers, and related staff such as auditors conduct workshops that progress through a series of structured steps for planning and designing a system. (Chap. 4)

Key   The field in a file format which uniquely identifies each instance of data (a record) in the file. An account number would be an example of the key for a customer master. (Chap. 8)

Leveling   An organization scheme used in preparing a Data Flow Diagram when the number of system components is too large to comfortably fit on a single page. Using the scheme, a high-level view of the system is prepared first (*see* Context diagram). The process components of the system are then decomposed to lower and lower levels in order to show more detail. The end of this process decomposition is typically the identification of processes which will become user tasks on the system's menu. (Chap. 7)

Life Cycle Process Model   An identification of the phases and subphases in software production and the transition criteria for progressing from one phase to another. (Chap. 1)

Lower CASE   Computer tools used to support the construction phases (programming and testing) of the software development life cycle. Typically these tools fall into two categories, code generators that produce 3GL programs such as RPG or COBOL, and 4GLs (4th generation languages) that compile machine-level programs directly from high-level specifications of the system requirements. (Chap. 1)

Methodology   An elaboration of the major phases identified in the Life Cycle Process Model, identifying an ordered set of detailed tasks to get from a starting point (a user request) to an end point (a deliverable product). (Chap. 1)

Method   This term has two meanings in software development. Used in the context of a software development methodology, it refers to a set of techniques, rules, and guidelines for tackling a problem, measuring the quality of a solution, and expressing the solution. Methods are the means of performing the tasks that make up the methodology. Used in the context of Object Oriented Design (*see* Object Oriented Design) a method refers to a procedure that operates on the data that is part of an object. (Chap. 1 and 9)

Normalization   The process of organizing data in its simplest form as part of the process of designing a database. Data is organized in the form of tables, with a key field such as an account number serving as the basis for grouping data related to the account such as customer name and address. (Chap. 1)

Notation   A means to organize and express an idea, such as a database design. A data Flow Diagram or a flow chart are examples of notations. (Chap. 1)

Object/Class/Instance   A term used in Object Oriented Design to identify a collection of data and the methods that operate on this data. If many objects have the same methods and data characteristics, they are identified as a class. The individual occurrences of objects that are a part of a class are then called instances. (Chap. 9)

Object Oriented Design (OOD)   A design philosophy which is geared to facilitating software development productivity by encapsulating data and the methods that operate into small chunks that can be reused. Much of the design philosophy evolving as part of OOD follows the concepts pioneered in the early 19th-century by the advocates of parts interchangibility for manufactured products. (Chap. 5)

Parieto Principle   Popularly known as the 80:20 rule, states that a small proportion of the cause is responsible for a disproportionate part of the results. Used in a software development context, this principle states that automating 20 percent of the functionality of a business process will typically provide 80 percent of the potential benefits. (Chap. 3)

Polymorphism   A term used in Object Oriented Design to describe the ability of two or more classes of objects to respond to the same system communication or signal, each in its own way. (Chap. 9)

Referential integrity   If a field in one record format serves as the primary key in the format of another file, there must be a matching value in the second file. An example is an account number. This field might be a data field in an order header record, and the primary key of the customer master. Referential integrity editing ensures that the order header record is not accepted if the account number entered as part of the order header does not match an entry in the customer master file. Where a data field in one file serves as the primary key for another file, it is called a foreign key. (Chap. 6)

Relational database   A technique for organizing the data structures used by an organization or a software system into its simplest form. The goal is to eliminate data redundancy so that information such as a customer name and address is only stored in one place. As a result, if there is a subsequent change in an address, it only needs to be updated in one place. The concept of a relational database is implemented by a Relational Database Management System (RDMS) which permits data to be stored in its simplest form and then retrieved and combined in more complex formats for use by the application programs which perform the business processing. (Chap. 6)

Structure chart   A hierarchical diagram which breaks a process solution down into its constituent parts. Typicaly this diagram is used for complex processes, and shows the program modules that are part of the solution, parameters passed between modules, and subroutines that have been incorporated into a module. (Chap. 11)

Structural component of software   A basic precept of Information Engineering is that the data in an organization is the stable component of business systems. As a result a well-designed database provides a stable structural foundation for all software development.

Structured Design   A process oriented approach to software development which emphasizes the decomposition of a system's procedural component down to a level where it can be programmed. Data analysis and the design of the database is not emphasized, and data definitions are considered to be subordinate to the processes that use the data. The techniques of Structured Design provide the basis for a number of formal methodologies that evolved in the late 1970s and early 1980s. The process focus of Structured Design is being superseded by the data focus of Information Engineering. (Chap. 5)

Timebox management A software development technique in which a large system is partitioned into small subsystems for independent development and installation. The basis for the partitioning is a time standard of three to six months. Within this time standard, a working version of the subsystem is to be developed and installed. Potential delays in installation are to be handled by reducing the functionality of the initial working version, not by extending the schedule or by adding development resources. Once the initial working version is installed and operational experience obtained, additional functionality required by the user is obtained by establishing new timeboxes to enhance the first working version of the subsystem. This management technique is comparable to the line item budgeting philosophy which has long been used in project and operations management. (Chap. 3)

Total quality movement A management approach which is based on the belief that quality is meeting the expectations of the user or customer and the way to achieve quality is to control the service or manufacturing process in order to prevent defects.

Transform analysis A term used in Structured Design to identify the formal steps in the functional decomposition of a business process into its primary components. These components are the afferent branch which includes the tasks needed to read data and transform it into a usable form (read a record stored on a disk) the efferent branch (the tasks needed to output the data, that is, printing a report) and the central transform (the tasks linking the afferent and efferent branches). (Chap. 8)

Upper CASE Computer tools, typically PC-based, that are used to support the analysis and design phases of the software development life cycle. (Chap. 1)

Virtual field A field which is not physically part of a data structure but which can be included in a view of that data structure by the Relational Database Management System (RDMS). An example might be a customer name which is not physically part of the order header. The RDMS can include customer name as a virtual field in a view of the order header (a joined logical view). This inclusion is possible if the order header structure includes as a field the account number (called a foreign key). The foreign key establishes a relationship between the order header and the customer master record (the foreign key in the order header is the primary key for the customer master record). (Chap. 6)

Waterfall model A software development life cycle model that specifies a formal set of phases to include analysis, design, programming, testing, and so on. Elaborate requirements and design documentation is produced as the output from the early phases. A significant feature of this model is a transition criteria that requires the completion of one phase as the criteria for entering the next phase. There is little provision for returning to earlier phases. To use a house-building analogy, details of the requirements such as the color to paint a bedroom would be specified before the next phase could be started such as digging the foundation. (Chap. 2)

Index